Freud
A to Z

Freud
A to Z

Sharon Heller, Ph.D.

WILEY

John Wiley & Sons, Inc.

Published by John Wiley & Sons, Inc., Hoboken, New Jersey
Published simultaneously in Canada

For general information about our other products and services, please contact our
Customer Care Department within the United States at (800) 762-2974, outside
the United States at (317) 572-3993 or fax (317) 572-4002.

Wiley also publishes its books in a variety of electronic formats. Some content that
appears in print may not be available in electronic books. For more information
about Wiley products, visit our web site at www.wiley.com.

Library of Congress Cataloging-in-Publication Data:

Heller, Sharon.
    Freud A to Z / Sharon Heller.
Includes bibliographical references and index.
ISBN 0-471-46868-1 (Paper)
        p. cm.
1. Freud, Sigmund, 1856–1939.   I. Title.
    BF109.F74H45 2005
    150.19'52'092—dc22

                                        2004015682

Printed in the United States of America

10 9 8 7 6 5 4 3 2 1

To James E. Wilson, my Freud,
and in memory of Teresa Benedek (1892–1977)
and Michael Franz Basch (1926–1996)

If I cannot move the heavens I will stir up the internal regions.
("Flectere si nequeo Superos, Acheronta movebo.")

—Sigmund Freud,
epigraph to *The Interpretation of Dreams*

Contents

Preface

Freud was trying to map the war zones of the heart, where air-raid sirens wail and bombs blast, and furtive souls scurry around in the half-light, frantically searching for a way back home. . . . In a world filled with psychological land mines, he thought, any step might trigger a memory that explodes one's self-esteem, and a small trip in the psychic rubble may lead to badly sprained emotions. We belong to our past, we are its slave and pet.

—Diane Ackerman, *The Natural History of Love*

In 1993, *Time* magazine ran a cover photo of Sigmund Freud with the headline "Is Freud Dead?" The answer was a resounding "Yes!" Freud had bungled many of his clinical cases and failed to prove the efficacy of psychoanalysis, and modern drugs rendered his talking cure obsolete.

What a bad case of throwing out the baby with the bath water. Freud *defined* the twentieth century. To the intellectual Harold Bloom, Freud is *the* consciousness of modern time. Every hour of every day, someone speaks of a "Freudian slip," an "anal" personality, a "phallic symbol," "dream symbolism," "unconscious motives," an "egomaniac," "repression," "inhibitions," and "defensive" or "conflicted" behavior. There are 1,247 entries for books written by or about Sigmund Freud on Amazon.com and 142,000 entries for him on the Internet. Other recent figures of great consequence—Charles Darwin, Karl Marx, Albert Einstein—have not commanded comparable attention to the details of their existences. Look in the index of most any book about human behavior and you might find more citations for Sigmund Freud than anyone else—that includes the thirteen references in my first book, *The Vital Touch: How*

Intimate Contact with Your Baby Leads to Happier, Healthier Develop-ment, a book barely relating to his work at all!

A century ago, Freud jolted our world, and it has never been the same. Love him or hate him, the inferences and reverberations of Freud's observations have irrevocably altered Western civilization. For thousands of years, people used the supernatural to explain the origins of behavior. Freud turned this belief on its head. Using the scientific tools he had at hand, his insights into the unconscious gave us a language to probe the uncharted territory of the human mind, changing how we conceptualize human nature. Today we take for granted that childhood experiences help mold our later emotional life, that our behavior often has disguised motives, and that dreams have symbolic meaning. People go for talk therapy as commonly as they previously went to confession, and sex is dis-cussed openly in the classroom, on *Oprah,* and more among one another. We tend to forget the world pre-Freud, where neuroses were poorly understood and many suffered needlessly with no use-ful treatment available; where a general framework in which to understand dreams and other unconscious processes didn't exist; and where sexuality was viewed as base and taboo.

Freud did not discover the unconscious mind. Poets and philosophers, writers such as Goethe and Schiller, whom Freud fre-quently quoted, looked to the unconscious mind for the roots of creativity. Freud provided a roadmap to navigate our psychic life. "Psychoanalysis was forced, through the study of pathological repression," Freud observed, to "take the concept of the 'uncon-scious' seriously"—to elucidate how our feelings, thoughts, fears, and actions are far more intricate *and* fascinating than they appear on the surface, as they emerge through our dreams, jokes, slips of the tongue, mistakes, and other actions. Arming us with a way to probe this heretofore inaccessible cavern of the mind, he gave us a way to alleviate human suffering.

Because most of Freud's theories, which were developed over a sixty-year career spanning the end of the nineteenth century through the first half of the twentieth century, are *presumably* passé, replaced by cognition, neuropsychology, and other modern domains in the field of psychology, his hold on our mindset is a conundrum. Why doesn't he just go away?

For one, many people relate to his basic premises. It's easy to see yourself, at times, as an *intrapsychic* mystery, in constant conflict with inner forces of good and evil, love and death, eros and thanatos—the proverbial angel on one shoulder whispering into one ear, "Carrot sticks," and the devil whispering into the other ear, "Chocolate chip cookies!" It's easy to sometimes feel baffled by the meanings and causes of people's simplest acts and experiences, silly mistakes, stupid comments, or seemingly senseless dreams, to feel that knowing another involves exposing and unraveling unconscious thoughts, motives, and feelings that underlay the inner deceits of daily life: jokes, slips of the tongue, dreams, repressed memories, displaced emotions, and so on.

As the most influential psychologist of the twentieth century, Freud's revolutionary theory of the person has left a mark on virtually all domains within psychology, from cognitive and perceptual psychology to psychotherapy and the study of abnormal behavior. Though Freud's basic theories have been largely discredited in the sixty-four years since his death, the modern theory of personality exists in large part as a result of the work of his disciples and critics to refute, support, argue, extend, dismiss, or incorporate new findings into his original theories. Nothing in psychology before or since has so stimulated research as Freud's ideas. Outside psychology his influence has been just as great. For example, the anthropologists Ruth Benedict, Clyde Kluckhohn, Margaret Mead, Gregory Bateson, and others collaborated closely with psychoanalysts in collecting and interpreting data, and some anthropologists were analyzed.

Political science, literature, literary criticism, art, and the cinema all acknowledge certain Freudian underpinnings and influences. Much fiction has been written with Freud as protagonist, such as *Freud, a Novel*, by Carey Harrison, and there are countless movies in which we see a patient lying on a couch, being psychoanalyzed by the stereotypical bearded analyst with a pipe. In the movie *The Seven-Percent Solution*, Sherlock Holmes works with Dr. Sigmund Freud to solve a crime. And recently, *The Talking Cure*, by Christopher Hampton, opened on Broadway, a story of Carl Jung's affair with an early analytic patient, Sabina Spielrein, and the decline of Jung's volatile six-year relationship with Freud. Woody Allen's Freudian jokes constitute some of his best material. In the movie *Annie Hall*, Alvie (Woody Allen) tells Annie Hall (Diane Keaton) he has to go see his analyst. "Oh, you're in analysis," she says. "Oh, only for fifteen years," replies Alvie. "I'm giving it one more year and then I'm trying Lourdes."

In addition to having created psychoanalysis, Freud begot numerous progeny. Freud's daughter Anna and the renowned psychoanalyst Erik Erikson, who was trained by her, refined and extended psychoanalytic concepts. Others left to form their own empires, as did Carl Jung and Alfred Adler. All have added immeasurably to our understanding of human nature.

Could Freud be resurrected? Indeed.

Freud started his career as a neurologist interested in the science of the mind. But with Victorian medical science unable to cure hysteria, a mysterious affliction that left patients inexplicably blind, paralyzed, mute, and so on, and some shut away in a psychiatric hospital, Freud felt forced to develop a theory to answer deeper questions about the mind. As patients began to make their way to his couch and free associate about their thoughts, wishes, dreams, and fantasies, the therapy of psychoanalysis became de nouveau. This technique spawned the revolutionary idea that, like the iceberg, the human mind was largely below the surface—a dark place concealing lust, aggression, sinister motives, self-deception, and dreams filled with hidden meaning. Inadvertently, Freud's path drifted from hard science; largely patient anecdotes replaced hard empirical data. Every psychoanalytic text, quipped W. H. Auden, should begin with: "Have you heard the one about . . . ?" Freud came under heavy criticism, and scientists dismissed the breezy speculations of psychoanalysis as more fiction than fact, noting that Freudian concepts such as repression, the id, or the Oedipus complex could not be put under a scientific microscope.

Further, drug intervention and shorter therapies such as cognitive-behavioral therapy started to replace psychoanalytic therapy, which often entailed the patient lying on the couch three to four times a week for years. These interventions were also more successful in treating conditions such as phobias or obsessive-compulsive disorder. Psychoanalytic theory and therapy seemed destined for the scientific trash bin.

Then came sophisticated tools such as the positron-emission tomography (PET) scan, which can map the neurological activity inside a living brain. Suddenly, neuroscientists began to discover that some of Freud's basic theories, especially the notion that much of our thoughts, feelings, and motivations lie beneath conscious awareness, have credibility. A small but influential group of researchers began to use Freud's insights as a guide to future research and in 1999 founded the journal *Neuropsychoanalysis*. "Freud's insights on the nature of consciousness are consonant with the most advanced contemporary neuroscience views," wrote Antonio Damasio, head of neurology at the University of Iowa College of Medicine. Research "is going on at the fundamental level where emotions are born and primitive passions lurk in the shadows of dreams."

Freud A to Z presents the magic of Sigmund Freud, his life, his theories, his progeny, and his legacy to psychology. And it includes his warts and foibles—how his inner demons led him down some erroneous paths. Freud's brilliance was to recognize that our unconscious mind contains a cavern of secret feelings, wishes, and fears. His shortcoming was his insistence, in spite of ongoing dissent, that such devious expression was necessary because at its core it contained forbidden sexual urges. Yet, even when Freud was wrong, he paved the way for later investigators, many who were his disciples, to refine and correct his theories. Freud remains a towering figure of modern history. If we see further today, it's because we sit on Freud's shoulders.

Acknowledgments

Of the many sources I used in writing this book, Louis Breger's balanced and penetrating biography *Freud: Darkness in the Midst of Vision* has been the most helpful. I have relied on his research, insights, and interpretations in many places and take this opportunity to acknowledge this unique and original work.

As always, I thank my agent, Mary Ann Naples, of the Creative Culture, for her ongoing diligence, warmth, support, and commitment to my work.

> Psychoanalysis confronted humans with the third of three narcissistic injuries: *Copernicus had displaced humanity from the center of the world; Darwin had compelled it to recognize its kinship with the animals; Freud showed that reason is not master in its own house.*

> —Sigmund Freud, *Introductory Lectures*

Allport, Gordon

A mere twenty-two and freshly out of college, Gordon Allport, who would become an influential academic American psychologist, wrote Freud a note announcing that while he was visiting Vienna, Freud would undoubtedly be delighted to meet him. Freud responded to his "callow forwardness" by inviting the brazen young traveler to his office. The "traumatic" visit, as Alfred Adler, a noted psychologist at the time, later described it, proved a pinnacle point in Allport's thinking of human behavior and in the development of his own important theories of personality.

Soon after Allport entered "the famous red burlap room with pictures of dreams on the wall," Freud appeared and summoned Allport to his inner office. Freud sat silent, waiting for Allport to state his mission. Unprepared for Freud's silence, Allport had to think fast about what to say to the great man and began to relay an episode on the tram car on his way to Freud's office. He told Freud about how a boy around four years of age "had displayed a conspicuous dirt phobia. He kept saying to his mother, 'I don't want to sit there. . . . Don't let that dirty man sit beside me.' To him everything was *schmutzig* (filthy)." To Allport, the child's dirt phobia seemed directly related to his mother's character, "a well-starched

Hausfrau, so dominant and purposive looking." Thinking Freud would make that association at the end of the story, Allport was flabbergasted when "Freud fixed his kindly therapeutic eyes upon me and said, 'And was that little boy you?'"

Allport was astounded at Freud's assumption, as he knew nothing of Allport or his past and was quite wrong in his interpretation. Freud's misunderstanding of Allport's motivation "started a deep train of thought. I realized that he was accustomed to neurotic defenses and that my manifest motivation (a sort of rude curiosity and youthful ambition) escaped him. For therapeutic progress he would have to cut through my defenses, but it so happened that therapeutic progress was not here an issue." Although depth psychology had its merits, the experience taught Allport that it may plunge too deep. He felt psychologists must recognize manifest motives before probing the unconscious.

America

To Freud, infused with old-world culture, America was a savage land of vulgar commercialism. He hated its informalities, like calling him by his first name. Yet it was America who gave Freud his first honorary recognition.

On September 10, 1909, Freud received the degree of Doctor of Laws, *honoris causa,* from Clark University in Worcester, Massachusetts. Long ignored by psychiatry in Europe, except for his small group of followers, he was thrilled and surprised. To most, Freud's ideas were shocking and outrageous. Fortunately, the president of Clark University, the psychologist C. Stanley Hall, was a bold, eccentric thinker who fostered controversy and novel ideas. "Something of a kingmaker," Freud called him. Hall had worked to popularize psychology, especially child psychology, in the United States. He had heard of Freud through Auguste Forel, the former director of the Burgholzli Mental Hospital in Zurich, who spoke of Freud's and Josef Breuer's work on hysteria. Hall continued to follow Freud's ideas, and in his book *Adolescence* in 1904, Hall favorably alluded several times to Freud's controversial ideas about sexuality.

The occasion was momentous. It was, said Freud, "the first official recognition of our endeavors," and he later described the visit to Clark University as the "first time I was permitted to speak publicly about psychoanalysis." Freud delivered five lectures in German to a rapt audience, delighted that in "prudish America one could, at least in academic circles, freely discuss and scientifically treat everything that is regarded as improper in ordinary life." In his autobiography written a decade later, he expressed the deep meaningfulness of his warm American reception: "In Europe I felt like someone excommunicated; here I saw myself received by the best as an equal. It was like the realization of an incredible daydream, as I stepped up to the lectern at Worcester." Clearly, "psychoanalysis was not a delusion any longer; it had become a valuable part of reality." Freud happily witnessed this testimony even on the boat to America; his cabin steward was reading *The Psychopathology of Everyday Life*.

A skilled and dynamic public speaker, Freud improvised his five lectures to his American audiences as was his custom. He launched the series by honoring Josef Breuer, who introduced him to the use of hypnosis for hysteria, as the true founder of psychoanalysis. By the end of the third lecture, he had familiarized his audience with the basic concepts of psychoanalysis: repression, resistance, dream interpretation, and so on. He devoted the fourth lecture to the touchy theme of sexuality, including infantile sexuality. Quite fortuitously, Sanford Bell, a fellow of Clark University, was present as his ally. In 1902, three years before Freud's *Three Essays on the Theory of Sexuality*, Bell had published a paper in the *American Journal of Psychology* describing having abundantly observed infantile sexuality, establishing its reality. Freud concluded the series with some cultural criticism and applied psychoanalysis, and gracefully thanked his audience for the opportunity to lecture them and for their genuine interest and understanding.

Freud's lecture was quite the happening, and leading figures in American psychology came to Worcester especially to meet him. William James, America's most celebrated and influential psychologist, was present. After the lecture, James and Freud took a momentous walk together, which Freud later described in his autobiographical study. Suffering from heart disease, which would kill him a year later, James suddenly stopped, handed Freud his briefcase, and asked him to walk on, as he felt an attack of angina pectoris coming on, and told Freud he would catch up with him as soon as it was over. "Since then," Freud, who long brooded on his own death, commented, "I have always wished for a similar fearlessness in face of the near end of life."

James had been following Freud's writings since 1894, when he came upon Freud and Breuer's "Preliminary Communication" on hysteria. Although skeptical, he was open-minded about and interested in Freud's intriguing new ideas. For James, to whom religious experience was the higher truth, Freud's greatest shortcoming was his open hostility to religion. Nevertheless, he remained graciously supportive. Bidding farewell to Ernest Jones in Worcester, who had accompanied Freud, as did Carl Jung and Sándor Ferenczi, Freud put an arm around his shoulder and, as if he were a seer, told him, "The future of psychology belongs to your work."

But it was another member of the audience who would champion psychoanalysis in the United States far more than James could. James Jackson Putnam, a Harvard professor and neurologist, gave Freud his wholehearted support. As early as 1904, Putnam had been treating hysterical patients at Massachusetts General Hospital and found the psychoanalytic method useful. His interest opened psychoanalytic ideas to American psychiatry. The Clark lectures, and his intensive discussions with Freud, convinced Putnam that psychoanalytic theories and treatment were valid. But no one, not Putnam, James, or Clark, could have predicted that psychoanalysis would grip the nation's psyche—that *Freud* would become a household word.

Anal Character

Aunt Margaret is rigid in her habits, overly clean, orderly, stingy, and stubborn; in short, she's anal retentive. According to Freud, she's fixated in the anal stage in the psychological and sexual development of the infant, the time of toilet training that lasts from one and a half years of age to about three, placing demands on the child for neatness, cleanliness, and bodily control. A part of her remains stuck in this stage because her mother enforced an early toilet training program before Aunt Margaret had the sphincter control and emotional maturity to handle holding it in until she made it to the potty.

Being anal retentive is used interchangeably with being obsessive-compulsive. Freud characterized his own son, Oliver, who was overly concerned about being orderly and with classifying, as anal retentive.

See **Childhood Sexuality; Obsession and Compulsion**.

Analysis of Self

Freud created psychoanalysis in part from the tales told by the troubled souls lying on his couch. But to grasp their demons, he knew he would first have to grapple with his own.

Saddled with depression, migraines, fainting, deep fears of dying, and unresolved issues with his mother and father, Freud, in the summer of 1897, began a lifelong self-analysis that employed the same inquiry that he was shaping with his patients. As he unearthed material from early memories and dreams, many shared in *The Interpretation of Dreams*, he translated these psychological traumas in letters to his close friend and confidant, Wilhelm Fliess. Had he not made this momentous step, and, as with most children, tucked away his dreams and early memories, we would probably be asking "Sigmund who?" and Western civilization would be radically different from how we know it today. But for Freud, these experiences, in turn intriguing and dangerous, would become grist for the psychoanalytic mill. His pinnacle discoveries reveal both the man and the origin of key ideas.

The overriding impetus for Freud's self-analysis was the death of his father Jacob Freud in October 1896. Freud felt strangely ambivalent for this man of "deep wisdom and fantastic light-heartedness." On the one hand, he felt profound loss. He wrote to Fliess about a feeling of "being torn up by the roots" that troubled him for some months, and four years later, in *The Interpretation of Dreams*, described his father's death as "the most poignant loss of a man's life." But following the funeral a dream made Freud question how sorry he really felt, and this provoked unexpected guilt.

In the dream, he saw a sign hanging in a barbershop that he visited every day, on which appeared either "You are requested to close the eyes" or "You are requested to close an eye." Which was it? Freud pondered, as each had its own meaning and led down a different path. It was the second.

> I had chosen the simplest possible ritual for the funeral, for I knew my father's own views on such ceremonies. But some other members of the family were not sympathetic to such puritanical simplicity and thought we should be disgraced in the eyes of those who attended the funeral. Hence one of the versions: "You are requested to close an eye," i.e., to "wink" or "overlook" [the simplicity of the services].

To Freud, the dream symbolized self-reproach for failing to provide the proper full-fledged funeral that his family wanted and expected. Simultaneously, the dream represented filial duty: the closing of his father's eyes at death. In a word image, the dream craftily condensed "failing to do your duty" with "filial duty."

But Freud suspected that the dream represented even deeper guilt. Could it be that he had not loved his father as much as he professed? The family thought so. On the day of the funeral, Freud had been detained in a barbershop and arrived late. His lateness, along with his wish for simple last rites for his father, showed lack of respect. Freud, too, worried that his behavior revealed ambivalent feelings toward his father.

Why was he hostile toward his father and why did he feel guilty? Freud exhaustively analyzed these questions. One troubling memory was a story the elder Freud told his son, then around eleven, on one of their walks together. "When I was a young fellow, one Saturday

I went for a walk in the streets of your birthplace. I was well dressed, and had a new fur cap on my head. A Christian came up to me and with a single blow knocked off my cap into the mud and shouted: 'Jew! get off the pavement!'" "And what did you do?" asked the son. "I went into the roadway and picked up my cap," replied the father. This struck Freud as "unheroic conduct." A father is supposed to be a "big strong man"; how else can he protect the young son?

This incident was a turning point in Freud's life. Although kind and loving, Jacob Freud was a weak, ineffective man who had lost the family's money and put them in poverty. Freud's mother, Amalia, dominated the family. Having lacked the security of the all-powerful father who would protect him from harm, Freud had to be very strong to compensate for his father's weakness. *He* would never grovel to a gentile. He would be like the intrepid Semite Hannibal, who had sworn to avenge Carthage no matter how mighty the Romans.

Freud was not only disappointed in his father's weak behavior, but some part of Freud doubted his father's love, evident in this humiliating incident that occurred when Freud was seven or eight and is recounted in *The Interpretation of Dreams*. The young Freud had urinated in his parents' bedroom. Infuriated, Jacob Freud blurted out, "The boy will come to nothing." This "terrible blow" to his "ambition" haunted Freud for years and continued to replay in his dreams. Whenever he recalled it, he enumerated his successes, as if to say to his father, "You see, I *have* come to something." Although Jacob Freud was proud of his firstborn and enormously supportive of his son's ambitions, Freud *felt* unappreciated and insignificant. When asked what he would change if he were to relive his life, Freud, one of the most original thinkers of the twentieth century, replied that he would wish for "a better brain," a telling remark of his basic feelings of worthlessness.

Freud's mixed feelings for his father gripped him all his life. In 1904, eight years after his father's death, Freud and his brother, Alexander, while vacationing in Greece, visited the Acropolis, where Freud experienced an overwhelming sensation of unreality, as if what he saw was not really there—a "splitting of consciousness."

Why Athens? Why the Acropolis? To Freud the child, Athens seemed unreal. Nor was he certain he would ever actually see it. Because his family was poor, going far away meant becoming successful enough to travel to distant lands. To achieve this meant feeling like a "hero who has performed deeds of improbable greatness." And Freud had a lifetime travel phobia. Being in Athens filled him with guilt, as if he had symbolically triumphed over his dead father: "The very theme of Athens and the Acropolis in itself contained evidence of the son's superiority. Our father had been in business, he had no secondary education, and Athens could not have meant much to him. Thus what interfered with our enjoyment of the journey to Athens was a feeling of *filial piety*." Torn between the need to be better than his father and his guilt for feeling this, Freud disassociated and temporarily lost his sense of self.

As Freud's self-analysis progressed, darker and more sinister depths of his unconscious spilled out beyond hostile feelings for his father. Freud discovered a sexual interest in his mother, jealousy of an older brother as his rival, and a wish for the death of a younger sibling—in short, the makings of Freud's own Oedipal stirrings and the fodder for his quickly evolving ideas of the then preposterous notion of childhood sexuality.

In October 1897, one fragment of a memory in particular came to him and opened the dam of his suppressed childhood sexuality: a memory of a woman, "ugly, elderly, but clever"—his very religious Catholic nanny who taught him much about "God Almighty and Hell," including a scary account of souls in hell, and was his "instructress in sexual matters." Coupled with this memory was a seemingly unconnected event: a train ride with his mother when he was two and a half (scholars place him at age four), that he described in a letter to his friend Wilhelm Fliess and is Freud's first awareness that the child experiences "sexual" impulses toward his mother:

My libido [sexual interest] was stirred up towards *matrem* [mother], namely on the occasion of a journey with her from Leipzig to Vienna, during which we must have spent the night together and I must have had an opportunity of seeing her *nudam* [naked].

By "sexual," Freud meant *all* pleasurable and affectionate interactions between mother and child (see **Childhood Sexuality**). Why did Freud connect the two memories? He probed the answer for years. The nanny of whom he was very fond, although he remembered her chiding him for being inept and clumsy, took over care of the young Freud when his mother was in the last stages of pregnancy with Freud's younger sister, Anna. Suddenly, the nanny disappeared, along with his mother, confined following the birth of Anna, and he felt at once abandoned by both mothers. Freud later discovered that his much older half-brother, Philipp, had the nanny arrested for stealing the young child's silver coins and toys, and she was sent to prison.

The nanny's disappearance, coinciding with his mother's absence, produced a vague, unpleasant memory that Freud managed to interpret only many years later. He remembered searching frantically for his mother and "screaming" his "head off." Philipp was holding open a cupboard and the young Freud peered in to look for her, but his mother was not inside. He began crying even more until his mother, "looking slim and beautiful," came in by the door.

Why should Philipp show the distressed young Freud an empty cupboard? In 1897, at the height of his self-analysis, Freud discovered the answer: when he had asked Philipp where the nanny had gone, Philipp said that she was *eingekastelt*—"boxed in"—a joking reference to her being in jail, where she remained imprisoned for ten months: "Now I must have thought that my mother had been too—or rather had been 'boxed up'; for my brother Philipp, who is 63 now, is fond to this very day of talking in this punning fashion."

In *The Psychopathology of Everyday Life*, Freud analyzed the incident in detail. The young Freud had requested that Philipp open the cupboard because he "had understood that the little sister (Anna) who had recently arrived had grown inside his mother." Full of hate for this new addition, he feared "that his mother's inside might conceal still more children." The cupboard symbolized his mother's inside, so the child insisted on looking. He turned to his big brother, who had taken his father's place as the child's rival, suspecting that Philipp had not only had the lost nurse "boxed up" but that he had introduced the recently born baby into his mother's inside. To Freud's relief, when she did appear, slim and beautiful, she was no longer with any other *unwanted* children.

Another of Freud's dreams, a brilliant example of the complexity of the verbal linkages we employ to defensively disguise threatening wishes, sheds further light on his discovery of Oedipal feelings for his mother. In his seventh or eighth year, he had dreamed of his mother with a "peculiarly peaceful, sleeping expression on her features." In the dream, he saw her being carried into a room by two or three people with birds' beaks and laid upon a bed. This dream has multiple meanings (see **Family, the Mother: Amalia Freud**). But one association in particular came to Freud's mind: the bizarre creatures were similar to the illustrations of bird-masked people in a particular edition of the Bible called the *Phillippson Bible*. Probing deeper, he associated the name Phillippson with a memory of an "ill-mannered boy" named Phillipp, who introduced the young Freud to the vulgar word for sexual intercourse—*vogel* in German, the proper form of which means "bird." Freud the master decoder uncovered a link from people with birds' beaks to the *Phillippson Bible* to the boy named Phillipp that revealed a sexual component to the dream images.

Further analysis led him deeper down an erotic path. The expression on his mother's face in the dream reminded him of his dead grandfather, who he had observed in a coma a few days before his death. But why, Freud pondered, would he depict his mother in a state similar to death? Surely he did not wish that his mother die. In fact, the nightmare awoke the young child who anxiously ran into his parents' room to wake his mother to confirm that she was still alive. Perhaps the anxiety over death was a disguise to cover a sexual longing *for his mother*. Freud had uncovered the basic shell of his sexual theory that entered the common parlance as the Oedipal conflict: ambivalence toward his father, the rival, and sexual longing for his mother.

The man who made *neurotic* a household word had another motive for undertaking his self-analysis: the discovery of his own neurotic symptoms. Freud had two lasting fears: he worried that he would die early, as he had some cardiac problems, and he had a lifelong travel phobia. His deep fear of dying started even before he fell into ill health. Upon departing on a trip, he would often say, "Goodbye. You may never see me again." His fear of death had a bit of paranoia; he fainted when, previous to boarding the ship for the United States, Jung went on about corpses (see **Fainting Spells**). It even led him down a path of superstition and the occult. He believed he would die on a certain day (see **Occult**).

Freud's travel phobia began at age three. Apparently he would often compulsively arrive at a railway station hours before his train was scheduled to depart so that he wouldn't miss it. But he would just as likely enter the wrong rail station or board the wrong train. He analyzed his conflicting behavior as possible anxiety about embarking on a journey. But it also indicated a fear of separation and abandonment, as did his fear of dying (see **Family, the Mother: Amalia Freud**).

Andreas-Salomé, Lou
(1861–1937)

In 1911, fifty-one-year-old Lou Andreas-Salomé, a notable novelist and essayist, was introduced to Freud at the Weimar Psychoanalytic Congress that she attended with her friend and much younger lover, the Swedish neurologist Poul Bjerre, who was married. Half a year after her first meeting with Freud, she went to Vienna to study psychoanalysis. A shining presence among the mostly neurotic men that constituted Freud's followers, Lou captivated Freud and his followers with her intelligence, depth of understanding, and warmth, and soon became part of Freud's inner circle and one of the first female psychoanalysts.

That Lou quickly enchanted Freud and his flock is no surprise. Energetic, beautiful, and seductive, she was a lover to half of intellectual turn-of-the-century Europe. She had been a close friend of Nietzsche's in the early 1880s, although to his great disappointment they weren't romantically involved. She became romantically involved with the poet Rainer Marid and later with Rilke, who may have been thirty-three-year-old Lou's first lover, and other distinguished men of the time. In 1887, she married Friedrich Carl Andreas, an orientalist, and remained married to him until her death. The marriage was chaste, and Lou, freed from bourgeois restraint and with a vast appetite for brilliant men, took lovers when and where she pleased.

From their first meeting, Freud felt Lou's effervescent magnetic pull. He wrote, "I missed you in the lecture yesterday. . . . I have adopted the bad habit of directing lecture to a definite member of the audience, and yesterday I fixed my gaze as if spellbound at the place which had been kept for you." He lovingly called her a muse. But surrounded by geniuses who sought her favor, Lou did not need to play a supporting role to even Freud. Her impressive writings, striking intelligence, and gift for absorbing new ideas made her feel at one with brilliance.

Fascinated with Freud's thoughts, she read everything and immediately showed, said the psychoanalyst Karl Abraham, who knew her in Berlin, a comprehension of psychoanalysis that he had never encountered. Freud called her "a female of dangerous intelligence" and later said to her, "You are an understander *par excellence.*" She seemed to view psychoanalysis, he said, as a "Christmas present" he had bought her. Lou stood out for the refreshing quality she brought to the group.

Not all her involvements in Vienna were purely intellectual. Rumors are that she had a brief affair with the much younger psychoanalyst Victor Tausk, one of Freud's strongest devotees, although he irritated Freud and later committed suicide. Nor was Lou totally intellectually faithful to Freud. Lou liked to play all hands at once, and at the beginning of her stay in Vienna, she toyed with the psychologist Alfred Adler's ideas, then already verboten in the Freudian camp. But Lou, long seeking her own god, eventually found it in Freud. She made psychoanalysis her religion, honoring Freud in her book *My Thanks to Freud*, and became fiercely loyal to him. He was, after all, the man who wrote of how society stifles one's instinctual urges and Lou had lived her life rebelling against such restraint, particularly of Eros. As the years went by and she began to practice psychoanalysis in Göttingen, she and Freud routinely corresponded in loving letters, and she became a surrogate mother to Anna Freud. Lou died in 1937, two years before Freud, who delivered her eulogy.

Anna O. (Case)

The birth of psychoanalysis emerged from two seminal events: Freud's self-analysis and the search for a meaning to the unexplainable behavior of a case that was not even his—Anna O.

In the fateful year of 1882, twenty-three-year-old Anna O. (whose real name was Bertha Pappenheim), a patient of the Viennese physician Josef Breuer, lay writhing in her bed with labor pains and the usual signs of advanced pregnancy. Anna O. bore no child. Her pregnancy was a "phantom pregnancy." Anna O. unconsciously believed that Breuer had impregnated her. The hysterical pregnancy was a symptom of her *hysterical neurosis*, a disorder recognized since antiquity.

The case of Anna O., however, did bear fruit beyond Breuer's imagination. From it sprouted a theory of hysteria, a method of psychological treatment that Anna O. named "chimney sweeping," and the epic theory of personality and psychotherapy that the young Sigmund Freud, enthralled by this case, was to almost singlehandedly formulate.

Charming, attractive, intelligent, poetic, and witty, twenty-one-year-old Anna O. was referred to Breuer in 1880 because of a severe and persistent cough that she developed while caring for her terminally ill father. She also began to refuse food, became weak and anemic, and developed even more bizarre symptoms of paralysis, muscle contractures, visual hallucinations, and loss of feeling in her hands and feet. No physical basis could be found for these symptoms; Breuer diagnosed her cough and other symptoms as hysterical neurosis.

Anna alternated between two states, or two selves. In one, she was aware of her surroundings, and although "melancholy and anxious," she seemed relatively normal. In the other state, she hallucinated and was "naughty"; she would throw cushions at people to the degree that her contracted limbs permitted movement, tore buttons off her clothes with the fingers that she could move, and other such behavior. Her moods changed rapidly: at one moment she had "temporary high spirits, and at other times severe anxiety, stubborn opposition to every therapeutic effort and frightening hallucinations of black snakes, which was how she saw her hair ribbons and similar things."

Other disturbing symptoms emerged. In conversation, she occasionally omitted necessary words until her speech became nonsensical. For two weeks she became mute; she struggled to speak, but no words came out. Next, Anna, whose native tongue was German, spoke only English. Apparently unaware of her changed speech, she was as oblivious to her unintelligibility as during her weeks of silence.

Nine months after these speech disturbances developed, Anna O.'s father died. "This was the most severe physical trauma that she could possibly have experienced. A violent outburst of excitement was succeeded by profound stupor which lasted about two days and from which she emerged in a greatly changed state." She again experienced loss of feeling in her hands and feet and paralysis, along with tunnel vision—her field of vision greatly narrowed, as if she were looking through a cylinder. For example, "in a bunch of flowers which gave her much pleasure she could only see one flower at a time." Unable to easily recognize faces, she had to say, "this person's nose is such-and-such, his hair is such-and-such, so he must be so-and-so."

During the day, Anna was acutely distressed; she hallucinated and talked incoherently. Toward afternoon, she became sleepy and quiet. By sunset, she fell into a deep trance, which she described in English as "clouds." She fantasized sad, poetic fairy tales that became even more tragic after her father's death. Typically, they involved an anxious young girl sitting near the bedside of a patient. When Breuer visited her in the evening, he would repeat several words or phrases from her mutterings. This triggered her to recount to Breuer her daytime hallucinations and stories; afterward, she became quieter, more logical, and even cheerful.

Breuer also tried to hypnotize Anna. Under hypnosis, he would ask what her thoughts were of a particular symptom. Some of Anna O.'s visual disturbances, language problems, hallucinations, and the paralysis of her right arm vanished after she was able to recount the story under hypnosis of a particularly long and frightening night vigil she had spent at her sick father's bedside.

> She fell into a waking dream and saw a black snake coming towards the sick man from the wall to bite him. . . . Her right arm, over the back of the chair, had gone to sleep and had become anaesthetic and paretic; and when she looked at it the fingers turned into little snakes with death's heads (the nails). When the snake vanished, in her terror she tried to pray. But language failed her: she could find no tongue in which to speak, till at last she thought of some children's verses in English, and then found herself able to think and pray in that language.
>
> . . . [O]n (another) occasion, when she was sitting by her father's bedside with tears in her eyes, he suddenly asked her what time it was. She could not see clearly; she made a great effort, and brought her watch near to her eyes. The face of the watch now seemed very big—thus accounting for her macropsia [tunnel vision] and convergent squint. Or again, she tried hard to suppress her tears so that the sick man should not see them.

Using hypnosis, Breuer discovered with Anna O.'s help that her hysterical ravings possessed a hidden emotional logic. The symptoms symbolized an unresolved conflict or problem that could be traced back to traumatic past experiences, some from childhood. Although no longer consciously remembered, these "strangulated emotions" survived unconsciously; pressing for release, they converted into bodily symptoms. While rambling in a hypnotic trance, Anna was in effect reliving the original experience, with the attended original emotions now "unstrangled." This "chimney sweeping," as the highly intelligent patient termed it, brought about a verbal catharsis. One by one, the symptoms dropped away, some permanently. Unknowingly, Anna O. and Breuer discovered a "talking cure."

During the almost two-year course of the treatment, an intimate and intense relationship developed between Breuer and Anna O.: Breuer's wife became jealous and Breuer began to feel guilty. He ended his treatment of Anna, now markedly improved, but after telling her, was fetched back to find her highly excited and as "ill as ever," in the now famous throes of false childbirth. As Breuer related to Freud years later:

> The patient, who according to him had appeared to be an asexual being and had never made any allusion to such a forbidden topic throughout the treatment, was now in the throes of an hysterical childbirth (pseudocyesis), the logical termination of a phantom pregnancy that had been invisibly developing in response to Breuer's ministrations. Though profoundly shocked, he managed to calm her down by hypnotizing her, and then fled the house in a cold sweat. The next day he and his wife left for Venice to spend a second honeymoon.

Breuer, of course, had no way of knowing that Anna had displaced her feelings for her father or some other highly significant other onto him—that the pseudopregnancy constituted the transference of feelings onto the analyst that would become the focus of a psychoanalysis, and the working through of these feelings the catalyst for the cure.

Upon terminating the case of Anna O., Breuer described the details to a greatly intrigued Freud, who questioned him incessantly. Freud pondered the strange case for ten years, obsessed with figuring out the riddle of hysteria. Their historic collaboration into the psychological roots of hysteria culminated in the landmark publication of *Studies on Hysteria* and launched psychoanalysis. In this book, Breuer presented the case of Anna O., while Freud presented four cases: Elisabeth von R., Emmy von N., Katharina, and Lucy R.

The two founders of psychoanalysis conclusively state that *"hysterics suffer mainly from reminiscences"*—from the memory of traumatic childhood events, the emotions of which convert to bodily symptoms. The physical symptoms of hysteria, said Freud, are like the monuments that people erect to commemorate important historical events.

Bertha Pappenheim eventually overcame her hysteria, if that is what she had. Today, her volatile emotions, terror, debilitating physical symptoms, depression, extreme mood shifts, and presence of multiple selves would point to a severe dissociative disorder. This condition is commonly seen in patients who have been traumatized or abused and suffer from posttraumatic stress disorder (PTSD), as it appears Bertha had. Of her three siblings, two had died of tuberculosis, and at the time of her breakdown, she was nursing her father, to whom she was very attached and who also appeared to be dying of tuberculosis.

Never marrying, Bertha Pappenheim became an active feminist, writer, and legendary figure in social work in Germany. Even in the depths of her illness as a young woman, she had looked after the poor and sick. In 1954, the West German government issued a postage stamp bearing her image. Ardently antireligious in her youth, she later became deeply religious and selfless. She died in March 1936, having escaped the Nazi nightmare.

See also **Breuer, Josef; Feminism; Hysteria.**

Antiquities

Long interested in archaeology and ancient or "dead" cultures, Freud began collecting antiquities in 1896, the year that his father died. Hunting down ancient artifacts would become a lifelong passion, and his collection eventually included Greek, Roman, Egyptian, Etruscan, and Far Eastern items.

Antiquities filled Freud's office, including artwork that revealed his ideas about unconscious motives. One piece was an engraving of Andre Brouillet's painting *La Lefon Clinique du Dr Charcot*, which shows Jean Charcot demonstrating a female hysteric to a rapt audience in the Salpêtrière Hospital. Sitting in his large armchair during therapy, behind the famous couch, Freud could eye a large picture of an Egyptian temple at Abu Simbel, a small reproduction of Ingres's painting of Oedipus interrogating the Sphinx, and a plaster cast of an antique relief, *Gradiva*. On the opposite wall, above a glass cabinet filled with ancient objects, was a picture of the Sphinx at Giza. Enthralled by Freud's ancient objects, the Wolf Man, one of Freud's case studies, commented: "There was always a feeling of sacred peace and quiet" in Freud's "two adjoining studies"; he was reminded not of "a doctor's office but rather of an archeologist's study. Here were all kinds of statuettes and other unusual objects, which even the layman recognized as archeological."

Freud's collecting was in a sense a metaphor for his life work. He told the Wolf Man that "the psychoanalyst, like the archeologist in his excavations, must uncover layer after layer of the patient's psyche, before coming to the deepest, most valuable treasures." In 1896, lecturing on the etiology of hysteria before his Viennese medical colleagues, Freud said that the student of hysteria is like an explorer discovering the remains of an abandoned city, with walls and columns and tablets covered with half-effaced inscriptions; he may dig them up and clean them, and, if lucky, "*saxa loquuntur!* [stones speak]" he cried out.

Writing his confidant, Wilhelm Fliess, Freud compared an analytic success he had just enjoyed to the discovery of Troy. With Freud's help, buried deep beneath fantasies, a patient had found "a scene from his primal period which answers all requirements and into which all left-over riddles flow; it is everything at once, sexual, innocuous, natural, etc. I still scarcely dare to believe it properly. It is as if Schliemann had dug up Troy, considered legendary, once again." In his preface to the case history of Dora, he compared the problems presented by the "incompleteness of my analytic results" to those faced by "explorers fortunate enough to bring to the light of day after long burial the priceless though mutilated remnants of antiquity."

Anti-Semitism

Freud, appalled that his father had groveled to a gentile in response to an anti-Semitic attack, decided that he would be like the intrepid Semite Hannibal, who had sworn to avenge Carthage no matter how mighty the Romans (see **Analysis of Self**). He stood his word. He responded to anti-Semitism by fighting it, even risking injury.

In 1883, traveling third class on a train between Dresden and Riesa, studious, reserved, short, and slight Sigmund Freud, who was twenty-three years old, nearly got into a fistfight to defend Judaism, the religion that he had long dismissed as myth. Angered by his opening the window for some fresh air, some roughnecks called him a "dirty Jew" and commented, "'We Christians consider other people, you'd better think less of your precious self,' etc.; and muttering abuses befitting his education, my second opponent announced that he was going to climb over the seats to show me, etc." Not in the "least frightened of that mob," Freud invited his opponents to step up and told one rabble-rouser in particular to take what was coming to him. "I was quite prepared to kill him, but he did not step up."

Freud showed similar chutzpah in 1901, his son Martin recalled, in the Bavarian summer resort of Thumsee, where Freud charged furiously with his walking stick at a gang of about ten men and some female supporters who had been shouting anti-Semitic abuse at Martin and his brother Oliver. Freud was prepared to be injured rather than cower submissively as his father had (see **Analysis of Self**).

From the first time Freud encountered anti-Semitism at the University of Vienna, he defied the insults. He refused to "feel inferior," as his gentile fellow students insolently expected him to be a stranger to the Austrian people "because I was a Jew. . . . I never understood why I should be ashamed of my descent or, as one was beginning to say, my race." With the same self-respect and "without much regret," he traded belonging for isolation, which served him better because it created "a certain independence of judgment."

Although an atheist, Freud felt a strong Jewish identity created partly by anti-Semitism: he believed Jews could never trust gentiles. He expressed his worries to his ardent follower Karl Abraham about the "hidden anti-Semitism of the Swiss" and felt it wise to acquiesce: "We must, as Jews, if we want to join in anywhere, develop a bit of masochism," even accept "a measure of injustice." "We are and remain Jews," he wrote to a Jewish correspondent; "the others will always simply exploit us and never understand or appreciate us." To Freud, this compromise was crucial: he had long feared that psychoanalysis, whose members were largely Jewish physicians, would be considered a "Jewish science" and lose its credence. Nor did he doubt that the resistance to psychoanalysis had the whiff of anti-Semitism. Freud resounded on the cost of his being Jewish to Abraham: "Be assured, if my name were Oberhuber, my innovations would have found, despite it all, far less resistance."

Freud's concern about the "hidden anti-Semitism of the Swiss" was not paranoia. In 1933, while Jewish psychoanalysts were being expelled, the Swiss psychologist Carl Jung accepted the presidency of the International Medical Society for Psychotherapy, which meant working with Matthias Heinrich Göring, Hermann's cousin. Threatening to resign on three occasions, Jung was eventually given a figurehead position of honorary president, which he held until 1940. Was Jung anti-Semitic? Although many would argue that he was a Nazi collaborator, the author Deirdre Bair in *Jung* believes that Jung, fitting in with his contradictory nature, was merely playing all sides. While he let the Nazis use him to legitimize their racial theories and he derided Freud—"insofar as his theory is based in certain respects on Jewish premises, it is not valid for non-Jews"—he also tried to help other Jewish analysts.

Anxiety

Angst—we all experience it: the beating heart, the twisted stomach, sweaty hands, rapid breathing, and a general feeling of distress. But what is anxiety exactly? Freud gave us the answer. We feel anxious when we don't know what we are anxious about; we feel fear when we do.

Freud originally proposed that anxiety results from repression of libido or psychic energy. He noticed that practicing *coitus interruptus*, sex without orgasm, a fairly common birth-control method in his time, made his male patients anxious. Using the hydraulic model of energy that was popular then, he theorized that blocked sexual arousal generates uncomfortable energy that seeks release: anxiety is dammed up energy that leaks out. If denied a sexual outlet, we will seek another way out, and in self-protection our ego devises defensive maneuvers.

Libido is not just sexual energy but life energy. Freud felt that the first moment of anxiety is birth, as stimulation exceeds the newborn's capacity to handle it. At the moment of birth, the newborn responds with all the changes we associate with anxiety: massive changes in heart rate and respiration; reddening; kicking and flailing; screaming or crying. Our first trauma becomes the prototype of helplessness in the face of danger. In a footnote to the *Interpretation of Dreams*, Freud wrote that "the act of birth is the first experience of anxiety, and thus the source and prototype of the affect of anxiety."

That anxiety resulted directly from repressed libido was initially considered by Freud to be one of his most important findings, as he stated in a footnote added to *Three Essays* in 1920: "One of the most important results of psycho-analytic research is the discovery that neurotic anxiety arises out of libido, that it is a transformation of it, and that it is thus related to it in the same kind of way as vinegar is to wine." Yet, it did not capture the essence of *Freud's* anxiety—his early fear of separation and loss of his own mother (see **Family, the Mother: Amalia Freud**)—and Freud faced an enigma: if repression created anxiety, what created repression?

Late in his career he realized that he had it backward: anxiety creates repression. In *Inhibition, Symptoms and Anxiety*, seventy-year-old Freud reversed his thinking: "It was anxiety which produced repression and not, as I formerly believed, repression which produced anxiety. . . . It is always the ego's attitude of anxiety which is the primary thing and which sets repression going. Anxiety never arises from repressed libido." Anxiety arises from the danger of losing the love object: "Anxiety arose originally as a reaction to a state of *danger* and it is reproduced whenever a state of that kind recurs. . . . [What are the dangers?] . . . when a child is alone, or in the dark, or when it finds itself with an unknown person instead of one to whom it is used—such as its mother. These three instances can be reduced to a single condition—namely, that of missing someone who is loved and longed for."

This revised theory remains unparalleled. Anxiety is our natural response to helplessness in the face of danger—real or anticipated—warning us to prepare our defenses. You feel anxious when the car in front of you swerves off the road—*real* danger. If you've been in a bad car accident, you may feel anxious driving your car down a quiet back road with little traffic—*anticipated* danger. Although we rarely experience real danger, brooding over what *might* happen is a common experience in our stressed-out, fast-paced world.

How does Freud's theory of sexuality fit in with the revised theory? Consider this example. Jane's parents had always told her that a good girl remains a virgin until marriage. When she was sixteen, she had alcohol at a party and had sex with her boyfriend. The next morning, she felt painfully guilty—her superego punished her for ignoring her parents' teachings and losing her virginity. The next weekend, when sober, the thought of losing herself again to passion made Jane's heart thump, her palms sweat, and her stomach twist—in short, she anticipated the wrath of her superego. To escape the discomfort of overstimulating anxiety, she might have repressed her sexual desire: anxiety creates repression. Or, more commonly, she might have only partially repressed her desire and hopped into bed with her boyfriend but failed to fully enjoy the experience because her brain was yelling, "I shouldn't be doing this."

See **Defense Mechanisms; Family, the Mother: Amalia Freud; Topographical Model**.

Atheist

See **Religion**.

Berggasse 19

In the fall of 1891, the Freuds moved to Berggasse 19, to an apartment on the first floor of an ordinary Viennese house with a butcher shop downstairs. Freud lived there for forty-seven years. A glass plate on the door read "Prof. Dr. Freud 3–4."

The consulting room where Freud saw his patients and his adjoining study overflowed with oriental rugs, photographs of friends, and plaques. The glassed-in bookcases were laden with books and covered with objects, the walls were covered with snapshots and etchings, and every available surface displayed his sculptures. His famous couch, a gift from a grateful patient, was piled high with pillows and had a rug at one end for patients to use if they were cold. It was also covered with a Persian rug, a Shiraz. The pillows placed patients in a comfortable reclining position facing away from Freud to help them focus inward. Freud didn't want people "to stare me in the face for eight hours a day." Freud's chow, Jo-Fi, to whom he was very attached, often sat in his office during analytic sessions throughout Freud's last decade. The dog would sit at the foot of the couch and arise at the appointed time to signal the end of the hour.

See **Antiquities**.

Beyond the Pleasure Principle

At one and a half years, Freud's eldest grandson, Ernst, played a strangely symbolic game. He would throw a toy wooden reel attached to a string in his curtained crib so that it disappeared into a corner of the room or under the bed and croon loudly the German word for "gone" (*fort*) with a peculiarly long, drawn-out "o-o-o-o" pronunciation. Immediately upon throwing his toys, Ernst would pull the reel back and joyfully say *da*—"there."

Freud deduced that Ernst's *fort-da* game symbolized disappearance and return—the infant's separation from and reunion with his mother. When she would leave, he was in a passive and helpless position and could do nothing to bring her back. But by making a symbolic game of her leaving, he translated passive to active: he obtained a sense of mastery over his situation by playing it out with his toy. From this small but significant observation, Freud suggested a model for children's play and, beyond this, for repetitive dreams and symptoms. Young children, as any parent knows, will endlessly repeat meaningful events. Such repetitious play, Freud suggested, helps them to feel the master of situations; events that were passively suffered are turned into active games and stories.

The theory of mastery coherently explained the repetitions encountered in neuroses and dreams. Neurotics seek help because they remain stuck on early unresolved traumas and they repeat them in meaningless cycles: for instance, having been rejected by her father, a woman repeatedly gets involved with married men. Such repetition limits her freedom and creates intense emotional turmoil. She repeats as if compelled. This is also the case with repetitive nightmares of a traumatic experience.

Freud concluded that the repetition compulsion contradicts the pleasure principle because the repetitive attempts are not at wishful gratifications but to master an anxiety-laden experience. To explain this behavior Freud had to go "beyond the pleasure principle." In his essay by that name, published in 1920, Freud found evidence in the repetition compulsion of a second instinct operating alongside Eros. He could only conclude that the death instinct, Thanatos, also rules human destiny.

Binswanger, Ludwig

In 1907, twenty-six-year-old Ludwig Binswanger, a psychiatrist who was later the director of Sanatorium Bellevue in Kreuzlingen, Switzerland, accompanied his friend and colleague Carl Jung to Berggasse 19 to meet the famous Viennese physician. Binswanger stood in awe of Freud's "greatness and dignity" but was neither frightened nor intimidated. His host's "distaste for all formality and etiquette, his personal charm, his simplicity, casual openness and goodness, and, not least, his humor," apparently banished all anxiety. At ease, the three men interpreted one another's dreams, sharing walks and meals.

Although Freud has been accused of being unreceptive to dissent and casting out those infidels who dared to differ with him, he maintained long friendships with people of vastly different perspectives, Ludwig Binswanger being one. When leaving Vienna after his second visit, Freud said to Binswanger, "Follow me as far as you can, and for the rest, let us remain good friends."

Biography

I felt an overpowering need to understand something of the riddles of the world in which we live and perhaps to contribute something to their solution.

—Sigmund Freud

The firstborn to the newly married Amalia Freud and Jacob Freud, Sigismund "Shlomo" Freud (Shlomo was his paternal grandfather's name) arrived on May 6, 1856, in Freiberg, Moravia, a small town in the Austro-Hungarian Empire surrounded by forests. Freud shortened his name to Sigmund after he entered the University of Vienna in 1873. Following a financial reversal in 1859, the family, which consisted of three-year-old Sigmund and Anna (an infant son had died in Freiberg in 1858), moved to Vienna. There Freud lived most of his life, although he despised the city and never ceased to miss the Freiberg countryside. One after another, Amalia and Jacob soon had five more children between 1860 and 1866: Rosa, Marie, Adolfine, Pauline, and Alexander.

Insecure, unhappy, desperately seeking to escape the poverty and humiliation of living in the Jewish ghetto, and wishing to transcend his father's weak character, Freud would proudly tell people that "an old peasant woman had prophesied to my mother, happy over her first-born, that she had given the world a great man." When Freud was eleven or twelve, a fortune-teller in a restaurant prophesied that he would become a minister of state. Convinced he was destined for greatness, Freud firmly believed in these prophesies and framed his life in heroic terms. At the age of twenty-eight, long before he would distinguish himself, he wrote to his fiancée that he had destroyed all his "notes of the last fourteen years, as well as letters, scientific excerpts, and the manuscripts of my papers. . . . As for the biographers, let them worry, we have no desire to make it easy for them. Each one of them will be right in his opinion of 'The Development of the Hero.'"

Though extreme for a poor Jewish boy, his aspirations were not unrealistic. Precocious and a brilliant, exemplary student with a retentive memory, the ambitious and *seemingly* self-assured adolescent had all the makings for a heroic figure. He was first in his class for seven years at the *Communal- Real- und Obergymnasium.* He completed his studies at the Gymnasium with honors. A voracious reader, he once ran up a bookstore debt beyond his means, as he fed his appetite for plays, poetry, and philosophy. This proved fruitful in his writings, where he often resorted to his favorite German classics, notably Goethe and Schiller, and to Shakespeare, whom he could recite at length in his near-perfect English.

The adolescent Freud held court in his family, who catered to his every need, happily fostering and reinforcing the idea of him being exceptional. To lose no time from his studies, he would eat alone in his tiny bedroom, as he had a room of his own from age seventeen, no matter how strained his parents' circumstances. Freud's five sisters, his brother, and their parents crowded into three bedrooms. If his sisters' needs or those of his brother conflicted with Freud's, his won out unquestionably. Unable to concentrate on his school books, he complained about the noise from Anna's piano lessons: the piano vanished forever.

At first, Freud thought that a political career might be his avenue to fame and, to this end, desired to study law at the University of Vienna in hopes of entering a political career. But then he decided that science would be the arena to perform "deeds of improbable greatness" and in 1873, seventeen-year-old Freud entered the University of Vienna to study natural science. He studied the anatomy of the brain, and from 1876 to 1882, worked in the laboratory of Ernst Brücke, an eminent physiologist whom Freud greatly admired and sought to imitate. Freud thrived in Brücke's laboratory and under Brücke's supervision. Forty years Freud's elder, nearly the age of Freud's father, Brücke was the first of Freud's many "intellectual" fathers. Freud described him as "the greatest authority that worked upon me." Following Brücke's death in 1892, Freud named his fourth child, Ernst, after him.

Brücke argued that the true scientist will explain natural phenomena in physical and chemical terms and used the machine as his model; superstition, mysticism, and the occult were all rubbish. This hydraulic model of energy was the conventional model in the late nineteenth century. Influenced by his mentor's teachings, Freud adopted this model in his own theories and argued that the human mind was an energy system—a machine fueled by "psychic" energy, or libido: psychic pressure builds up, bursts out, or gets diverted into other channels. Metaphors abound in the notion of built up energy that seeks release: bottled up; ready to explode; flipping our lid; venting our anger; letting off steam; blowing our stack. For years, Freud would struggle with having deviated from the physiology of the brain to the psychology of the brain, from hard-core science to what many considered more fiction than fact.

Freud's early interests lay in research. But shortly after graduating from medical school in 1881, he was struck with a dilemma: to follow his scientific interests or to earn the money he needed to marry Martha Bernays by becoming a practicing physician. Love won and six weeks after he had committed himself to Martha, who he married in September 1886, he joined the General Hospital in Vienna. For three years, in what we would now term a medical internship, he tried out various medical specialties, from surgery to internal medicine, ophthalmology, dermatology, psychiatry, and nervous diseases, and gained experience in Theodor Meynert's psychiatric clinic. Need for money ultimately decided his interest in neurology. "From a practical perspective," Freud later wrote, "brain anatomy was certainly no advance over physiology. I took material considerations into account by starting the study of nervous diseases."

In the late 1870s, Freud met the Viennese physician Josef Breuer, who befriended him. In 1882, Breuer told Freud of a patient, Anna O., whose hysterical symptoms Breuer had succeeded in curing through hypnosis. The case greatly intrigued Freud, who found that some of his patients displayed symptoms that defied neurological sense. A patient might feel her hand paralyzed, but no sensory nerve was damaged that would numb the entire hand and nothing else. Freud wondered whether their cause might be psychological rather than physical. Seeking an answer set Freud's mind on a path destined to alter human self-understanding—his discovery that beneath our conscious mind and seeming volition lurk unconscious wishes and needs that motivate our behavior: free will is a myth.

His voyage of discovery began in 1885 with a traveling grant to Paris to attend the lectures of Jean Martin Charcot, the legendary neuropathologist at the renowned Salpêtrière Hospital. Investigating the symptoms and causes of hysteria, Charcot induced hysterical paralyses by direct hypnotic suggestion and then removed the symptoms, demonstrating apparent psychological roots of nervous disorders. Fascinated, impressed, and intrigued by Charcot's theatrical demonstrations, Freud began to ponder the power of mental forces hidden from conscious awareness.

Upon returning from Paris and excited about what he had learned, Freud attempted to share Charcot's remarkable findings with the Viennese Society of Physicians, and in October 1886 he read his paper, "On Male Hysteria." The reception was cool, unpleasant, and close to hostile. Afterward, he was excluded from working in Meynert's laboratory and from working with other physicians in the hospital. These were the first of many slights that would become the norm upon Freud presenting his ideas. But Freud was too interested in understanding this curious condition of hysteria to be deterred from his investigations and thereafter took on a me-against-them attitude—one he knew all too well as a Jew in a gentile world. He resigned from the General Hospital and devoted himself fully to a private practice he had opened earlier that year upon returning from Paris.

He treated nervous ailments largely with electrotherapy, which he eventually abandoned as useless, and, following Charcot's lead, as well as that of the French physician Hippolyte Bernheim, whose lab he had visited in Nancy in 1887, began using hypnosis. Freud would prompt his patients to talk freely of their symptoms while hypnotized and discovered that some responded openly and at times became quite agitated. Similar to the relief that he witnessed with Charcot's patients, their symptoms would often thereby lessen or even disappear.

But hypnosis had some inherent problems. Although some patients' symptoms disappeared under hypnosis, the effects didn't last, and they would quickly relapse. And not all patients could be hypnotized. At the prompting of his patients, Freud began to let them speak freely about what came to their mind, regardless of how bizarre, evil, unnatural, or forbidden the thought—to free associate. Soon, he shifted totally from hypnosis to the cathartic talking cure: psychoanalysis was born. By 1892, the outlines of psychoanalytic technique—close observation, fitting interpretation, free association unencumbered by hypnosis, and working through—were in place. By the time he and Breuer published *Studies on Hysteria* in 1895, Freud was developing the psychoanalytic ideas and vocabulary that Western culture would embrace in the twentieth century.

As Freud carefully listened to and observed his mostly middle-class Jewish neurotic female patients, saying, as he had instructed them, whatever came into their minds, he discovered that what was on the minds of these supposedly unsullied Victorian women was sex—their feelings, their fears, their desires, and more than that, something quite disturbing: their terror from having been seduced, often by their fathers. Had Freud heard these stories a few times, he may have dismissed them. But he heard them repeatedly. What else could he deduce but that hysterical and neurotic behavior emanated from early sexual trauma or conflict? His seduction theory was born and shocked the proper, moralistic, and rigid Victorian mores of that time. As he began to lecture on and publish his findings, he was more and more ostracized from the Vienna medical community, shunned by his university colleagues, and rejected by patients. Although he felt alone, he was convinced that what he observed was real and tenaciously dug deeper into the dangerous waters of the unconscious mind, as if their hostility had strengthened his determination. This move was truly heroic. Freud was not only challenging psychiatry as it was then practiced but was proposing ideas that rocked the very foundation of nineteenth-century society.

Freud also gained strength and determination by attaching himself to brilliant men as surrogate father figures, starting with Ernst Brücke. In the midst of such overwhelming rejection from peers, he had Breuer, with whom he collaborated to understand hysteria. But following the publication of *Hysteria*, Freud broke off his friendship with Breuer. By this time, he had become intimately attached to Wilhelm Fliess, a Berlin nose-and-throat specialist who he met through Breuer and who became his confidant and most intimate friend. When the world rejected him, Freud wrote his heart out to Fliess. For example, in April 1896, Freud lectured to experts on deviant sexual behavior at the local Society for Psychiatry and Neurology on "The Etiology of Hysteria": his seduction theory as the cause of hysteria. If any of his colleagues would be receptive to his risqué theories, it would be this educated, professional audience. But as usual, his eloquence fell on deaf ears. "The donkeys gave it an icy reception," he wrote Fliess, who could reassure Freud of the brilliance of his theories.

Nevertheless, recalling these years always left him sad: "For more than a decade after my separation from Breuer, I had no adherents," he wrote a quarter-century later. "I stood wholly isolated. In Vienna, I was shunned. Abroad, no one took notice of me." But ever the iconoclast, Freud accepted his "splendid isolation" and pushed on. He continued to seek out a select circle of men who would welcome him "regardless of my audacity." In 1897, he joined the lodge "Wien" of the Jewish organization B'nai B'rith and began giving popular lectures to the brethren.

Devastated by the death of his father in October 1896, Freud began the painstaking process of his self-analysis. During the process, he pieced together snatches of childhood memories that fueled his pioneering discovery that childhood laid the foundation for all later experience, and he analyzed his own dreams, the basis for the groundbreaking *The Interpretation of Dreams*, published in 1900, when Freud was forty-four years old.

The Interpretation of Dreams was Freud's masterpiece and put psychoanalysis squarely on the map. In this seminal work, Freud demonstrated dreams to be the "royal road to the unconscious" and declared his basic theories of identity, memory, childhood, and sexuality. Yet *Dreams* was initially "hardly reviewed in the professional journals." His first lecture on dreams on May 14, 1900, a turning point in Western civilization, was attended by three people: Mr. Hans Konigstein, Miss Dora Teleky, and Dr. Marcuse (first name unknown).

What kept Freud going? To start, he was tenacious. No matter how controversial or irreverent his ideas, Freud, throughout his long career, defied conventional wisdom and followed his observations of his patients and insight from his self-analysis to build his theory of psychoanalysis, the public and scientific community be damned. And he was immensely curious; his mind never rested. No sooner had *The Interpretation of Dreams* hit the press than Freud's mind was stirring with what would be his most revolutionary, controversial idea—one that would ultimately shatter Victorian thinking but would also be his nemesis: the nature of sexuality. "Things are working in the lowest floor, strange to say," he told Fliess in October 1899. "A theory of sexuality may become the next successor to the dream book." The following January, Freud reported that he was "collecting for the sexual theory and waiting until the piled-up material can be set aflame by a rousing spark." He had been contemplating childhood experience and the controversial Oedipus complex since his own uncovered Oedipal feelings during his self-analysis, and, as early as the fall of 1897, he announced this momentous idea to Fliess. In *The Interpretation of Dreams*, Freud elaborated upon the as-yet-unnamed idea of the universal male passage of love for the mother and hate for the father. By 1900, Freud's long-held ideas about sexuality were coming together in a comprehensive theory.

But Freud's mind, contrary to popular belief, was not only on sex. While working on his book on sexuality, other ideas were rolling off his pen. In 1901, he published *The Psychopathology of Everyday Life*, a book about how our dreams, accidents, and the mistakes we make in daily life have important psychological meaning and can be traced back to unconscious conflicts and instinctual urges. He was also working on the intriguing case of Dora, a young hysteric, which reads like a masterful detective story, and on the psychoanalysis of jokes, which became the subject of a book published in 1905.

Nevertheless, the main event of 1905 was the publication of *Three Essays on the Theory of Sexuality*. Complex and multilayered, *Three Essays* explores several areas related to human sexuality: sexual practices, preferences, and roles; the development of masculine and feminine gender and identity; the development of infantile and childhood sexuality as it progresses through stages designated as oral, anal, and phallic, before reaching maturity in adolescence; and bisexuality, masochism, and sadism. When it finally caught on, it hit like a bombshell and turned Victorian Europe on its back—or at least that was the prevailing fear. Many accused him of being "a dirty-minded pansexualist." They called him a "Viennese libertine," his psychoanalytic papers "pornographic stories about pure virgins," and the psychoanalytic method "mental masturbation." He was accused of writing about sex for monetary gain and of having sex with his patients, who were rapidly dwindling in number.

Yet in spite of all the controversy his theories generated, Freud, who turned fifty on May 6, 1906, had reason to celebrate. Since the turn of the century, he had formulated the basic psychoanalytic ideas that ultimately brought him fame; the dream book and his book on parapraxes started to attract attention, and his reputation began to grow. He had freed himself from his need for a father figure, having broken off ties to Breuer and with Fliess in 1902, and overcame his lifelong travel phobia to visit Rome. In 1902, his ten-year isolation from the Viennese medical community ended. Freud, himself now becoming a father figure, gathered a group of like-minded physicians together to study and discuss psychoanalysis. A small group was beginning to recognize him as a man of heroic proportion, and for his birthday presented him with a medallion with his portrait in profile on one side and Oedipus solving the riddle of the Sphinx on the other. The inscription in Greek, drawn from Sophocles's *Oedipus Rex*, read: "He divined the famous riddle and was a most mighty man." The moment held deep meaning for

Freud. As a student at the university, Freud had fantasized that one day his bust would stand in the courtyard among other departed greats, inscribed with the words on the medallion.

As his followers steadily grew, his "Wednesday Psychological Society" expanded and later extended to other countries: Switzerland in 1907; the United States in 1911. In the meantime, notables such as Eugen Bleuler, the head of the psychiatric clinic of the University of Zurich and the renowned expert on schizophrenia, and his associate, Carl Jung, were applying Freud's ideas. Jung was a pivotal person in Freud's life. Meeting for the first time in 1907, Freud immediately regarded the impressive Swiss as his "intellectual heir." Freud felt that Jung being Aryan and not Jewish would save psychoanalysis from becoming a "Jewish national affair." The two men enjoyed a close relationship until 1911, when Jung, differing with Freud on the central role of sexuality in the neuroses, as did so many others, split with Freud to eventually form Jungian psychology.

On September 10, 1909, Freud received the degree of Doctor of Laws from Clark University in Worcester, Massachusetts. He was delighted and surprised. Although he had his small group of followers in Vienna and others were popping up in Zurich, Berlin, Budapest, London, and even New York, they constituted a small, besieged minority in the psychiatric profession. To most, Freud's ideas remained scandalous, and hurtful rejection continued to come from across Europe and the United States. In 1910, Professor Wilhelm Weygandt, who wrote an unflattering review of *The Interpretation of Dreams* in 1901, declared to the Hamburg Congress of Neurologists and Psychiatrists that Freud's theories were not for scientific debate but "for the police."

Freud was similarly assaulted from overseas. In April 1910, following a vicious attack by a professor of psychiatry in Toronto, Ernest Jones feared that "an ordinary reader would gather that you [Freud] advocate free love, removal of all restraints, and a relapse into savagery!" On April 5, 1912, the *New York Times* reported that the American neurologist Moses Allen Starr, who had briefly worked with Freud in Vienna during the 1880s, denounced Freud's theories at a meeting of the Neurological Section of the Academy of Medicine, describing Freud as "the Viennese psychologist, whose conclusion that all the psychological life of human beings is based on the sex drive has gained considerable hold on American physicians." Starr informed the audience that "Freud was not a man who lived on a particularly high plane. He was not self-repressed. He was not an ascetic," and, Starr thought, "his scientific theory is largely the result of his environment and of the peculiar life he led."

By 1911, however, Freud was partially vindicated. After seventeen years of anxious waiting, he finally received a professorship at the University of Vienna, which entitled him to the prestigious title of Herr Doktor and to give lectures. What took the academic community so long to recognize the man who would forever alter twentieth-century thinking? Apparently his colleagues had finally transcended both anti-Semitism, which was rising in Austria during this period, and the fear of stigma from his scandalous theories on sexuality and the neuroses.

The year 1914 brought World War I, which darkened Freud's outlook and reinforced his anxieties about death and humans' destructive tendencies. Never rich, Freud constantly worried about money, and the devaluation of European currencies at the end of the war wiped out his life savings. All three of his sons were in the Austrian army, and although none was killed or maimed, Freud had been understandably anxious about their welfare. Unable to explain or treat the "shell shock" of some of the soldiers, some medical doctors began applying psychoanalytic theory and technique. Freud's theories were taking hold. At the Fifth International Psychoanalytic Congress in 1918, near the war's end, a hot topic was how to apply psychoanalysis to the psychological war casualties. Freud was elated that his theories were finally being embraced by the world and would not die with him. "I am swimming in satisfaction. I am light hearted, knowing the problem child, my life's work, is protected and preserved for the future."

As Freud entered his mid-sixties in the 1920s, his status as an original thinker—a titan—worthy of respect, recognition, and admiration, was finally guaranteed. Psychoanalysis was now sweeping European and American culture as a new psychic religion, changing sexual mores, exploding in new forms in art, and being talked about in newspapers, novels, plays, and eventually the movies. Many educated people took up psychoanalysis; in New York, it became fashionable to be "psyched."

In spite of psychoanalysis's difficult birth, Freud had now produced many prodigious progeny. The European psychoanalytic institutes and their counterparts in the United States were training more and more psychoanalysts. New journals of psychoanalysis were published in England, the United States, and somewhat later in France and Italy, while Freud's own works became available in languages other than German. With a strong following now in place, Freud freely left the organizational and administrative tasks to others and focused his energy on doing psychoanalysis—he still saw five to six patients a day—and writing.

At last, Freud was deified, as had been his ambition. But he could not fully enjoy his hard-won status. As psychoanalysis was flourishing, Freud was deteriorating. Old, ill, and often betrayed by friends and followers, he felt increasingly more disheartened and pessimistic about people and even about the therapeutic value of psychoanalysis. Freud's daughter Sophie, his "Sunday child," had died of post-war influenza in 1920. He felt horrible that he had outlived her; years later, he seemed relieved when his mother died before him. In 1923, Sophie's son and Freud's favorite grandson, Heinz—"Heinele"—died, and Freud, a longtime cigar smoker, learned of his cancer of the jaw and mouth from which he would eventually die. As his cancer advanced, he endured chronic pain and thirty-three operations on his mouth, and he was forced to wear a prosthesis, which made talking difficult. In constant pain and forced increasingly into convalescence, he withdrew from society and psychoanalytic functions. Nevertheless, Freud continued to see patients, keep up with his correspondence, and write more noteworthy essays.

Beyond the Pleasure Principle, published in 1920, shortly after the war's end, reflected his illness, losses, and deep pessimism of humankind following the barbarism of World War I. In it, Freud presented his new and extremely controversial ideas about death instincts, suggesting that humans unconsciously desire their own death and often project this desire outward in aggressive, even murderous, behavior toward others. Whereas previously he had felt that libido had driven all behavior, he now identified two basic instinctual urges as the underlying motivators of all behavior and experience: life instincts, expressed directly in sexuality; and death instincts, expressed in aggression.

His pessimism about humankind was reinforced in *Civilization and Its Discontents*, published in 1930. Freud concluded that the potential for happiness will always be restricted by our socially repressed sexuality and aggressivity. "If civilization," he wrote, "imposes such great sacrifices not only on man's sexuality but on his aggressivity, we can understand better why it is hard for him to be happy in that civilization." Still, although his life was cheerless and the book pessimistic, Freud could take heart in its astonishing popularity; within a year, *Civilization and Its Discontents* sold out at twelve thousand copies.

The man whose theories had been ridiculed, ignored, and derided in middle age now unwittingly found himself a cause célèbre but was too ill to rejoice. In 1932, for his seventy-fifth birthday, celebrations broke out, as he wrote his longtime friend, Lou Andreas-Salomé, like a "flood." An avalanche of letters arrived from friends and strangers, psychoanalysts, psychiatrists, and other admirers. Telegrams poured in from organizations and dignitaries, and Berggasse 19 was strewn with flowers. A German congress of psychotherapists scheduled papers in his honor, and supporters in New York organized a festive banquet at the Ritz-Carlton, with speeches by the eminent American psychiatrist William Alanson White and A. A. Brill, the founder of the New York Psychoanalytic Society, seconded by celebrities like Theodore Dreiser and Clarence Darrow. "Men and women recruited from the ranks of psychoanalysis, medicine and sociology," read the telegram the celebrants sent to Freud, "are assembling in New York to honor themselves by honoring on his 75th birthday the intrepid explorer who discovered the submerged continents of the ego and gave a new orientation to science and life." The Herzl Club greeted Freud "reverentially" as "the son of our people, whose seventy-fifth birthday is a day of joy and pride for all of Jewry," while Viennese institutions such as the Psychiatric Neurological Clinic and the Association for Applied Psychopathology and Psychology sent their warmest greetings.

Freud took some of these tributes coolly, even resentfully. When he learned in March that to celebrate his seventy-fifth birthday the Society of Physicians proposed to make him an honorary member, he bitterly recalled the humiliations the Viennese medical establishment had visited on him decades before. In a letter to the psychoanalyst Max Eitingon, Freud called the nomination repellent, a cowardly reaction to his recent successes; he thought he would accept it with a curt, distant acknowledgment.

Although still active, Freud at seventy-five was increasingly incapacitated. In mid-July 1936, his surgeon, Dr. Hans Pichler, operated on him for the third time that year and found a recurrence of cancer. In December, Pichler operated once more, and on the twenty-fourth Freud recorded in his terse manner, "Christmas in pain."

The political situation mirrored Freud's deteriorating state. In a letter written to Freud in March 1933, the Hungarian psychoanalyst Sándor Ferenczi, one of Freud's closest followers, urgently implored Freud to leave Austria as the Nazi threat escalated. Old, ill, and dependent on his physicians, Freud refused. Freud consoled himself and Ferenczi that it was uncertain "that the Hitler regime will also overwhelm Austria. It is indeed possible, but everyone believes that things here will not reach the height of brutality they have in Germany." He concluded firmly, "Flight would be justified, I believe, only if there were a direct danger to life."

That became ever more a threat when on March 12, 1938, Freud sat by his radio listening to the sound of Germans taking over Austria. Partly shielded by his international reputation and his tenacious friends, Freud was spared most of the terror that ensued in the following days but not all of it. On March 15, the day after recording Hitler's arrival in Vienna, both the office of the psychoanalytic publishing house at Berggasse 7 and Freud's apartment at Berggasse 19 were invaded by the Nazis. They searched the files of the *Verlag* and held Freud's son, Martin, prisoner all day, but luckily failed to find some of the compromising documents stored in the office: Freud's will, kept there, would have revealed that he had funds abroad. At the apartment, storm troopers confiscated $500.

Freud, at age eighty-two, finally agreed to exile. Arriving in London in early June 1938, he wrote, "The feeling of triumph at liberation is mingled too strongly with mourning . . . for one had still very much loved the prison from which one has been released." Four of Freud's five sisters were left behind in Vienna when the family escaped to London, and they were all killed in concentration camps in 1942.

Sigmund Freud died in London in 1939. He was eighty-three. Martha Freud died in London in 1951.

Breuer, Josef
(1842–1925)

An intimate friend and a hated enemy have always been necessary requirements of my emotional life. I always knew how to provide myself with both over and over.

—Sigmund Freud, *The Interpretation of Dreams*

In the late 1870s, while studying at the University of Vienna, Freud was befriended by Josef Breuer, an affluent, respected, highly cultivated, and prominent Jewish physician who had made some important contributions to physiology. Sensitive, generous, and compassionate, Breuer, who was fourteen years Freud's senior, grew very fond of Freud and took a strong interest in him as well as his career. Their relationship grew warm and intimate, and Breuer became Freud's next father figure, following Ernst Brücke. Freud admired Breuer and referred to him as "the ever-loyal Breuer" to his fiancée, Martha Bernays. In 1882, twenty-six-year-old Freud, who was about to marry Martha and begin a family, worried about his financial position as a neurologist. Breuer helped a reluctant Freud to get established as a private physician in Vienna, a more financially rewarding position than research scientist. When Freud was short on cash, Breuer repeatedly loaned Freud money without expecting it back.

In 1882, Breuer introduced Freud to the case of Anna O. and the cathartic method, or the "talking cure" as Anna phrased it. This famous case was the embryo that hatched psychoanalysis, and in Freud's speech at Clark University in 1909, Freud acknowledged Breuer as the true founder of psychoanalysis. Their work culminated in the landmark publication of *Studies in Hysteria*.

The collaboration between the two founders ended in a bitter feud sometime in the 1890s. Freud and Breuer disagreed about the proper role of sexuality in the etiology of hysteria and other mental disturbances: Freud, wishing to risk putting all his fertile eggs in one basket, claimed all neuroses have a sexual component; Breuer, more cautious in his conclusions, disagreed. Freud believed that Breuer had betrayed him and the two parted as enemies, never again to meet as friends—a pattern Freud would compulsively repeat.

See **Anna O.**

Cancer and Cigars

Just short of Freud's sixty-seventh birthday, his internist, Felix Deutsch, discovered a suspicious lump in Freud's mouth. Deutsch removed it, and it proved cancerous. Hans Pichler, an excellent surgeon who had done reconstructive surgery on the mouths of soldiers wounded in the war, removed Freud's entire upper jaw and palate on the right side. To be able to eat, speak, and, yes, still smoke, Freud was forced to wear a prosthesis in his mouth—"the monster"—for the rest of his life. Although the surgeon appeared to have removed the cancer, for the last sixteen years of Freud's life, he endured chronic pain and thirty more operations to remove precancerous tissue. Many who saw him commented on Freud's courage in the face of pain and incapacitation.

Some have speculated on why Freud developed cancer of the jaw. Wilhelm Reich postulated the cancer as a result of Freud's unhappy sex life with his wife. Of course, the more likely explanation was Freud's cigar chomping year after year. Even at that time, carcinoma of the mouth was thought to be caused by pipes and cigars.

Freud was fatally addicted to his cigars, smoking twenty a day for years. He had begun smoking at age twenty-four, at first cigarettes, but soon only cigars. He claimed that this "habit or vice" greatly enhanced his capacity for work and his ability to muster self-control. His father was also a heavy smoker and "remained one until his eighty-first year."

Two or three times, beset by nasal catarrh, Freud reluctantly gave up his beloved cigars on Fliess's orders. But he chided Fliess that to outlaw cigars was only too easy as his one "defect" was that *he* did not smoke. But Freud could not sustain abstinence for long and defiantly would quickly lapse. "I am not observing your ban on smoking," he told Fliess in November 1893. "Do you think it's such a glorious fate to live many long years in misery?" The only time in his life that he refrained from smoking his cherished cigars was during a time of somewhat superstitious worry over the possibility of an early nicotine-aggravated death. Yet when stricken with cancer of the mouth years later and facing a certain horrible death, he fervently clung to his cigars.

Freud the cigar smoker was far from alone in those days. For the weekly gatherings at his house of the Psychoanalytic Society, cigar and cigarette smoke filled the air, and the maid scattered ashtrays across the table, one for each guest. Late one Wednesday night after one of these meetings had adjourned, Freud's son Martin got a whiff of the atmosphere. The room "was still thick with smoke and it seemed to me a wonder that human beings had been able to live in it for hours, let alone to speak in it without choking." When Freud's nephew Harry was seventeen, Freud offered him a cigarette, and when Harry refused, his uncle told him, "My boy, smoking is one of the greatest and cheapest enjoyments in life, and if you decide in advance not to smoke, I can only feel sorry for you." Of course, the psychoanalyst in Freud prevailed. In 1897, sharing an intuition he never developed into a paper, he told Fliess that addictions, including tobacco, are only substitutes for the "single great habit, the 'primal addiction,' masturbation." Yet Freud also supposedly said, "Sometimes a cigar is just a cigar." He ignored his own insight and never gave up smoking.

Freud would have attributed his addiction to oral fixation and being driven by the death instinct. Today his smoking would be seen as a form of self-regulation. Freud suffered apathy and depression, indicating a low level of arousal—like being stuck in the drowsy state. He needed stimulation to make him alert enough to function in the world. He found it through nicotine. The cigar that he found essential to help him work was actually boosting his arousal into a more optimal zone so that he could focus and concentrate. Cocaine, a stimulant that he used early in his career, served the same purpose. In addition, sucking helps the eyes to focus. His cigars may have killed him, but they may have saved psychoanalysis from a premature death.

Case Studies

See **Anna O.; Dora; Elisabeth von R.; Emmy von N.; Katharina; Little Hans; Lucy R.; Rat Man; Wolf Man**.

Catharsis

Following a trauma, such as having been seriously injured in a car accident, the event is consciously intolerable and we may repress the memory. If recalled later in therapy, as under hypnosis, we may experience concomitant emotional release and relief—a *catharsis* or abreaction. A Greek word, catharsis means "cleansing" or "purifying." Aristotle used the word to describe the emotional release and purification engendered in the audience during their viewing of a tragic drama.

How does catharsis operate? When traumatized, the system produces large quantities of excitation beyond normal coping. According to the constancy principle proposed by Freud and his colleague Josef Breuer, this excitation must be discharged to return the system to an optimal state of minimal arousal. The cathartic method or abreaction was the essential treatment in hysteria, as Freud first witnessed in Anna O., Breuer's patient (see **Anna O.**).

Charcot, Jean-Martin
(1825–1893)

Charcot was a famous neuropathologist in Paris at the renowned Salpêtrière Hospital investigating the symptoms and causes of hysteria. Through hypnosis, Charcot was able to induce and then remove many hysterical symptoms. Further, he was able to document that these symptoms were not related to physical abnormalities but to the patient's peculiar *ideas*. For instance, a patient who was in a frightening horse-drawn carriage accident but was unhurt might exhibit the symptoms of paralysis from having *expected* to become so afflicted.

In 1885, Freud spent four months attending Charcot's lectures. Profoundly influenced by Charcot's work, Freud wrote to his future wife: "Charcot . . . is simply wrecking all my aims and opinions;" "I sometimes come out of his lectures . . . with an entirely new idea of perfection;" "no other human being has ever affected me in this way." In 1889, Freud named his first son, Jean Martin, known as Martin, after Charcot, a tribute that the master acknowledged with a brief courteous reply and "all my congratulations."

See **Biography; Hysteria**.

Childhood Sexuality

Before Freud's *Three Essays on the Theory of Sexuality* burst on the scene in 1905 to shock a bourgeois, Victorian European society, sex was assumed unquestionably to begin at puberty. That children innocent and pure could have sexual wishes, fantasies, and pleasures, especially about their parents, was unimaginable. Freud courageously argued that children are sexual beings who exhibit early sexual behavior, such as uninhibited masturbation, similar to what polite society calls "perversions" in adults. "Infantile amnesia" prevents most from recalling these early sexual experiences, but even casual observation of the infant's pleasure at suckling from the nipple or fondling his genitals points to sexual-sensual behavior as beginning almost at birth, and later emotional life likely has roots in this early sex life. Freud's bold assertions of infantile sexuality as normal and universal helped free the twentieth century from the chastity belt of Victorian hypocrisy and repression that infused the rampant sexual pathology of the time.

Psychosexual Stages

Freud theorized that the sexuality of children passes through a succession of developmental stages in the first thirteen or so years of life, each stage centering on an erotogenic zone that dominates the given age. This journey, the parents' responses to these stages, and how the child deals with those responses, Freud argued, have lifelong effects.

The psychosexual stages of childhood are not discrete but overlap, unconsciously laying down continuing themes in subsequent stages. Further, the time periods are approximate and variable.

Oral

During the first year or so of life, pleasure centers on the mouth—first, by that obtained from feeding, then by purely sensual, nonnutritive sucking, like that of the thumb. As the libido is centered in the oral zone, sucking at the mother's breast is the "starting point of the whole of sexual life, the unmatched prototype of every later sexual satisfaction," to which fantasy recurs in times of need. Adult kisses, caresses, oral sex, and other forms of foreplay recapture the early pleasurable sensuality of nursing at the mother's breast. Since the infant's own body provides sensual pleasure, this period is "autoerotic."

The earliest bodily pleasures of children are "polymorphously perverse" (literally, "many-formed perversity") in that if the same means of obtaining pleasure prevailed in adulthood, they would he labeled "perverse"—for instance, sucking one's thumb or masturbating in public. Although these bodily pleasures are nongenital, Freud termed them "sexual" because they contain the seeds of adult sexuality and center on genital pleasure and the wish for contact with another: "No one who has seen a baby sinking back satiated from the breast and falling asleep with flushed cheeks and a blissful smile can escape the reflection that this picture persists as a prototype of the expression of sexual satisfaction in later life."

Feeding gets negotiated in different ways. A mother may feed her infant on demand or on schedule; allow thumb sucking or put gloves on the child's hands; let the child dictate when she is ready to wean from the breast or bottle, or force her to give it up prematurely. If feeding became equated with frustration and battles with the mother, the child may become fixated at the oral stage, stunting and distorting the subsequent sequence of development, and the person will lag behind in her maturing sex drive. For instance, she may develop an eating disorder such as anorexia, bulimia, or overeating. Of course, during times of stress, most of us regress to this earlier stage and head for the refrigerator. But these are only temporary regressions; they don't guide our behavior. Another way that oral fixation manifests is a preference for oral sex over sexual intercourse.

Anal

When my friend Sam was visiting his daughter, his two-year-old grandson, Jack, opened the bathroom door as Sam was urinating. "Good boy, Grandpa!" said the child, clapping. Jack was in the process of toilet training.

To Freud, the major task for the toddler period is toilet training. The child wants to immediately "let go"; the parent wants the child to learn to tolerate the discomfort and "hold it in."

Though Freud rarely faulted parents for their children's problems—one of his major shortcomings—some Freudians later assigned a strong parental responsibility to a child's emotional development. To them, the greater the parents' insistence on toilet training, especially if the child is too young to easily accomplish sphincter control, the greater the child's fight for autonomy and independence, and the child may refuse to use the toilet. Eventually, the child will give in but will later become fixated on the anal pleasures that were forcibly and prematurely denied him. As an adult, he may be compulsively stingy—not letting go—or compulsively concerned about filth. Having learned that failing to put things in their proper place resulted in punishment, he reduces anxiety by rigidly controlling his environment. In the extreme, the person becomes obsessive-compulsive. The toddler is also learning another important lesson that will have lifelong consequences, sexually and emotionally: her body and its functions are natural and acceptable, or disgusting and shameful.

Freud saw the roots of sadism in the anal period. When denied what they want, two-year-olds will bite, push, and hit. During this stage, Freud believed that the sexual and aggressive instincts become linked and later lead to sadistic and masochistic sexual fantasies and behaviors.

Phallic

Young children are fascinated with their sex organs and, not yet knowing shame, will guiltlessly exhibit their genitals; some will masturbate, which is pleasurable. But the hottest topic of conversation during this period of "sexual researches" is the penis: who has it, who doesn't, and why not. As the little boy explores his body and gets caught fondling his penis, the shocked mother, at least the Victorian mother, likely stops him from such "perversity," making the boy feel guilty for masturbating. Perhaps she even threatens to cut off his penis or to have the father do so—a common threat in Freud's day. The boy might not believe her threats until he discovers the "castrated" female genitals, then fears the threats are real; he is beset with castration anxiety. As for the little girl, her discovery of the boy's penis leaves her feeling forever castrated and inferior; she is beset with *penis envy*.

This scenario is played out consciously. But, Freud believed, something more profound is playing out in the psyche: the Oedipus and Electra complexes. Lurking deep in the little boy's unconscious is a desire to possess his mother. But his father, who the child fears will castrate him, stands in the way. He must kill his father so that he can have his mother to himself. Likewise, the little girl wishes to be rid of her mother, who she believes is responsible for her castration, and marry her father.

How do the Oedipus and Electra complexes get resolved? The young boy must learn to relinquish his mother as his exclusively and reconcile his contradictory feelings of love for and anger at his father; the young girl must learn to relinquish her father as her love object and reconcile the love and anger she feels for her mother.

If the Oedipal conflict does not get resolved, either because of castration anxiety, or penis envy, and the child continues to feel hostile toward the same-sex parent, he becomes fixated in this stage. This can take different forms. Both men and women may become sexually inhibited; masturbation, if engaged in, may be more satisfying than sex. A man may become a Don Juan, aggressively using his penis to dominate the woman, whom he devalues as he flaunts his masculine superiority. A woman may grow to feel inferior and become passive and submissive to men, or she may resent her mother and become masculinized. For a critique of Freud's Oedipus and Electra complexes, see **Contributions and Critique**.

Latency

Many of us remember in grade school how girls played with girls, boys played with boys, and never did the two sexes meet. Previous infatuation with the opposite sex goes underground until puberty.

From infancy, sexual drives and activities become increasingly more suppressed. Around age six or seven, they get repressed, although they're still lurking in the unconscious: libidinal impulses become latent and obscured by learned shame, disgust, and morality.

Genital

As puberty hits the child, the sudden wave of hormones breaks the repression barrier and frees sensuality/sexuality. The adolescent moves from autoeroticism to the fantasies and desires of shared sexual pleasure. The girl must now face the crucial task of completely resolving the Oedipal complex by relinquishing her erotic attachment to her father for a partner she can desire and love, and vice versa for the boy. At puberty, the girl discovers her vagina and becomes feminine by forsaking clitoral masturbation of the vagina. If she does not make this transfer, she will never accept her lack of a penis and will become neurotic (see **Vaginal and Clitoral Orgasm**).

Psychosexual Stages Today

Today the emphasis on development is not on Freud's *psychosexual* stages but on interpersonal development. One popular theory is that of the psychoanalyst Erik Erikson, who proposed *psychosocial* stages of development that roughly parallel Freud's stages but extend to cover all of development: trust versus mistrust (oral); autonomy versus shame/doubt (anal); initiative versus guilt (Oedipal); industry versus inferiority (latency); identity versus role confusion (genital). His psychosocial stages are widely employed by psychologists to understand the child's development.

In psychoanalytic psychotherapy, the analyst still focuses on your childhood issues, but rather than concentrating on how well you negotiated your Oedipal conflict, the analyst is more likely to focus on your feelings as a child—on whether you felt appreciated and validated, approved of and supported, and confident that your parents would be there when you needed them, issues to which we all relate.

See **Anal Character; Oedipal Complex; Sexuality, Freud's**.

Civilization and Its Discontents

> *Civilized society is perpetually menaced with disintegration through this primary hostility of men towards one another.*
>
> —Sigmund Freud

Civilization and Its Discontents, published in 1930, begins with a dialogue with Romain Rolland, a French novelist and winner of the

Nobel Prize, who corresponded with Freud from 1923 to 1929. Rolland disagreed with Freud's characterization of religion as childish worship of a powerful father figure. He argued that his faith was not tied to a specific doctrine but experienced as an "oceanic feeling," a sense of being at one with the universe. Freud argued that Rolland's experience was nothing more than the infantile wish for oneness with the mother.

Written when Freud was old, embittered, and ill, *Civilization and Its Discontents* paints a bleak picture of humanity: driven by unconscious sexual and aggressive impulses, we battle constantly with society, which demands that we repress these survival impulses. From nursing onward, sexual desire butts horns with civilization, which links sexual pleasure with disgust, shame, and immorality, while the aggressive instincts make "human communal life difficult and threaten its survival." The result? Humans tend to be anxious, miserable, and often neurotic.

To exist in society, both men and women must repress sexual desire. The woman forgoes sexuality for mothering and caring for the home, while men forgo sexual pleasure to make their mark in the world—they "sublimate." Three thousand years before Freud, Plato advised readers in *The Symposium* to curb their sexual appetite and their need to give and receive love. They should concentrate all that energy on higher goals—that is, sublimate.

Projecting personal biases and his Victorian view of gender, Freud lumps *all* men and women into rigid, traditional roles:

> Women soon come into opposition to civilization and display their *retarding* influence. . . . Women represent the interests of family and sexual life. The work of civilization has become increasingly the business of men. . . . Since a man does not have unlimited quantities of psychical energy at his disposal, he has to accomplish his tasks by making an expedient distribution of his libido. What he employs for cultural aims he to a great extent withdraws from women and sexual life. His constant association with men, and his dependence upon his relation with them, even estrange him from his duties as husband and father. [emphasis added]

Freud didn't have to look far to see the shortsightedness of his thoughts. Not all women devote all libido to mothering and cleaning, as his daughter Anna and his close friend Lou Andreas-Salomé aptly demonstrated. Nor are all men estranged in their roles of husband and father, at least not to the degree that Freud was. His friend Josef Breuer was not; his close associate Karl Abraham was not; nor were many of the other men in Freud's inner circle.

The overall themes in this book seem to reflect Freud's personal state. Not only was he disillusioned about life but he was caught his whole life by his desire for the close, "oceanic" feeling of early connectedness coupled with a dread of reexperiencing the helplessness and terror associated with his early childhood—of being engulfed by his overwhelming need for his mother's love (see **Family, the Mother: Amalia Freud**). To cope, he became moralistic, dutiful, hardworking, and abstinent most of his life; in short, "civilized" and in control of *his* impulses.

In spite of Freud's pessimism, *Civilization and Its Discontents* drew our attention to the tension between biological impulses and social well-being, reminding us of our potential for evil.

Climate of the Times

To understand and appreciate Freud and his theories, we must view him in the context of the time and the place in which he lived— a world that no longer exists in many respects.

Sigmund Freud was born into an aristocratic, extremely oppressive world dominated by kings and queens and empires and run largely by the conservative Catholic Church: women were second-class citizens; anti-Semitism was widespread; homosexuals were degenerates.

Born at the tail end of the Romantic Age, its ethos greatly influenced Freud's thinking. The Romantics, and later Freud, viewed the individual in hostile and constant conflict with a society that demanded conformity to ensure social order, stifling the uniqueness of the self. To transcend such oppression, the Romantic seeks freedom through passionate quests such as art and love. Goethe's Faust was willing to sell his soul to the devil to seek self-fulfillment. The Romantics celebrated the emotional and irrational aspects of human nature over reason, and they believed humans to be ruled by impulses and emotions both wicked and sublime—you can't get much more Freudian.

But Freud was also a rational scientist whose puritanical views reflected the Victorian Age in which he was educated. Although sex and aggression drive behavior, Freud felt these unconscious instincts must be channeled into socially acceptable expressions or neither the human being nor society will survive, as he explicated near the end of his life in *Civilization and Its Discontents*. This more scientific, rationalistic, and moralistic worldview coincided with the increasing industrialization, urbanization, and nationalism at the end of the nineteenth century. In the Victorian mind, advances in science and technology, such as railroads and steel mills, coupled with hard work, would transform modern life. With numerous reform societies—missionary societies and temperance leagues abounded—the passage of major social bills emphasizing individual rights and privileges in England and elsewhere, and the emphasis on high standards of moral behavior and decorum in the Victorian court, the Victorian Age characterized moral reform and rectitude.

But this preoccupation with behaving "appropriately" and doing good works, although improving the lives of the middle and working classes, repressed the passion that the Romantics had celebrated—that is, sexuality. Mysterious and frightening, sex was subjugated to the higher callings of rational duty. This splitting of the self into a public respectable one and a debauched private one gave rise to the neuroses of the day, particularly hysteria. That Freud had the courage to doggedly pursue his sexual theories within such a repressive climate was truly heroic.

See **Childhood Sexuality; Seduction Hypothesis; *Three Essays on the Theory of Sexuality***.

Cocaine

Of those who seek to discredit Freud as a neurotic scientific charlatan, a popular attack is that Freud had been a cocaine addict. This is doubtful. Although Freud did experiment with the drug, he mistakenly declared that "repeated doses of coca produce no compulsive desire to use the stimulant further; on the contrary one feels a certain unmotivated aversion to the substance."

In the spring of 1884, Freud wrote his fiancée of an interest in a little-known drug called cocaine that a German army physician had been using to boost his soldiers' endurance. He intended to experiment with its possible uses in alleviating heart trouble and nervous exhaustion, as occurs during morphine withdrawal. At that time, the addictive properties of cocaine were unknown. In June, he completed a paper, "On Coca," which was published in a Viennese medical journal the following month. This paper and other papers published shortly afterward established Freud's name in Viennese medical circles as well as abroad.

Freud experimented with cocaine to alleviate depression and low energy, and it worked. "I take very small doses of it regularly against depression and against indigestion, and with the most brilliant results," he wrote Martha. Not knowing it was addictive and excited about this "magical" drug as a mood enhancer, he sent some to Martha "to make her strong and give her cheeks a red color. . . . When I come, I will kiss you quite red and feed you till you are plump. And . . . you shall see who is the stronger, a gentle little girl who doesn't eat enough or a big wild man *who has cocaine in his body.* In my last severe depression, I took coca and a small dose lifted me to the heights."

In his enthusiasm, Freud began giving it freely to patients, friends, and even to his sisters. But he started to notice individual reactions to the drug, some of them negative. A friend of his, Ernst Fleishl, to whom he gave it to alleviate intractable pain, became delirious and hallucinated that white snakes were creeping all over his skin. The medical establishment soon condemned cocaine as a new plague, the same as opium, and Freud stopped dispensing it and cut down his own use. But he continued to use it occasionally for at least ten years when Wilhelm Fliess, who was doing his own experimenting with cocaine, prescribed the drug to treat Freud's depression.

Contributions and Critique

Freud should be placed in the same category as Darwin, who lived before the discovery of genes. Freud gave us a vision of a mental apparatus. We need to talk about it, develop it, test it.

—Jaak Panksepp, neurobiologist at
Bowling Green State University

Because we have learned so much about human behavior since Freud's original conceptualizations, we tend to dismiss him as a neurotic, dirty old man who overemphasized the role of sexuality in human motivation and painted a conflicted, bleak, overdetermined perspective of human personality. We forget the world before Freud and his immense influence in modern-day thinking.

Before Freud created psychoanalysis, the closest thing to therapy was confessing to a hidden priest or bending the ear of a barkeeper. Hysterics were readily locked up in institutions. In addition to spawning many different types of therapy, Freud's depth therapy has given birth to numerous takes on psychoanalysis—from a full-term "talking cure" to short-term psychotherapy; from child therapy to adult therapy; from one-on-one therapy to family and group therapy. And long-term contemporary psychoanalysis, in its emphasis on the self and interpersonal relations, still remains the therapy of choice for many of the educated with the time, money, and desire to probe their soul and restructure their character.

Before Freud, there was little notion that the child is father to the man. Today, Freud's ideas that childhood prototypes are fore-runners of adult personality are common knowledge, although psychologists disagree on how much they influence later behavior. Before Freud, sexuality was assumed to emerge with the onset of puberty. Freud's idea that sexuality appears in infancy and runs throughout childhood has been borne out—even newborns get erections and infants routinely masturbate. Before Freud, the sexual identity of adults or preferences for different sexual practices or types of partners, were considered moral choices, or perversions. In contrast, Freud viewed homosexuality, bisexuality, fetishism, fixations on particular body parts or practices, sadism, and masochism as results of interactions between inborn predispositions—he believed we are all born bisexual—and life events, developing and changing over the years.

Before Freud, there was no coherent, workable theory explaining the nature and function of dreams, a central aspect of psychoanalytic therapy. A century after *The Interpretation of Dreams* broke new ground in elucidating the mystery of our nocturnal dramas, Freud's theories of dream interpretation still inform how we think of dreams. Dreams of being naked in public and feeling embarrassed, of needing to use the bathroom but being unable to find a toilet, of being late to take an examination, or frozen in our steps, are familiar to most and are a few of the situations that Freud analyzed as symbolic of inner rumblings. For instance, being unable to move when faced with danger symbolizes being caught between two conflicts. His sexual symbols, although joked about, have become common knowledge. Few could dream of snakes without conjuring the penis.

At the same time, much of what Freud said has been proven wrong. That *all* dreams disguise and fulfill wishes, as Freud believed, has been disputed by new ideas about why we dream: for instance, to sort and filter the happenings of the day. Slips of the tongue can often be explained cognitively: sometimes word choices compete in our memory network, like wanting to say "My niece is nice" and having it come out as "My nice is niece." And history, as Jerome Kagan noted in *Unstable Ideas: Temperament, Cognition and Self*, has knocked down the cornerstone of Freud's theory—that sexual repression causes psychological disorder: sexual repression has diminished since Freud's time, but psychological disorders have not.

Some of Freud's views were not only wrong but damaging, as were his distorted views of women. Believing in the natural superiority of men, Freud related femininity to "passivity" and "masochism," and masculinity with "activity" and "sadism." To him, all women experience "penis envy" upon discovery that they lack one, and this shapes their sense of self and morality. Biology is destiny, and the woman is a second-class citizen. Such demeaning views clashed greatly with the women's movement for equality between the sexes. Still smarting, some women dismiss all of Freud's theories as bosh.

Freud's pessimistic views left our psyche programmed for negative self-appraisals. Take his idea of a death instinct to drive behavior. The idea of aggressing against ourselves as instinctive behavior led generations to frame addictive behavior—smoking, drinking, overeating, and so forth—as self-destructive and to feel weak and lacking control; in short, a failure. For instance, overeating is considered a regression to the oral stage of development where our needs for sucking were left unsatisfied. If you eliminate the idea of a death instinct and see all behavior as essentially self-preservative, which is the evolutionary perspective, a different theory of behavior emerges that better fits how the brain operates. At every moment in time, the brain evaluates a sensation as safe, dangerous, or neutral to ensure *survival*, not *death*. What appears to be self-destructive behavior is a starved nervous system's need to go to an extreme to self-regulate.

Seeing all human motivation as driven by unconscious instincts of sex or aggression also overanalyzes behavior as governed by psychic motivation, rather than from something physical, neurological, or psychophysiological. For instance, although I am athletic and coordinated, I've lost almost every match of racquetball and tennis that I've played. I naturally assumed that I must have a fear of failure—or success—and sabotaged my matches. In fact, I have visual-spatial processing problems. I lost on the court because my eyes couldn't focus properly on the ball! Take another example. The Freudian view of morning sickness is that it represents the woman's loathing of her husband and her unconscious desire to abort the fetus orally. The biologist Margie Profet has posited that morning sickness might serve some evolutionary benefit. Hundreds of studies have supported her hunch that nausea protects women from eating or digesting foods with toxins that might harm the developing fetus.

Here's another example close to home: Freud's biographers, assuming all behavior to be first and foremost psychologically motivated, may have misinterpreted certain aspects of Freud's behavior. For instance, Freud had a well-known aversion to music. Upon entering a restaurant with a band playing, Freud would have "a pained expression on his face" and "quickly his hands would go over his ears to drown the sound." His biographers interpreted this reaction as Freud's need to keep his emotions under control, as music evokes strong emotions. I suggest his behavior more strongly suggests noise sensitivity. Were Freud's behavior purely emotional, he might have described his antipathy verbally rather than reacting as if in pain and physically trying to shut out the sound.

Critics also argue that Freud's belief that constraints of civilization preclude happiness, that one's best hope was for psychoanalysis to "transform hysterical misery into common unhappiness," is not only negative but not true of the experience of all. The common ethos in psychology today is that while we experience some conflict, we are not passive, conflicted, essentially unhappy entities but creatures actively driven to master our environment, to explore our world freely, and to become self-fulfilled.

But the critics' greatest beef with Freud's theories is their lack of predictability and testability. How do you prove or disprove the existence of abstract unconscious thoughts, of an id, ego, or superego? You don't, say the psychoanalysts. This method of scientific inquiry is not applicable to psychoanalysis, which lends itself to case histories, nor did Freud ever allege that psychoanalysis is a predictive science. Yet as the theory does not lend itself to scientific scrutiny, it is more metaphorical than scientific, say the critics. Of course, that doesn't prove that the tenets are wrong.

Let's look closely at how Freud's theories have passed or failed the test of time.

Infantile Sexuality

One of Freud's most creative and significant findings that has greatly helped change how we parent our infants was his discovery that sexuality runs through childhood. In the Victorian Age, the body was thought to contain evil sexual impulses. In 1906, around the time that Freud published his landmark *Three Essays on the Theory of Sexuality*, Margaret Morley warned parents to watch their children carefully almost from birth lest children sin against themselves and lose their sexual purity. In 1914, *Infant Care*, a publication of the U.S. Department of Labor, cautioned that the infant has "strong and dangerous impulses" that easily "grow beyond control." Mothers must fight their children's sinful nature by preventing masturbation, or children could be "wrecked for life." They recommended that the mother tie the baby's feet to opposite ends of the crib so that he could not rub his thighs together, and to pin his nightgown sleeves to the bed so that he could not touch himself. The baby's own movements may provide dangerous pleasures, or he may be seduced into them with pacifiers to suck or having his genitals stroked by the nurse. Thumb sucking was severely restricted.

Thanks to Freud's landmark discovery that deriving pleasure from playing with the genitals is normal infantile behavior, by the 1940s, when psychoanalysis was part of the Western canon, touching of the genitals no longer caused panic. Now *Infant Care* described touching the genitals as normal exploration—the same as the toes, the ears, or a toy. The solution was not tying down but diverting—if the baby has a toy to play with, he will not play with his genitals. Buttressing Freud's theory of infantile sexuality was the discovery by René Spitz, an early psychoanalyst, that infantile genital play is not only normal exploration but a sign that a baby is well mothered. When mothering was optimal, Spitz found virtually all infants played with their genitals. When mothering was inadequate, genital play was rarer. And infants reared in families exhibited genital play approximately two months earlier than those cared for in nurseries.

Oral Stage

Freud was correct that oral needs play a crucial role in the infant's development, that our sensual/sexual life begins with the breast or bottle, and that suckling the breast or sucking the thumb, which is driven by libido, or sexual energy, reduces tension from over-stimulation. In fact, oral activity is the infant's first means of self-regulation and remains primary throughout life. We head for the cookie jar when stressed, because sucking, swallowing, chewing, and chomping give us quick somatosensory input into our nervous system to organize our behavior into a comfort zone. We seek tension reduction not only when overstimulated and anxious but also when understimulated and bored. Every second of our lives, our brain maintains order by avoiding or approaching sensory stimulation until we reach an optimal level of arousal, the midpoint between boredom and anxiety.

Freud was incorrect that oral needs comprise the center of the mother–child relationship, the notion of which influenced parents for decades to believe that our babies (and our pets) attach to us because we feed them. The mother is the "prototype" for all later love relations because she *nurtures* her baby, not because she *feeds* her: it is the mother's comforting arms, not her breast milk, that is the core of mother–baby attachment. When infants are fed but not nurtured, they don't survive. Spitz studied infants in orphanages, most of whom died. While fed enough, these infants were mostly left in their cribs; they didn't flourish because of "contact hunger." Harry Harlow's work in the late 1950s with rhesus monkeys definitively demonstrated the infant's crucial need for contact comfort in order to feel secure in the world; food is secondary. Harlow took rhesus newborns from their mothers and placed them in a room with a cold wire monkey with an attached bottle and a warm, soft terry-cloth mother. The infant monkeys would go to the wire mother surrogate only when hungry. They spent most of the rest of their time clinging to the soft warm cloth monkey for contact comfort. Touch as the core of mother love would have surprised Freud, who believed, as did many of his generation, that "too much petting" produces anxiety in the child; he was not affectionate with his own children. In fact, as long as you follow your infant's cues for closeness, you cannot hold, stroke, or cuddle an infant "too much," as I demonstrate in my book *The Vital Touch*.

Whereas Freud emphasized the psychosexual development of the infant, post-Freudians emphasize the interpersonal aspect of the mother–child relationship. Among the most influential is the psychoanalyst Erik Erikson, who theorized *psychosocial* stages of development. In infancy, the relationship with the mother determines the extent to which the infant will experience *basic trust*, or security, versus *basic mistrust*, or insecurity. This notion has become gospel and spawned a plethora of research into the mother and infant relationship.

Anal Stage

To Freud, the central concern in the anal stage is "holding in" and "letting go" of feces. In extending the issues of the toddler into the psychosocial realm, Erikson outlined the toddler's primary task as autonomy and exploring independence that goes beyond toilet training. "No!" is a pronouncement to most anything the parent might request, as the child's emerging autonomy is pitted against adult authority. In fact, in some modern households and in societies relaxed about toilet training, there is no conflict because there is no toilet "training." When the child is ready, he starts to use the toilet, or the potty, or goes behind a bush. Struggles over toilet training exist primarily in societies that emphasize cleanliness and obedience to parental demands and that portray urine and feces as dirty and disgusting.

The child psychoanalyst Margaret Mahler, a Viennese pediatrician who immigrated to the United States in the 1930s, digs deeper into the two-year-old's dilemma: the child is faced with wanting closeness to the mother for protection and wanting to freely explore the world. If the mother does not lovingly support the child's need for both autonomy and closeness, later the person remains to some extent locked into a lifelong struggle between abandonment and engulfment, as was clearly Freud's dilemma and informed so much of his thinking (see **Family, the Mother: Amalia Freud**).

Oedipus Complex

The greatest controversy regarding Freud's theories was his insistence on the universality of the Oedipus complex. Actually, anthropological evidence from folktales supports the phenomenon of universal Oedipus feelings and fantasies in boys but not girls.

As Freud outlined in *Totem and Taboo*, a custom common to all societies is the incest taboo. It must be so for the species to survive. Explains Gardner Lindzey, a social psychologist trained in behavior genetics, inbreeding would have produced offspring less well fitted for survival than outbreeding; thus, only societies that forbade incest would have survived.

Research by the anthropologist John Whiting offers further evidence of the Oedipal conflict in rituals. In some polygamous cultures, mother and baby sleep together the first year, and the father sleeps apart. In these cultures, the initiation rites for adolescent boys are more severe than in other cultures, and they often involve considerable pain, including genital mutilation. Unconsciously, perhaps the father is getting his revenge for being pushed out of the conjugal bed by symbolically castrating his son.

While anthropological evidence from folktales supports the phenomenon of universal Oedipus feelings in boys, girls' Electra feelings are far different from how Freud envisioned them. As we would assume, the father, not the daughter, most often initiated incestuous actions, as Freud himself discovered in his early work with hysterics. The daughter rarely reciprocated the father's interest and did not see the mother as a competitor. The girl, however, probably does experience Oedipal-like jealousy, but of the *father*, with whom she competes for *mother's* attention.

In all cultures, young children are at times possessive of their mothers and jealous of their fathers. But the explanation is not sexual. Around age three, the child realizes that she is not the center of Mommy's world; something goes on behind the bedroom door that has nothing to do with her, and this creates conflict with the father for access to the mother's affection, attention, and nurturing. And if Mommy has had another baby, the girl has two rivals with whom to contend. Children protest Mommy's attention to the other rivals much the same way they protested weaning. This theory sheds light on why so-called Oedipal feelings are as common in girls as in boys, while avoiding the absurdity that little boys unconsciously want to have sex with their mothers.

As boys mature sexually, they may indeed feel sexually competitive with their fathers, but not for the mother. In many societies, fathers compete with their sons for sexual partners, and in polyga-mous societies, the son might compete for the same women.

Freud's Oedipal theory was erroneous in another way. He pos-tulated that conscience and gender identity form as the child resolves the Oedipus complex. Research in developmental psy-chology reveals that children gain gender identity earlier and will do so even without a same-sex parent present in the household. In fact, a girl brought up by two homosexual men and a boy brought up by two lesbians are not more likely to later show same-sex orientation.

Latency

Freud asserted that the sexual impulses become dormant when the child is around six, even without cultural pressures, because the phenomenon of latency is biologically determined. Anthropo-logical observations do not confirm Freud's theory of a universal latency period. In cultures that are open about sex and nudity and permit masturbation, children play out adult sex, including inter-course, throughout their childhood.

Genital

Freud declared that, starting at puberty, the girl must relinquish cli-toral masturbation for vaginal penetration because only vaginal orgasms are "normal." He was wrong. Female infants and little girls are aware of their vaginas and experience intense pleasure from the orgasms that result from fondling their clitorises or vaginas. Furthermore, as Masters and Johnson reported in *Human Sexual Response* in 1966, clitoral and vaginal orgasms are indistinct and orgasms alway have vaginal contractions. They state: "From a bio-logical . . . [and] anatomic point of view, there is absolutely no dif-ference in the responses of the pelvic viscera to effective sexual stimulation, regardless of whether the stimulation occurs as a result of clitoral-body or mons area manipulation, natural or artificial coition, or for that matter, specific stimulation of any other eroge-nous area of the female body."

Freud's faulty thinking caused many women to feel, incorrectly, that they were sexually maladjusted. His ghost still resides under the bedcovers every time a woman feels reluctant to ask her partner to stimulate her clitoris during intercourse (or to do so herself), believing that she should experience an orgasm from intercourse alone.

Freud would be fascinated to learn how neuroscience is now mapping the adolescent brain. Although we originally thought that teens are sex crazy because of raging hormones, this is only half the truth. They are sex crazy because their limbic system, the emotional brain—the *id*—where sex hormones are especially active, is *extremely* active during adolescence. At the same time, their prefrontal cortex, the decision-making part of the brain—the *ego*—has not yet matured enough to allow them to make wise decisions about sexual activity. This part of the brain is not mature until around age twenty-five, the average age today for getting married. This is why teens seem so id driven.

Neuroscience

Freud's psychological map may have been flawed in many ways, but it remains the most coherent and, from individual experience, meaningful theory of the mind. One hundred years after Freud published the groundbreaking *Interpretation of Dreams*, modern neuroscience has confirmed many of his insights, as *Newsweek* reported in 2002 in "What Freud Got Right."

Unconscious

Was Freud right? Is thinking largely like an "iceberg" and mostly underwater? Indeed. Modern technology has confirmed what Freud proposed over one hundred years ago: much of our everyday thinking, feeling, and acting operate outside conscious awareness. We are not masters in our own psychological household.

In studying automatic processing, subliminal priming, implicit memory, heuristics, right-brain processing, instant emotions, nonverbal communication, and creativity, cognitive science is revealing an intriguing unconscious mind. It's not quite the Freudian state of mind reflected in the tripartite division of id, ego, and superego, but Freud didn't have the sophisticated tools we have today, such as the MRI (magnetic resonance imaging), to study brain processes. Rather, it appears to be what researchers call dual processing—thinking, memory, and attitude operate on two levels: the conscious/deliberate and the unconscious/automatic.

In the unconscious/automatic lay forbidden feelings, as Freud postulated. For instance, in one experiment on unconscious processing, researchers demonstrated that "dirty" words have a higher threshold for stimulus recognition than comparable words that lack sexual or other taboo connotations. Subjects were shown words on a screen. The exposure time was varied to determine how much time a subject needed to recognize a particular word. The exposure time required for taboo words (e.g., bitch, fuck, Kotex, cancer) was indeed longer than for words lacking taboo connotations. Interpreting the findings in terms of Freudian defense mechanisms, particularly repression, the authors concluded that the taboo words were perceived subconsciously and censored from consciousness because their appearance would have elicited anxiety. The part of the brain implicated in the forbidden psyche is our gut emotional brain—the limbic system/"id"—where fear, lust, and anger overtake us before our logical neocortex/"ego" steps in to say, "Calm down. His bark is bigger than his bite," or, "Count to ten before you whack him."

Other brain researchers have found strong evidence for the unconscious mind. Candace Pert at Georgetown University School of Medicine has discovered receptor sites for neuropeptides (brain chemicals) that reveal the "brain" and its functions, including our emotions, to actually be located all over the body. Functioning as messengers between cells and various organs and other mechanisms in the body such as the immune, endocrine, and gastrointestinal systems, these neuropeptides, or "molecules of emotion," create a transit system to and from the brain to systems throughout the body and form a dynamic information network—a finding that supports Freud's idea of unconscious processing. "If we accept the idea that peptides and other informational substrates are the biochemicals of emotions," wrote Pert, "their distribution in the body's nerves has all kinds of significance, which Sigmund Freud, were he alive today, would gleefully point out as the molecular confirmation of his theories. The body is the unconscious mind! Repressed traumas caused by overwhelming emotion can be stored in a body part, thereafter affecting our ability to feel that part or even move it." Molecules of emotion explain the paralysis, blindness, and so on of hysteria that so baffled Freud and others a century ago. In fact, both Anna O. and Elisabeth von R., two of the prominent cases in *Studies on Hysteria*, were highly traumatized. Both became symptomatic while nursing their dying fathers, to whom they were strongly attached, and both experienced more than their share of deaths and losses of people close to them (see the cases of **Anna O.** and **Elisabeth von R.**).

A leader in the field of neural science, Joseph LeDoux also argues for Freud's idea of the unconscious: "Absence of awareness is the rule of mental life, rather than the exception, throughout the animal kingdom. If we do not need conscious feelings to explain what we would call emotional behavior in some animals, then we do not need them to explain the same behavior in humans. Emotional responses are, for the most part, generated unconsciously. Freud was right on the mark when he described consciousness as the tip of the mental iceberg."

Drives

For the past half-century in psychology, neuroscience has focused on rational processes in conscious life and downplayed the role of unconscious universal drives. But in mapping out the brain, researchers have discovered evidence that Freud's drives really do exist. Their roots lie in a primitive part of the brain operating mostly outside of consciousness: the limbic system. More commonly called "emotions," five basic drives have been identified: rage, panic, separation distress, lust, and a variation on libido that is sometimes called seeking. Freud presaged this finding in 1915, when he wrote that drives originate "from within the organism" in response to demands placed on the mind "in consequence of its connection with the body." Drives, in other words, are primitive brain circuits that control how we respond to our environment: foraging when we're hungry, running when we're scared, and lusting for a mate.

The seeking drive is proving particularly fertile to researchers. Although like the others it originates in the limbic system, it also involves parts of the forebrain, the seat of high mental function. In the 1980s, Jaak Panksepp, a neurobiologist at Bowling Green State University in Ohio, became interested in a place near the cortex known as the ventral tegmental area, which in humans lies just above the hairline. When Panksepp stimulated the corresponding region in a mouse, the animal would sniff the air and walk around, as though it were looking for something. It wasn't hungry; the mouse would walk right by a plate of food, or for that matter any other object Panksepp could think of. This brain tissue seemed to cause a general desire for something new. "What I was seeing," he said, "was the urge to do stuff." Panksepp called this "seeking."

To the neuropsychologist Mark Solms of University College in London that sounds very much like libido. "Freud needed some sort of general, appetitive desire to seek pleasure in the world of objects," says Solms. "Panksepp discovered as a neuroscientist where Freud discovered psychologically."

Dreams

Since the 1970s, neurologists have known that dreaming takes place during REM (rapid eye movement) sleep that is associated with a primitive part of the brain known as the pons. Dreaming, they proposed, was a low-level phenomenon of no great psychological interest; it was mere random scraps of memory flickering through the sleeping brain. But when Solms, who has been studying dreams for some fifty years, looked into it, he discovered that the key structure involved in dreaming is actually the ventral tegmental, the same structure that Panksepp had identified as the seat of the "seeking" emotion. Dreams, it seems, originate with the libido, just as Freud proposed.

Daily Life

Freud lived by the clock, a habit that served him well in his constant quest for self-mastery and productivity. He awoke at seven and saw psychoanalytic patients from eight to twelve. At the stroke of one o'clock, the household assembled around the dining room table for the midday dinner, the largest meal of the day. During family meals, Freud was generally silent and concentrated on his food. This would disconcert visitors who wished to converse with the great man. After the midday meal, Freud took a walk. The route and time remained almost the same daily. Those who knew him could predict where and what time to find him in his stroll for a word or two. Freud's focus on his food and walking after eating were healthy habits to help digest food and probably contributed to his enormous stamina and productivity.

At three, he had consultations and then saw more analytic patients, often until nine in the evening. He then had supper. After the evening meal, he played a short game of cards with his sister-in-law Minna, or took another walk with his wife or one of his daughters, often to a cafe, where they read the papers or ate an ice in the summer. The rest of the evening he read and wrote, often letters. Freud was a prolific letter writer—it's estimated that he may have written more than twenty thousand letters during his lifetime—and answered each one within a day or two of receiving it. Although his reading was largely related to psychoanalysis, occasionally he read a novel, a poem, or a play for pleasure. When he needed to relax, as when recuperating from surgery later in life, he enjoyed murder mysteries by such classic detective story writers as Agatha Christie and Dorothy Sayers. In 1907, responding to a questionnaire from his publisher, Hugo Heller, asking for a list of ten "good" books, Freud named books by Gottfried Keller, Conrad Ferdinand Meyer, Anatole France, Emile Zola, Rudyard Kipling, Lord Macaulay, Dmitri Merezhkovski, Multatuli, Theodor Gomperz, and Mark Twain. At one in the morning, he retired to bed, getting on average six hours' sleep a night.

On Wednesday evenings, the meeting of the Psychoanalytic Society lasted from nine to past midnight. One night a week from seven to nine, he held a seminar for students, from beginners to advanced, many of whom were nonmedical. Freud suggested the subject for discussion. On Saturdays from five to seven, Freud lectured, as usual without notes, at the University of Vienna, which gave him the opportunity to bring basic psychoanalytic ideas such as slips and errors, dreams, the theory of neurosis, and psychoanalytic therapy to a wider audience. From these lectures emerged *Introductory Lectures on Psychoanalysis*, published in 1916 and 1917. Afterward, he went to his friend Leopold Konigstein's house for his weekly game of tarock, an old card game for four that was long popular in Austria and Germany and that Freud played his whole life with a regular group of nonpsychoanalytic lifelong friends. On Sunday mornings, he visited his mother and then wrote letters.

During the summer, Freud often recuperated from his hectic and fatiguing schedule at a spa. His parents, his wife and six children, and Minna would stay in a quiet hotel in the mountains at Bad Gastein in Austria, or at Berchtesgaden in Bavaria. Some of their favorite activities were to hunt mushrooms, gather strawberries, go fishing, and take long walks. Freud, though not one for strenuous sports, enjoyed long, hefty mountain walks. In August and early September, Freud would often explore Italy with his brother Alexander or a close colleague like Sándor Ferenczi.

Death

To us he is no more a person now but a whole climate of opinion.

—W. H. Auden, "In Memory of Sigmund Freud," 1940

An exile in London, by 1939 Freud was gravely ill. The ulcerated wound in his mouth smelled so fetid that his beloved chow Jo-Fi would cringe from him and refuse to come near its master. Tortured by constant pain, exhausted, and barely able to eat, Freud suffered greatly in these last days. The nights were especially hard, and ever needing to remain in control, he refused sedation. But he could still read. How fitting that his last book would be a metaphor for his shrinking time and his withering skin—Balzac's mysterious tale of the magical shrinking skin, *La Peau de Chagrin*. Freud spent the last days in his study downstairs looking out at the garden.

On September 21, Freud could endure no more. As Max Schur, Freud's personal physician from 1928 to 1939, sat by his bedside, Freud took his hand and said to him, "Schur, you remember our 'contract' not to leave me in the lurch when the time had come. Now it is nothing but torture and makes no sense." Holding Freud's hand, Schur nodded. Freud sighed with relief and, holding Schur's hand, said, "I thank you." He hesitated slightly, then added, "Talk it over with Anna, and if she thinks it's right, then make an end of it." His daughter, Anna, wanted to wait, but Schur convinced her that it was time.

On September 21, Schur injected Freud with enough morphine for Freud to sink into a peaceful sleep. The next day, he administered the final injection. Freud lapsed into a coma and died at three in the morning, September 23, 1939, weeks after the onset of World War II.

Defense Mechanisms

Life can be cruel. To protect the ego from the slings and arrows of a sometimes harsh reality, we erect defense mechanisms— unconscious strategies of the ego to distort reality and lessen anxiety. For instance, if we feel we are lazy, we might unconsciously attribute laziness to a coworker in self-protection. This defense mechanism is called *projection*. Many of the defense mechanisms that Freud identified, such as "denial" and "rationalizing," are part of our everyday parlance. Though we all use them, they become a problem when used excessively or inflexibly, as in the neuroses.

Freud focused on repression as an all-inclusive defense, the cornerstone on which psychoanalysis rests. Later, his daughter Anna in *The Ego and the Mechanisms of Defense* of 1936, still a classic psychoanalytic text, expanded and systemized the defense mechanisms. Following are some of the most common.

Repression

To reduce anxiety, our brain shunts from consciousness—*represses*—a dangerous impulse, idea, or memory. For example, a man forgets to attend the nuptials of his brother to a woman to whom he was attracted, repressing his continued romantic interest in her. In another example, a student of mine had, over a two-year period, cared for her terminally ill husband, to whom she had been happily married for twelve years, but after his death she had no memory of getting married or of her life with her husband before his illness. Photos of her marriage and their life together seemed like a dream or something from a past life; they jiggled no recall of the photographed events. Her husband's long illness and death had been so traumatic that she had to repress the good times, because she couldn't bear to think about the happiness she had lost.

Freud believed that repression explains why we do not remember the childhood lust for our mother or father that he hypothesized to exist in our unconscious. At the same time, this lust is incomplete, and the repressed urges seep out in dreams and slips of the tongue.

Projection

Projection is a means of attributing one's own unacceptable and disturbing thoughts and impulses to others. "The thief thinks everyone else is thief," says an El Salvadoran proverb. A man preoccupied with doubts about his own heterosexuality may become homophobic and frequently accuse others of being homosexual. In addition to explaining homophobia, projection explains racial prejudice when one group accuses another of its own unacceptable impulses or characteristics.

Denial

While repression blocks internal thoughts from conscious awareness, *denial* blocks external events whose perception threatens our ego. For instance, as the husband lies dying, the wife continues to set his place at the table; she denies his impending death. All of us deny reality to some extent. Smokers and junk food eaters deny the potential health risks of their habits. Gamblers keep taking chances that the slot machine will pour out thousands of quarters or that one of the hundreds of lottery tickets they purchased will be the winner, denying the extremely slim likelihood of winning a fortune. While denial can be dangerous, as in continuing to smoke or overeat, it can also be adaptive. Denying that you have terminal cancer may keep your mood more upbeat and might actually facilitate healing rather than allowing you to become deeply depressed and lose all hope.

Reaction Formation

When people overemphasize the opposite of a dangerous impulse, they are employing *reaction formation:* "I love him" becomes "I hate him"; timidity becomes daring; inadequacy becomes conceit. For instance, a man who is terrified of his dependency says he doesn't need anyone. Some nuns and priests may have entered the clergy in reaction to a fear of their own sexual urges.

Rationalization

We all devise extremely reasonable explanations of our behaviors to protect our self-esteem. For instance, we go off our diet and eat a huge slice of birthday cake at our friend's birthday party *rationalizing* that we don't want to be rude. We down three martinis to be "sociable." A wife explains her husband's repeated infidelity as a result of his unfortunate upbringing or an overly seductive environment.

Regression

Regression means retreating to an earlier, more primitive form of behavior to avoid pain or threat. Freud made this comparison to "a stream of water which meets with an obstacle in the river bed, is dammed up and flows back into old channels which had formerly seemed fated to run dry." Whenever confronting a tough decision or a threatening situation, a friend's mother lapses into baby talk with her grown daughter, for instance, telling her that she has to "go pee pee." After a fight with your husband, you lap up a pint of ice cream, regressing to the early oral phase of development. A person has sexual difficulty in a relationship and retreats to masturbation, regressing, according to Freud, to the phallic stage of development.

Displacement

We all have experienced shifting or *displacing* an impulse from a threatening to a nonthreatening object. For instance, a husband angry at his boss because of a demotion goes home and argues with his wife.

Sublimation

Living in civilized society requires that we channel socially unacceptable impulses into acceptable, even admirable behavior that we *sublimate*. The surgeon channels aggressive energy into constructive medical work; the artist employs the libido to produce a masterpiece. And of course there's all the screaming, yelling, and chest pounding at the Sunday football game. Freud viewed Leonardo da Vinci's painting of the Madonna as a sublimation of his longing for intimacy with his mother, who left when he was very young.

Depression and Mourning

All of us experience loss. But while most of us get depressed, grieve, then get over it and on with our lives, some people fall into a major depression and get stuck in that black hole. Freud was struck by the similarities between depression—"melancholia"— and mourning, which he explored in his 1917 essay "Mourning and Melancholia." Both involve loss of a love object, painful dejection and sadness, loss of interest in the world, low energy, and inability to love. But whereas the bereaved experiences the *world* as "poor and empty," the depressed person feels *herself* "poor and empty."

Depression, Freud ingeniously concluded, was "frozen anger," or "anger directed against oneself," replete with reproaches, low self-esteem, and even self-hate and self-attack. While grief and preoccupation with loss serves to hold onto the lost person, in depression the self splits: "one part of the ego sets itself over against the other, judges it critically, and, as it were, takes it as its object." This is in effect conscience—the superego—and illustrates how we keep punitive authority figures alive in us and still beating us up.

The idea of depression as anger against self is one with which the depressed person can easily identify. The neuroscientist Robert Sapolsky commented, "Suddenly the loss of pleasure, the psychomotor retardation, the impulse to suicide all make sense. As do the elevated glucocorticoid levels. This does not describe someone too lethargic to function; it is more like the actual state of a patient in depression, exhausted from the most draining emotional conflict of his or her life—one going on entirely within."

Why does such depression happen? All love relationships contain ambivalent feelings; mixed in with love is some hate. When we normally mourn a person's loss, we can resolve these mixed feelings: we lose; we grieve; we recover. But when we get depressed— melancholic—ambivalence dominates and feels irreconcilable. Thus, asserted Freud, melancholy is the internal conflict spawned by this ambivalence. As you have both lost your love and any chance to resolve your conflicts, you grieve doubly and become obsessed with the intensely mixed feelings. You ruminate on "only ifs": "If I hadn't said that"; "If I had only said this." But it's too late. You will never know if things could have been different.

Alongside intense grief in a major depression is another uncomfortable emotion: intense guilt. If along with love you harbored intense anger toward the lost person, some part of you is celebrating as well as grieving. "He's gone . . . thank God. I can finally do as I please, grow up, find someone worthy." In the next second comes the reproach: "How can I feel relief in this sad time? I must be an unfeeling monster." Guilt!

How does the melancholic person resolve such ambivalence? You begin to take on some of the traits of the lost loved/hated one—you "introject the lost object." To undo the loss, you behave as if the lost person is now a part of you; he lives on inside. And what traits do you assume? Invariably those you found most annoying, as if to justify that you were right to be irritated: "If I'm now impossible to put up with, imagine how hard it was to have put up with your constant complaining." This introjection, Freud thought, helps you fend off the loss and also express the angry side of the ambivalence.

Freud believed that he discovered the concept of introjecting and identifying with the lost object in his case of a young homosexual girl. He analyzed the girl as desperately wanting a baby with her father. Her mother became pregnant, and the girl felt betrayed and furious at all men and hostile and competitive toward her mother. Freud analyzed her homosexuality as a way to become like her father by loving women. While Freud originally conceptualized introjection of the lost object to occur only in pathological grieving, in *The Ego and the Id* he conceded that this was a universal response to mourning the lost object. In fact, introjecting the good qualities of the lost person—for instance, through comforting memories and fantasies—may greatly help to resolve the devastation of the loss.

Freud's insightful work in understanding mourning and melancholy contributed greatly to our understanding of human suffering, and his findings have become among the best understood and most thoroughly explored therapeutic tools.

Dissenters

*He was a man possessed by a daemon—a man vouchsafed
an overwhelming revelation that took possession of his soul
and never let him go.*

—Carl Jung

Freud's inner circle was a hotbed of conflict. This was inevitable.
As psychoanalysis assaulted the conventional wisdom of the time,
those attracted to its tenets tended to be creative, unconventional
thinkers. While in deference to Freud most initially concurred with
his unwavering insistence that the origin of *all* neuroses lay in sexual conflict, eventually many would challenge the sacred psychoanalytic text and defy the word of the father to go out in the world
and develop their own creative psychologies. Over the years, a son
would leave or be cast out, in classic Oedipal fashion. Some dis-
sented and blazed an entirely different trail to break new ground in
psychology. Alfred Adler, who became Freud's archenemy; Otto
Rank, who Freud took in like a son and then banished him; and
Carl Jung, Freud's greatest hope and then his greatest disappointment, were the three most notable dissenters.

Alfred Adler

Adler met Freud in 1902, and, although skeptical of Freud's theories
from the start, he became quickly active in psychoanalytic circles.
In 1910, he became the first president of the Vienna Psychoanalytic
Society but quickly lost tolerance for Freud's orthodoxy and, fol-
lowing a succession of bitter disputes, severed his relationship with
Freud a year later.

Publicly denying that sexuality was at the center of instinctual
life, Adler argued for a basic motive of aggression, a stance that
Freud would ironically take some twelve years later in his reformu-
lation of human motivation to include both life and death
instincts. To Adler and many other neo-Freudians, the childhood
tensions that are crucial for personality development are largely
social, not *sexual*. Struggling to overcome childhood illnesses and

accidents, Adler proposed that behavior is driven largely by an effort to conquer childhood feelings of inferiority—feelings that trigger our need for love and security. Adler put forth the idea of the "inferiority complex," which has become instilled in our cultural psychic niche. He formed his own group and eventually attracted followers worldwide.

After immigrating to the United States, Adler wrote Freud to implore him to reconsider his position. By downgrading the sexual component, he found American professional physicians and psychiatrists far more willing to accept psychoanalysis. Freud was enraged. If the goal was to be "acceptable," Freud wrote back, then the whole psychoanalytic movement had better pull down the blinds and go home.

Freud never forgave Adler for his infidelity, and from 1911 on, there was bitter enmity between the two men; when Adler died in June 1937, Freud felt gratified that he had outlived him. In *Civilization and Its Discontents*, Freud wrote of failing to understand the Christian order to universal love; many people were detestable, especially those infidels (implying Adler and Jung) who became famous by taking advantage of public dissent to his libido theory.

Otto Rank

Alfred Adler introduced Freud to Otto Rank, who became initially one of Freud's most favored sons. Adler was Rank's family physician and introduced him to Freud's writings, which Rank devoured. A trained machinist, short, unprepossessing, and in ill health, the highly intelligent Rank escaped from the miseries of his impoverished and deeply unhappy Jewish family—he had been neglected by his mother and terrorized by his alcoholic father—by an infinite appetite for learning. Rank read everything.

In the spring of 1905, twenty-one-year-old Rank gave forty-nine-year-old Freud a manuscript of his book, *The Artist*, in which he applied to culture and the arts psychoanalytic ideas, demonstrating a mastery of Freud's work. Freud quickly recognized Rank's potential and took him under his wing. He made him secretary of the Wednesday Psychoanalytic Society, employed him as his assistant for the revision of his writings, and provided financial and emotional support for Rank's doctoral work. Freud felt paternal toward Rank, affectionately calling him "little Rank," and Rank almost became a member of the Freud household. Before the Wednesday evening meeting of the psychoanalytic club, Rank dined with the Freud family. Freud may have even hoped that Rank would marry his daughter, Anna. Although the men were close, their relationship was father to dutiful son. Rank revered Freud and courted his favor. At meetings, he would gladly fetch a glass of water for Freud or light his cigar.

Rank was drafted into the Austrian army in 1915 to serve during World War I. When he returned from duty, he was transformed from the timid, deferential Freud gofer to a strong-willed, independent adult. He fell in love, married, and became a practicing psychoanalyst, as well as the managing director of the International Psychoanalytic Press.

From 1920 on, signs hinted that Rank was developing his own ideas apart from Freud's. He coauthored a book on psychoanalytic technique, *The Development of Psychoanalysis*, with Sándor Ferenczi, another Freud disciple. In the book, the two authors advocated an "active therapy" that was radically different from classical psychoanalysis. Far from the analyst as a stern father, she was a "midwife" who assisted the patient to create a new personality. The focus in therapy was not on reconstructing the past but on reliving emotional relationships.

Although Freud accepted the publication of this book with reserve, the coup d'état came in 1924 with the publication of Rank's *The Trauma of Birth*, which held that life in the womb was the prototype of pleasure and security and that separation from the mother at birth was the primary source of anxiety. Rank traced many later conflicts and neurotic symptoms to this original trauma. He dedicated the book to Freud—"Presented to the Explorer of the Unconscious and Creator of Psychoanalysis"—and said that his thesis originated with Freud's statement: "We shall take as our guiding principle that all anxiety goes back originally to the anxiety at birth" (an aside in *The Interpretation of Dreams*).

In *The Trauma of Birth*, Rank argued that the birth trauma was the central emotional constellation in psychological development, neurotic and normal. In one fell swoop, he dethroned the Oedipus complex and sexual strivings from their primacy. To Freud, Rank's ideas threatened his psychoanalysis; he repudiated them and banished Rank from the Psychoanalytic Society.

Breaking with his surrogate father was profoundly traumatic for Rank, who returned to Vienna and went into analysis with Freud as a last attempt at reconciliation, confessing that his book came from "neurotic" motives. Freud urged him to write a letter stating this to the committee, an elite group of Freud's closest followers in the Psychoanalytic Society, which Rank did, as if brainwashed: "From a state which I now recognize as neurotic, I have suddenly returned to myself. . . . I was able to understand the type of reaction and its mechanism from my childhood and family history—the Oedipus and brother complexes."

But eventually Rank got the courage to break completely with Freud. Freud's followers labeled Rank crazy—in his biography of Freud, Jones described the break with Freud as evident of "psychotic manifestations"—and his theories a product of mental illness, while Freud vacillated between describing Rank as unhinged and childishly rebellious. In fact, Rank lived a productive life, including a new love. Nor did he later express bitterness toward Freud.

Carl Jung

> If ever you should rid yourself entirely of your complexes
> and stop playing the father to your sons and instead of aiming continually at their weak spots took a good look at your
> own for a change, then I will mend my ways and at one
> stroke uproot the vice of being in two minds about you.
>
> —Carl Jung to Sigmund Freud

In April 1906, a month short of Freud's much celebrated fiftieth birthday, thirty-one-year-old Carl Jung, a Swiss clinical and experimental psychiatrist living in Zurich, sent Freud a copy of *Diagnostic Association Studies* that he had edited, including an important paper of his own. Freud was impressed. The two corresponded for a year, then met in Vienna on March 3, 1907. Large, strong, eloquent, and brimming with vitality and a sparkling intellect, Jung was instantly appealing to Freud, and Freud immediately asked Jung to be his gentile "scientific son and heir" to defend his "Jewish science" and carry forth the psychoanalytic torch. Seeking a prominent father figure, Jung felt flattered, and the two men quickly developed an intimate relationship, but it lasted only five years. In 1911, Jung, as did so many others, broke with Freud over the role of sexuality in the neuroses.

In 1910, not long before their final break, Freud requested of Jung: "Promise me never to abandon the sexual theory. . . . We must make a dogma of it, an unshakable bulwark." Against what? Jung asked. "Against the black tide of mud . . . of occultism." How ironic. Jung would later launch psychology into the mystical and set in motion the New Age spirituality that has overtaken the modern ethos.

The son of a pastor, Jung was born into the occult. His mother, who suffered delusions, hysteria, and a split personality, believed their house was haunted by ghosts. His cousin ran family séances in which he participated. Jung, biased toward the existence of the paranormal, chose it as the subject of his dissertation: "On the Psychology and Pathology of So-Called Occult Phenomena." From an early age, he had mystical visions—one included God dropping "an enormous turd" on a cathedral—and throughout his life was beset by religious crises. Jung always saw himself as essentially two people. One part of him chose to be a physician and make science his life; the other was preoccupied with the occult, fascinated with religions, and lived a rich and dream-filled fantasy life. Freud and Jung's relationship was doomed from the start.

Jung was introduced to Freud by his mentor, the eminent Eugen Bleuler, the director of the Burgholzli sanatorium, which served as the psychiatric clinic for the University of Zurich. Shortly after his arrival at the sanatorium, Bleuler asked Jung to report to the staff on *The Interpretation of Dreams.* Jung was intrigued and soon incorporated ideas from Freud's dream book, the early papers on hysteria, and, after 1905, the case history of

Dora, into his own researches and into his understanding of schizophrenia, the psychosis in which he specialized and made his reputation. In the summer of 1906, in the preface to his much-praised monograph *On the Psychology of Dementia Praecox*, he singled out the "brilliant conceptions" of Freud, who had "not yet received his just recognition and appreciation." He also did innovative experimental work that buttressed Freud's conclusions, and in 1906, in a remarkable book on word association, he offered ample experimental evidence to support Freud's theory of free association.

In March, almost a year after they had begun to exchange letters, Jung visited Freud at Berggasse 19, accompanied by his wife Emma and his young colleague Ludwig Binswanger, an early existentialist. The two men talked extensively in between a meeting of the Wednesday Psychoanalytic Society and family meals. Martin Freud recalled that Jung was full of himself and his case histories. He "never made the slightest attempt to make polite conversation with mother or us children but pursued the debate which had been interrupted by the call to dinner. Jung on these occasions did all the talking and father with unconcealed delight did all the listening." Jung recalled the discussion between himself and Freud as more evenly matched and endless. They talked, he remembered, for thirteen hours, virtually without stopping. Jung struck the Freuds as exploding with vitality and, Martin Freud wrote, endowed with "a commanding presence. He was very tall and broad-shouldered, holding himself more like a soldier than a man of science and medicine. His head was purely Teutonic with a strong chin, a small mustache, blue eyes and thin close-cropped hair." He appeared to enjoy himself enormously.

Once initiated, their friendship flourished. They politely exchanged letters and discussed the place of sexuality in the genesis of neuroses, exchanged books, and traded vignettes from cases that particularly intrigued them.

In his letters to other intimates, Freud repeatedly praised Jung for doing "splendid, magnificent" work in editing, theorizing, or smiting the enemies of psychoanalysis. Jung guaranteed that psychoanalysis would survive its founder's demise, to Freud's delight.

In the summer of 1908, he told Jung he was coming for a visit and planned to "install" Jung as the analyst who would continue and complete "my work." As a "strong, independent personality, as a Teuton," Jung seemed best equipped, Freud told him frankly, to enlist the sympathetic interest of the outside world on behalf of their great enterprise. Jung was not Viennese, not old, and, best of all, not Jewish—Jung was irresistible.

Jung basked in Freud's glowing approval. "I thank you with all my heart for the proof of your confidence," he wrote in February 1908 after Freud had first addressed him as "Dear Friend." This "undeserved gift of your friendship signifies for me a certain high point of my life, which I cannot celebrate with noisy words." He asked Freud "to let me enjoy your friendship not as that of equals but as that of father and son. Such a distance appears to me appropriate and natural." As the appointed heir to Freud's magnificent legacy, chosen by the founder himself, Jung felt a call to greatness.

Jung continually reassured Freud of his "unconditional devotion" to Freud's theories and his "no less unconditional veneration" of Freud's person. "You may rest assured," he had written Freud in 1907, "that I shall never abandon a piece of your theory essential to me—I am far too committed for that." Two years later, he reassured Freud once again: "Not only for now but for all the future, nothing Fliess-like will happen." Freud wasn't convinced. Jung's "veneration" had a "religious" enthusiasm, and Freud knew that a religious transference was doomed; nor did he feel worthy of such reverence and tried to dissuade Jung from such worship, as "I am unsuitable to be a cult object." Soon, the crown prince turned into the prince of darkness and would agree.

Jung had long struggled in applying Freud's theories to an understanding of schizophrenia. Gradually, he came to question some of Freud's cherished practices and beliefs, particularly the inordinate importance given to sexuality. This theoretical conflict created strong feelings in Jung, who, intensely creative, had to seek his own identity and be true to his own ideas.

The turning point may have come with Freud's misinterpretation of a crucial dream of Jung's—one of the most important of

Jung's life. He was in an unknown house of two stories, but he knew it belonged to him. The upper floor was furnished in rococo style with fine oil paintings; the ground floor was "much older," dark, with medieval overtones. Behind a "heavy door," he found a stone stairway that led down to a cellar, a beautifully vaulted room that was incredibly ancient, dating perhaps from Roman times. Set in the floor of the cellar was a ringed stone slab that revealed another stairway when lifted, which led to a low cave cut into the rock. "Thick dust lay on the floor, and in the dust were scattered bones and broken pottery, like remains of a primitive culture." Here were two very old and half-disintegrated human skulls.

When told of the dream, Freud immediately focused on the two skulls and repeatedly asked Jung whether he could uncover any "wish" connected with them. Jung knew that Freud was fishing for a secret death wish; to not disappoint Freud, he lied and said they reminded him of his wife and his sister-in-law. A newlywed, Jung felt no death wish against his wife, but Freud "seemed greatly relieved" at the reply, as this explanation fit his theories. This was a turning point for Jung. Freud's quick acceptance of his glib interpretation revealed Freud's theoretical myopia.

To Jung the house represented the psyche; the top floor with its "inhabited" feeling referred to consciousness, while the ground floor stood for the "first level of the unconscious." The deeper he went, the more alien and dark the scene became, with the cave representing the very lowest level of the unconscious. Here the skulls and the other remains of a primitive culture symbolized the world of primitive man existing in the deepest layers of the mind. To Jung, the successive levels of the house and the increasing antiquity that each level revealed struck him as a history of the evolution of the conscious and unconscious mind. The top level was the consciousness of this lifetime; the other floors reflected aspects of consciousness laid down in earlier human history.

Jung was beginning to play with archetypal images and the collective unconscious, which contains images derived from our early ancestors' experience explaining why spirituality is deeply rooted for many people and certain myths and images are universal:

mother/earth mother/Virgin Mary/church/godmother symbolizes nurturance; hero/Christ/Abraham Lincoln symbolizes overcoming humble birth with superhuman powers; shadow/Satan/devils/aliens/Hitler symbolizes the dark half of personality.

In 1911, he wrote *Symbols of Transformation* and formulated his own theories on schizophrenia, as well as plunging into research in religion and mythology. To Jung, the loss of reality in schizophrenia "cannot be reduced to repression of libido—defined as sexual hunger. Not by me at any rate." Jung wrote Freud that he disagreed that all anxiety can be traced back to castration threats during the Oedipal conflict, because his own research had convinced him of the power of mothers, as revealed in mythology: Jung and Freud now locked theoretical horns. It was only a matter of time before Jung's thinking would radically divert from Freud's. He would come to believe that the key to decoding neurotic symptoms lay within the history of civilization and mythology; sexual repression and family issues were of secondary importance. As Freud considered any disagreement of his sexual theory infidelity, Jung's fate was sealed. In little time, Freud disinherited him, losing the perfect son/heir, while Jung lost the strong and loving father/idol he never had.

They attempted reconciliation. But ultimately their friendship ended in enmity and insults. Freud called Jung "crazy" and his ideas "abnormal"—"fairy tales," "spookery," and "occultism." Some psychoanalysts still dismiss Jung's theories as "mystical" in contrast to Freud's "scientific" theories.

After the break, Freud, backed by his entourage of followers, quickly regained equanimity. Jung fell apart and struggled for years in a near-psychotic state. In Jung's words: "After the break with Freud, all my friends and acquaintances dropped away. My book was declared to be rubbish; I was a mystic, and that settled the matter . . . a period of inner uncertainty began for me. It would be no exaggeration to call it a state of disorientation." He felt panic, terror, intense guilt, suicidal impulses, images of death and dying, and a disorienting loss of reality. Even worse, he described being "menaced by psychosis . . . the ground literally gave way beneath my feet, and I plunged down into dark depths."

For all his seeming self-confidence and vibrant, forceful personality, Jung was vulnerable, highly sensitive, and intensely emotional, vacillating between intense joy and intense fear of the world. Since childhood, he felt that he was in reality two people: a child and an authoritative wise old man who had lived in the eighteenth century. So convinced was Jung of his ancient roots that occasionally while doing school work he would write "1786" rather than the real date. In childhood, several experiences convinced him that he was two people. One involved a game that Jung frequently played with a large stone jutting from the garden wall on which he would sit:

> I am sitting on top of this stone and it is underneath. But the stone could also say "I" and think: "I am lying here on this slope and he is sitting on top of me." The question then arose: "Am I the one who is sitting on the stone, or am I the stone on which *he* is sitting?" This question always perplexed me, and I would stand up, wondering who was what now. The answer remained totally unclear, and my uncertainty was accompanied by a feeling of curious and fascinating darkness.

Jung had hoped that Freud and psychoanalysis would help him integrate his different sides. With Freud, he could entrust his dreams, emotions, and ideas. Psychoanalysis became for him his belief system—"the myth in which you live." When he lost Freud, he lost the thread that kept him together, and he unraveled.

Jung overcame his "madness" and created his own psychoanalysis and his own fame that continues to increase in popularity as Freud's continues to decline. The Jungian concepts of archetypes, like anima and animus, and the collective unconscious heralded today's New Age of spiritual growth, while his two dimensions of personality, extroverted and introverted, which came to him when he compared the reserved Alfred Adler to Freud's more outgoing social personality, and man's four basic functions—thinking, feeling, sensation, and intuition—are widely used in a personality test devised for job applicants.

The story of the two historic figures has long captured public attention. Recently, *The Talking Cure,* a play by Christopher Hampton, directed by Howard Davies and performed in London in 2003, opened on Broadway, telling the story of Carl Jung's affair with an early analytic patient, Sabina Spielrein. A well-educated Russian eighteen-year-old whom he began treating in 1904, Spielrein went on to study with Freud and became a gifted psychoanalyst herself. In the play, Spielrein goes back and forth between the two saviors, as Hampton depicts the decline of Jung's volatile six-year relationship with Freud and his transformation from the "heir apparent of psychoanalysis" to the alienated traitor.

Writes John Lahr in his review of the play in the *New Yorker* (January 27, 2003): "Both geniuses appear spectacularly brilliant and spectacularly misguided. When Jung challenges Freud's authority, Freud faints; when Freud challenges Jung's appropriateness, Jung lies. 'I let her become a friend,' he tells Freud. 'But eventually I realized she was systematically planning my seduction.'" Later, Jung admitted to Freud that he, not Sabina, had been the seducer. He ended their sexual intimacy and helped and supported Sabina, who overcame her psychosis and became a psychoanalyst, joining Freud's group in Vienna and eventually returning to her native Russia.

Dora (Case)

On October 14, 1900, Freud told his friend Wilhelm Fleiss of a new, fascinating case: Dora, whose real name was Ida Bauer. "It has been a lively time," he wrote, "and I have a new patient, a girl of eighteen: the case has opened smoothly to my collection of picklocks." Three months later, Dora ended the therapy, robbing Freud of the chance to unlock the secrets of her mind. Freud was shocked and hurt: "Her breaking off unexpectedly, just when my hopes of a successful termination of the treatment were at their highest, and her thus bringing those hopes to nothing—this was an unmistakable act of vengeance on her part." Freud, however, discovered this case to indeed contain jewels that he quickly mined, propelling his theory forward. In January of the following year, Freud wrote his short but crucial case: "Fragment of an Analysis of a Case of Hysteria."

Dora, a girl "in the first bloom of youth of intelligent and engaging looks," was deeply unhappy, irritable, and melancholy. She suffered from breathing difficulties, recurrent headaches, fainting spells, and violent attacks of nervous coughing that often led to a loss of voice—all symptoms of *hysteria*. Dora argued incessantly with her parents and left them a note saying that she could no longer endure life. Alarmed by her deterioration, Dora's father, a wealthy industrialist and a former patient of Freud's, insisted that she see Dr. Freud for therapy.

Although estranged from her neurotic mother, a compulsive house cleaner who made Dora's life miserable, she had felt close to her father but was now angry at him. For years, he had been having an affair with Frau K., a surrogate mother figure for Dora. Apparently, Herr K. knew of the affair and considered the teenage Dora fair exchange for his wife. He made two sexual advances to her. When Dora was thirteen, Herr K. had suddenly embraced her and kissed her on the mouth at his place of business. Experiencing a "violent feeling of disgust," Dora broke loose from Herr K. and ran into the street. Two years later, as they walked back to a vacation house from a visit to an Alpine lake, Herr K. again grabbed Dora and kissed her on the mouth. Dora slapped his face. She told her mother of the incident, and her mother told her father, who confronted Herr K. He denied the event ever happened and said that Dora was obsessed with sexuality and probably fantasized the whole incident. Her father believed Herr K.

Freud interpreted these two sexual attacks as the traumatic roots of her hysterical symptoms. As Herr K. was a handsome man, Freud reasoned that the disgust Dora felt when Herr K. first kissed her disguised her sexual interest—a typically "hysterical" reaction. Further, Freud interpreted disgust as a common, although neurotic, "means of affective expression in the sphere of sexual life," especially as the male sexual organ reminds the woman of urination. Her nervous cough came from displacing the positive sensation of sexual arousal from her genitals to her thorax and mouth. Since the incident, Dora had occasionally hallucinated that she felt Herr K.'s embrace on the *upper* part of her body. Freud speculated that when Herr K. embraced her, he had an erection that Dora felt in the *lower* part of her body. This "perception was revolting to her" and thus "dismissed from memory, repressed, and replaced by the innocent sensation of pressure upon her thorax, which in turn derived an excessive intensity from its repressed source."

Freud's leap from mouth to genitals fit with his newly developing libido theory in which the mouth was the first erogenous zone. A thumb sucker for many years, Dora had a memory of sitting contentedly on the floor as a child, sucking her thumb as she tugged at her brother's ear. Freud theorized that Dora continued to derive sensual pleasure from sucking through her middle childhood years and speculated that she unconsciously fantasized oral sex between her father and Frau K. Apparently, Dora believed that her father was frequently impotent and that Frau K. used oral stimulation to satisfy him sexually. These sexual fantasies produced an oral symptom of hysteria: her persistent cough. After Dora "tacitly accepted" Freud's interpretation, the cough disappeared.

Dora's therapy revolved around the following recurrent dream:

A house was on fire. My father was standing beside my bed and woke me up. I dressed myself quickly. Mother wanted to stop and save her jewel-case; but father said: "two children will be burnt for the sake of your jewel-case." We hurried downstairs, and as soon as I was outside I woke up.

Dora first had this dream for three successive nights following Herr K.'s first kiss. As she recounted the incident to Freud two years later, the dream returned. Freud was intrigued. He asked Dora to let her mind wander and to report her stream of thought. She told him of a recent argument between her father and mother about locking her brother's bedroom door. Dora's mother wanted to lock the door at night, but her father objected, worried that "something might happen in the night so that it might be necessary to leave the room." Something like a *fire*, Freud guessed; Dora agreed. Then

Dora remembered that two years ago at the lake her family and the K.'s were staying at a small wooden house that her father feared might easily burn down. This was precisely the time that she first dreamed the dream.

Dora remembered returning from a walk with Herr K. to the wooden house at noon and taking a nap on a sofa in one of the bedrooms. Shortly after lying down, she awoke, startled to see Herr K. standing beside her (as her father had awakened her and stood at the foot of her bed in the dream). She was furious, but Herr K. told her that he was "not going to be prevented from coming into his own bedroom when he wanted." So Dora secured a key for the bedroom, but Herr K. stole the key. After that, she always *dressed quickly* in the bedroom, as she did in the dream, fearful that Herr K. would break in. On one level, then, the dream brought to resolution Dora's problem with Herr K. In the dream, her father *saved* her from the fire by whisking her through the unlocked door of her bedroom so that she could escape. In so doing, her father symbolically saved her from the "fiery" sexual advances of Herr K.

The sexuality in the dream, argued Freud, is apparent in the *jewel-case*—Freud believed that receptacles symbolized the vagina. Among other things, Freud pointed out that "jewel-case" (*Schmuckkästchen* in German) is a common slang word for a virgin girl's *genitals*. Dora retorted, "I knew you would say that," a response that Freud remarked is "a very common way of putting aside a piece of knowledge that emerges from the repressed."

Freud interpreted the dream as Herr K.'s wish to make Dora's jewel-case his own—to have sexual intercourse with her—and Dora's wish to both repel him and give in, offering her jewel-case/genitals as a love "gift." Freud then argued that her father/savior in the dream also represented the object of Dora's own romantic/sexual longings—her Electra complex. Her father was a composite of both her father and Herr K.—both of whom Dora loved, feared, and occasionally resented. Her mother was a composite of both her mother and Frau K.—both of whom she resented but wished on some level to be. Although her mother rejected her father's gifts, Dora would happily accept the bracelet from her father and give him the gift of her jewel-case/vagina. Her dream was the Electra complex in disguise.

But Freud didn't stop. Once he got on the Oedipal bandwagon, he rode it until he exhausted all avenues. Freud reminded Dora of an old folk belief that children who play with matches (fire) tend to wet their beds (water). Dora said she had not heard of it. Freud continued. Dora's first association in the dream of her father's fear that "something might happen in the night so that it might be necessary to leave the room" suggested both fire and bedwetting. In fact, both Dora and her brother were bedwetters to the point that her parents called in a doctor when she was about seven. As in the dream, her father may have occasionally woken her up in the middle of the night to take her to the toilet.

Freud associated bedwetting with *masturbation*. Dora denied any memories of childhood masturbation. But after discussing the topic, she showed up wearing at her waist a small *reticule* (a purse-like bag) that "she kept playing with, . . . opening it, putting a finger into it, shutting it again, and so on." To Freud, the jury was in: the reticule was a substitute for the vagina. He surmised that Dora masturbated frequently as a child of age seven and eight, when she was an inveterate bedwetter, and that she felt guilty about both behaviors, regarding them as *dirty* and associated with sexuality. In fact, all sexuality was dirty, since her father, Dora learned at an early age, had contracted a *venereal disease* before marrying. Her mother's obsession with *cleanliness* was a reaction to being dirtied by her husband's venereal disease.

Freud concluded that Dora blamed her father for her illnesses, unconsciously believing that she too had a venereal disease that she inherited from him. Although there was no medical evidence of the disease, Dora nonetheless believed this to be true. She cited as evidence recurrent *catarrh*—an infectious secretion manifested in periodic vaginal discharges, about which she felt great shame and disgust. Freud asserted that unconsciously the catarrh was one of Dora's psychological "proofs" that her problems were her father's fault. Not only had he "handed her over" to Herr K., but he had also given her a dirty sexual disease. All sexual phenomena were dirty and disgusting to Dora, explaining why, in part, Dora felt disgust, not sexual excitement, when Herr K. first kissed her.

Was it any wonder that Dora quit therapy? She probably went to see Freud in the hope of a sympathetic ear to her position as pawn in an adult chess game of sexual trade-offs. Instead, she was told that she unconsciously wanted to bed the scoundrel who had taken advantage of her innocence and who repelled her. But the person she really wished to have sex with and marry was her father!

Read today, Freud's domineering and unsympathetic attitude toward Dora seems outrageously insensitive. But despite its therapeutic failure, Dora's breaking off the treatment after three months, her anger with Freud, and her claim that he had not cured her led Freud to formulate his theory of transference. He later speculated that Dora was unconsciously transferring dynamics from her interactions with Herr K. and her father onto the therapeutic relationship—relating to Freud as father/lover/enemy. When interpreting what he believed to be her pleasure at Herr K.'s kiss, he assumed that "indications . . . seemed to point to there having been a *transference* on to me . . . the idea had probably occurred to her one day during a sitting that she would like to have a kiss from me." And Freud may have been unwittingly countertransferring some of his own unconscious feelings about young neurotic women onto Dora. When she stopped the treatment, he believed she was taking revenge on him, just as she wished to do with her father and Herr K. Admittedly, by not recognizing and dealing with this transference, he had allowed her to act out her feelings. While this transference of feelings initially seemed a major obstruction in this case, Freud's recognition of it eventually enabled him to better understand the dynamics underlying a patient's and an analyst's behavior, and the *transference* became a powerful therapeutic tool that advanced his new science.

Despite the shortcomings in Freud's therapeutic technique and his outlandish gender biases, Freud's analysis of the case, which reads like a Sherlock Holmes detective story, is impressive. The Freud scholar Steven Marcus marvels at the "over one hundred pages of dazzling originality, of creative genius performing with a compactness, complexity, daring, and splendor that seem close to incomparable in their order."

Dora returned to Freud's office fifteen months after terminating treatment to tell him that she had confronted Frau K. and her father about their affair and Herr K. about his inappropriate conduct. A year later, she married, then bore her only child, a son. In an odd turn of events, Dora visited another psychoanalyst, Dr. Felix Deutsch, in 1922 for treatment of hysterical symptoms, announcing that she indeed was Dora, the famous patient of Freud's case. According to Deutsch, Dora never recovered from her neurosis. Her cough and asthma still plagued her twenty years after her last meeting with Freud. As an adult, she repeatedly accused others— her husband, her son, her few acquaintances—of persecuting and betraying her. In Deutsch's view, her husband was "slighted and tortured by her almost paranoid behavior." Dora apparently lived an extremely unhappy life. She died of colon cancer in New York City in 1945 at age sixty-three.

Dreams

See **Analysis of Self;** *Interpretation of Dreams, The*.

Drives

See *Beyond the Pleasure Principle;* **Instincts.**

Ego and the Id, The

A *New Yorker* cartoon by Roz Chast from 1983 displays four captions: the Voice of Reason (a maternal woman) says, "It's not such a big thing; just put the galoshes on"; the Voice of Conscience (a maternal woman) says, "Mom will be mad if you don't put them on"; the Voice of Practicality (a paternal man) says, "It's raining. Why don't you just wear them?"; the Voice of Binky (a clown) says, "Toss them out the window." The Voices of Reason and Conscience, a maternal woman, were the *ego*; the Voice of Practicality, a paternal man, was the *superego*; the Voice of Binky, the clown, was the *id*.

In *The Ego and the Id*, published in 1923, Freud revamped how the mind is organized. Early on, Freud had proposed a neurological model of the mind (see **Project for a Scientific Psychology**) that would portend the neurological advances of the second half of the twentieth century, although it was soon abandoned. In chapter 7 of *The Interpretation of Dreams*, he proposed a *psychological* model of the mind divided into three separate systems: conscious, precon-scious, and unconscious (see **Topographical Model**). But this sys-tem didn't fit with Freud's notion of the mind as being in unremitting conflict. In this new theory, he concluded that the mind can be broken down into three independent structures for-ever at war: id, ego, and superego.

Each of the three agencies exists for a different purpose. Housing the basic survival instincts, the *id* strives for immediate satisfaction. The *ego* seeks to control these primal instincts by seek-ing realistic ways to express them. The *superego* censures and tries to block instincts that are unacceptable by society.

Id

Completely submerged in the unconscious—the part of the iceberg underneath the water, in Freud's famous analogy of the mind—the primitive *id* (*das Es* in German, or "the it") houses the instinctual impulses of sex and aggression and their primal wishes. It is a chaotic "seething cauldron of desire" inhabited by selfish, sexual, destruc-tive, and barbaric emotions that constantly threaten to break loose. Governed by the *pleasure principle*, the id demands immediate gratification: "I want it now!" Today, we would identify the id as the primitive, reptilian "gut" brain housed in the brain stem, along with the "emotional" limbic brain. Sexual hormones are especially active in the hypothalamus of the limbic system, the part of the brain that controls basic survival functions such as breathing and heart rate.

A bundle of primitive instinctual urges, the baby is born "all id" and governed by *primary process thinking*—irrational, timeless, immoral instinct-driven thought that fails to distinguish fantasy from reality, wish from action. As the child learns that she must attend to and learn the rules of the real world or pay the consequences, primary process thinking becomes less prominent. After all, if we remained id driven and took what we wanted when we wanted it, we would all be in jail. Unbridled id strivings must be tamed.

And so, beginning in infancy, a second structure of the mind emerges out of the id: the ego (*das Ich* in German, or "the I"), or conscious self.

Ego

Representing "what may be called reason and common sense, in contrast to the id, which contains the passions," the ego works diligently to arbitrate the blind demands of the id and the restrictions that the external world imposes. It helps us survive safely in the world by obeying the *reality principle*—"I may want it now but I know I have to wait"—and by relying on the power of *secondary process thought*—sensible, logical thinking about the consequence of eating that candy bar before dinner. The ego is the part of the brain that we may now refer to as the prefrontal cortex, our thinking brain and home of the executive functions: planning, setting priorities, organizing thoughts, suppressing impulses, weighing the consequences of our actions.

Whereas the id is totally unconscious, the ego is partly conscious—the tip of the visible iceberg. Consciously, our ego helps us function rationally and make wise decisions. Unconsciously, our ego helps us cope with the inevitable conflicts that arise in daily life through defense mechanisms (see **Defense Mechanisms**). Note that Freud's definition of the ego is far different from the jargon use as overinflation of self. As Freud conceptualized the ego, the more we are ego dominated, the more we are able to make wise decisions in life: we gain control of our *actions* which is far different from being blinded by *pride*.

Superego

The superego (*das Oberich* in German, or "the over-I"), our conscience, emerges at the end of the Oedipus complex. When the id shouts, "Give me all the chocolate ice cream! No one else can have any," the superego wags its finger and sternly replies, "No! Absolutely not!" It is also the part of ourselves that tells us that we must be perfect—our ego-ideal. If we give in to id demands and selfishly eat too much ice cream and go off our diet, the superego punishes us with guilt.

Freud's conceptualization of the inception of the superego was ingenious. Initially, we had to obey our parents or get punished. But as we matured, we identified with our parents and internalized the norms and prohibitions that they taught us, as if our parents were a homunculus or little voice inside the self. Although the concept seems simple, Freud's theory of the superego broke new ground.

Freud's theorizing about the superego began with his attempt to explain why certain people suffer from an overly severe conscience—why they were subjected to extreme and unrealistic self-criticism and self-attack. He explained this by describing an internal voice—the superego—that judges, condemns, rewards, and punishes, a part of the personality that is built up from one's actual experiences with childhood authority figures. Children identify with the important figures in their lives, with their father's power—do it or die—and authority, with their mother's love and care, and internalize these qualities as part of their developing selves.

The Warring Mind

As the three agencies jockey for position, inevitable conflict arises that we are forever trying to resolve. In Freud's famous analogy, the id is the horse with its power and superior strength; the ego is the rider who must guide it down socially appropriate paths. The more in control the rider—the ego—the healthier the person.

People who remain governed by the pleasure principle and are largely id driven have little to no conscience—they are hedonists without regard for others, and if necessary, will lie, cheat, steal, rape, or kill with little or no remorse. Those driven largely by the superego have a rigid, guilt-ridden personality—like the religious moralist who feels compelled to deny passion.

In an oversimplification of the complex issues of obsessions and addictions, we can see id forces and the ego's struggle to control it if we have ever dieted, tried to stop smoking, or tried to get out of an unhealthy relationship and faced sleeping alone. According to Freud, if we don't find another sex partner soon but repress our need for sex, ultimately tension will build up and burst out in the form of hysterical or neurotic symptoms. In the drug addicted, the id's need for gratification so overpowers the ego's resistance that one's quest for drugs becomes the soul purpose of life. And while psychoanalysis can be quite successful in helping the garden-variety neurotic come to terms with unconscious desires, it can do little to help the drug addicted when id forces dominate the mind.

Ego Psychology

In Freud's structural model of the mind, the ego was the executive of the personality, but it was weak and lacked confidence. Caught between the eternal battles, instinctual demands and moral and societal constraints, the ego struggled to constantly resolve conflicts and thereby reduce anxiety to tolerable levels.

Ego psychologists, or neo-Freudians, accepted Freud's basic ideas of the personality structures of id, ego, and superego and the importance of the unconscious, the shaping of personality in childhood, and the dynamics of anxiety and the defense mechanisms. But they assigned the ego—the conscious mind—much more muscle in its struggle with the id, superego, and outside world. More than just coping with the slings and arrows of outrageous fortune, they argued that the ego, as the CEO of thinking, memory, and perception, has much say in adapting to life's demands. Further, they deemphasized sex and aggression as all-consuming motivations and placed more emphasis on grander motives, such as developing what Erik Erikson called our "ego identity," and on social interaction.

See **Freud, Anna; Hartmann, Heinz**.

Electra Complex

The female . . . acknowledges the fact of her castration, and with it, too, the superiority of the male and her own inferiority; but she rebels against this unwelcome state of affairs.

—Sigmund Freud, *Female Sexuality*, 1931

If the greatest conflict in a boy's life is the Oedipus complex, the comparable conflict for the little girl, thought Freud, is the Electra complex. For the boy, the Oedipus complex was dissolved by the real or fantasized threat of castration. The girl, in contrast, already feels castrated. Upon first seeing a boy or man and discovering that her clitoris, the stimulation of which has given her much pleasure, is not a penis, she feels penis-less and inferior: "She makes her judgment in a flash. She has seen it and knows that she is without it and wants to have it." The result is "envy of the penis," and a "wound to her narcissism [and] she develops, like a scar, a sense of inferiority." Desiring to be a boy dominates her life: "her whole development may be said to take place under the colors of envy for the penis." As her mother is also castrated, she blames her mother for having deprived her of the penis and its pleasures and turns against the inferior, penis-less mother. Freud expanded on this thought in his 1916 essay "The Exceptions."

Women regard themselves as having been damaged in infancy, as having been undeservedly cut short of something and unfairly treated; and the embitterment of so many daughters against their mothers derives, ultimately, from the reproach against her for having brought them into the world as women instead of men.

This hostility intensifies when a sibling is born.

What the child grudges the unwanted intruder and rival is not only the suckling but all the other signs of maternal care. It feels that it has been dethroned, despoiled, prejudiced in its rights; it casts a jealous hatred upon the new baby and develops a grievance against the faithless mother.

Penis envy initiates the girl's Electra complex—thus, Freud's statement, "Anatomy is destiny." How does the little girl resolve the hostility she feels toward her mother? She turns to her father to obtain that which is rightfully hers and wishes her father to give her a baby. Ultimately, the girl resolves the Electra complex by repressing her attraction to her father and identifying with her mother. Freud did not consider what happens when a girl identifies more closely with her father, as did his own daughter Anna.

Elisabeth von R. (Case)

In 1892, Freud ran up against a roadblock with the cathartic method. A new patient, Fraulein Elisabeth von R., his fourth case in *Studies on Hysteria*, could not be hypnotized. How could he get her to open up and discuss her symptoms without hypnosis? Freud turned to his newly found method of free association with success, increasing his confidence in its effectiveness. But treating Elisabeth von R. yielded more than the efficacy of this new treatment. It contributed greatly to his newly evolving theory of how our unconscious erects mental defenses in self-protection.

Elisabeth experienced hysterical symptoms of intense pain in her legs and inability to stand or walk for long periods while nursing her father following his heart attack. For a year and a half, she dutifully slept in his room, attending to his needs around the clock and trying to appear cheerful and encouraging, but then her pains made her a bedridden patient as well. Two years after her father's death, the unbearable pains returned. She could not walk and felt depressed and fatigued. She sought Freud's help.

Her father's death hit hard. Like Bertha Pappenheim, who had also nursed her father throughout his fatal illness, Elisabeth was bright, sought intellectual stimulation, and felt choked by the constraints imposed on women at that time. She felt close to her father, with whom she identified, and who had encouraged her, "jokingly calling her 'cheeky' and cock-sure." His death devastated the family, causing social isolation. Other tragic losses followed. Her mother became ill, one sister died in childbirth, and the other sister deserted the family. Within a few years, Elisabeth had lost those most important to her and became almost totally isolated, and, as she couldn't walk, an invalid.

Although taken by Elisabeth's heartbreaking tale, Freud could not connect it with the cause of her hysterical symptoms. He was stymied. Increasing his frustration were Elisabeth's often cutting remarks about "his treatment as not helping alleviate her symptoms." He suspected that Elisabeth's hysterical symptoms were connected with some experience that she did not feel free enough to recall—Freud at this time had only started experimenting with the use of free association. How could he get her to do so?

Then Freud remembered something remarkable that he had observed Hippolyte Bernheim do while visiting his clinic in Nancy, France. Bernheim had suggested to one of his hypnotized patients that he was no longer present in the room, then made threatening gestures in front of the subject's face, but the patient truly behaved as if Bernheim no longer existed. Bernheim told her not to remember anything of what had transpired. But after awakening the patient, he demonstrated that she *could* recall what had happened, despite the hypnotic amnesia, if he strongly, urgently, and convincingly insisted that she did so. To aid her recall, he placed his hand on her forehead, pressing firmly. To Freud's surprise, she *did* recall the events of the hypnotic session.

Freud decided to try this new strategy. When Elisabeth responded "I don't know" to his query of "How long have you had this symptom?" or "What was its origin?" he placed his hand on her forehead or held her head between his hands and said: "You will think of it under the pressure of my hand. At the moment at which I relax my pressure, you will see something in front of you or something will come into your head. Catch hold of it. It will be what we are looking for. Well, what have you seen or what has occurred to you?"

To his delight, after a long silence, Elisabeth began to spill forth *without hypnosis* a romantic tale. One evening, a young man she had known for a short time had escorted her home from a social affair. They had talked of marriage, but as he was unable to support a wife and as Elisabeth was obligated to care for her ailing father, she would wait to marry him until they both were independent. She felt deeply torn between her feelings for this man and her responsibility for her father. The night that they had walked home together, she resented having to return home to nurse her father and arrived late. She found her father quite ill and blamed herself for neglecting him for her own pleasure. She never again left him for a whole evening. Thereafter, she saw her young man only rarely, and after her father died, she lost touch with him.

Freud believed that Elisabeth's spontaneous thoughts were not random but related to her neurotic symptoms. But how? To start, Freud observed that Fraulein Elisabeth's feelings for the young man and her father *conflicted*. Her symptoms must be a *defense*, thought Freud. To protect herself from the conscious awareness of her painful conflicting emotions, she unconsciously converted her psychic pain into a painful bodily manifestation. Eureka! Elisabeth now knew why her leg pains always began at the same point on her thigh: *This was where her father rested his leg every morning while she changed the bandages on his swollen leg.* Clearly, the pain in her legs symbolized her father's painful leg. As Freud and Elisabeth discussed this interpretation, the pain in her legs intensified, or as Freud put it, "Her painful legs began to 'join in the conversation.'"

And there was more. Under the pressure of Freud's hands, Elisabeth recalled a whole series of other emotionally painful events, each connected with her legs or with walking. For the pain she felt while standing, she remembered standing at the door when her father was brought home after his heart attack and freezing in place with fright. Freud asked her what else "standing" meant to her, and she remembered standing "as though spellbound" by her sister's deathbed.

Yet, Elisabeth still seemed to hesitate, to resist recalling certain feelings, desires, or events. Freud was stymied. Was the new concentration technique a failure? Or was *another* psychological process at work?

Freud noticed that when nothing had occurred to Elisabeth, her face seemed tense and preoccupied, as if ideas *had* come to her, but for some reason she did not want to reveal them to him:

> I could think of two motives for this concealment. Either she was applying criticism to the idea, which she had no right to do, on the ground of its not being important enough or its being an irrelevant reply to the question she had been asked; or she hesitated to produce it because—she found it too disagreeable to tell.

Freud took a chance. He told Elisabeth that he knew she had thought of something under the pressure of his hand, and if she continued to hide it, her pains would never go away. His risk paid off. When he again questioned her about the origins of her pains, she began to chatter about the summer resort where she had stayed just before her sister died in childbirth.

Elisabeth had gone on a walk with her brother-in-law, who had wanted to remain with his sick wife. They talked freely and intimately, and Elisabeth enjoyed the afternoon tremendously; for the first time, she felt someone really understood her. A few days later, she returned to the place in the woods where they had been together and fantasized finding a man like her brother-in-law to make her as happy as her sister. She arose from the reverie with her legs in pain. Elisabeth's hidden conflict was revealed: she desired her brother-in-law; this made her feel guilty, especially as her sister was so ill and helpless and died several months later.

> At that moment of dreadful certainty that her beloved sister was dead without bidding them farewell and without having eased her last days with her care—at that very moment another thought had shot through Elisabeth's mind, and now forced itself irresistibly upon her once more, like a flash of lightning in the dark: 'Now he is free again and I can be his wife.'

What psychological force, pondered Freud, kept Elisabeth from willingly recalling her desire for her sister's husband or her guilt feelings? Freud reasoned that a motivated amnesia for unacceptable impulses, ideas, or events that created intense anxiety was at work—*repression*. But although repression consciously removes conflicts, they continue to operate *unconsciously*, producing symbolic symptoms to replace the conflict's psychological pain: the conflict continues unconsciously but in distorted form. The symptoms of pain in Elisabeth's legs and the inability to walk or stand were symbolic of *standing* alone; of *standing* in shock by her dead sister's bed; of *walking* with her young man while she could have been caring for her father; of her father having placed his *leg* on her *thigh* to be bandaged.

Elisabeth von R., who had been born Ilona Weiss in Budapest in 1867, later described Freud as "just a young, bearded nerve specialist they sent me to." He had tried "to persuade me that I was in love with my brother-in-law, but that wasn't really so." Yet her daughter added that Freud's account of her mother's family history was substantially correct.

Emmy von N. (Case)

In May 1889, Freud had a new patient: Emmy von N.—the Baroness Fanny Moser—Freud's first case study in *Studies on Hysteria*.

As Freud entered the room, Frau Emmy was lying on a couch. After greeting Freud properly, Frau Emmy blurted: "Keep still!—Don't say anything!—Don't touch me." She exhibited several tic-like facial twitches in response to insults or criticisms—virtual "slaps in the face"—punctuated by grimaces of disgust and fear that contorted her pleasant face with each repetition of her bizarre utterance. Frau Emmy had a tendency to stutter, and her speech often included a smacking sound. Freud first suspected that Frau Emmy was practicing some form of protective ritual to ward off a repetitive hallucination.

Since the death of her husband fourteen years earlier, Frau Emmy had suffered from animal phobias, hallucinations, and intense stomachaches, which Freud noticed to coincide with each new animal terror. Freud would carefully quiz Frau Emmy under hypnosis regarding the possible origin of these stomachaches. One day, she grew impatient with Freud's careful probing and examination of each new symptom and "rather grudgingly" responded to his probing that "she did not know. I requested her to remember by tomorrow. She then said in a definitely grumbling tone that I was not to keep on asking her where this and that came from, but *to let her tell me what she had to say*" [emphasis added].

Freud took the hint and let Frau Emmy direct the conversation. Thus began the birth of the technique of *free association*—a turning point in Freud's burgeoning psychoanalytic treatment. Eventually, the "fundamental rule" of psychoanalysis was to say everything that came to mind with no attempt to edit the stream of thought.

Rich, intelligent, sensitive, and literary, Frau Emmy was a forty-year-old widow trailed by death. She was the thirteenth of fourteen children, of whom only four survived. Her "over-energetic and severe mother" died when she was nineteen. At twenty-three, she married an older, wealthy industrialist. After giving birth to her second daughter, her husband, who had been sitting beside her reading a newspaper, suddenly got up, looked at her strangely, "took a few paces forward and then fell down dead." If this wasn't traumatic enough, her family blamed her for his death, and her relations with her older daughter became strained.

Images of death filled her memories: "When I was five years old . . . my brother and sister often threw dead animals at me . . . when I was nine I saw my aunt in her coffin and her jaw suddenly dropped." At fifteen, she found her mother, who had a stroke, on the floor, and at nineteen came home to find her mother dead, her face distorted. Given this background, it's not surprising that Frau Emmy would feel anxious should one of her daughters get sick and repress that fear, as Freud, ever the astute detective, discovered.

One morning, Frau Emmy felt agitated. She had recommended to the governess that her children use the elevator at the hotel where they were staying and now worried that it might be faulty. But when Freud questioned her under hypnosis as to the reason for her anxiety, he found, surprisingly, that she recounted worries not about her children's welfare but that her massage treatments would have to stop because her menstrual period might begin. Freud was puzzled. Is it possible, he thought, that the mind, for self-protection, distorts and obscures connections between anxiety-arousing ideas by rearranging the correct sequence of ideas? Freud had already suspected that some of the material revealed during hypnosis might be a cover-up of more threatening material. For instance, the unconscious might falsely connect one memory with another to obscure the real connections between thoughts. Going on this hunch, he was able to decipher the meaning of Frau Emmy's jumbled thought train.

Frau Emmy's real concern was for her oldest daughter, who was having some difficulty walking because of a severe attack of ovarian neuralgia. That morning Frau Emmy had asked the governess if the girl had walked down the stairs. Then, erasing the actual source of her anxiety—her daughter's illness—Frau Emmy recalled only worry over the elevator. Displacing her anxiety to the least threatening part of the sequence—the elevator—transformed the thought sequence: not afraid of consequences of the daughter's illness but afraid that the elevator might fall.

Freud realized that her anxiety had not only been displaced to another thought but was displaced along logical lines: daughter's menstrual problem—her own menstrual problem—elevator fear.

Seven weeks after the beginning of treatment, Frau Emmy's condition was markedly improved. But her "cure" was short-lived. Seven months later, Frau Emmy told Josef Breuer that her daughter's ovarian difficulties returned, along with a "severe nervous illness." To Frau Emmy, Freud was responsible because he had treated her daughter's illness lightly during therapy, and she relapsed into her early twilight state. Breuer convinced her that Freud was not at fault, and a year later she revisited Freud.

Frau Emmy arrived emaciated, refusing to eat meals and drinking little. Freud insisted that she increase her food intake, and the two argued. Under hypnosis, Frau Emmy revealed the reason for her self-inflicted semistarvation (anorexia), a story that eerily reverberates the stories that anorexic women of the latter twentieth century would tell of their childhood.

When she was a child, she often refused to eat her meat "out of naughtiness." Her mother would become furious and would threaten to punish her. She would force Frau Emmy to eat the meat, which had been left standing on the same plate for two hours. By this time, "the meat was quite cold . . . and the fat was set so hard (she showed her disgust). . . . I can still see the fork in front of me . . . one of its prongs was a little bent. Whenever I sit down to a meal I see the plates before me with the cold meat and fat on them." Many years later, she lived with her brother, who was an officer and had a venereal disease. Knowing that it was contagious, she was "terribly afraid of making a mistake and picking up his knife and fork [she shuddered] . . . and in spite of that I ate my meals with him so that no one should know he was ill. And how, soon after that, I nursed my other brother when he had consumption so badly. We ate by the side of his bed, and the spittoon always stood on the table, open . . . and he had a habit of spitting across the plates into the spittoon. This always made me feel so sick, but I couldn't show it, for fear of hurting his feelings."

In Frau Emmy's reminiscences, Freud discovered the phenomenon he called *overdetermination* that he would pick up again in dream interpretation. Each symptom, Freud discovered, had multiple threads woven into a single pattern—the overt symptom. Her refusing to eat symbolized disgust for the act of eating cold meat and fat; fear of contracting a "foul" disease through shared eating implements; and revulsion at witnessing her brother spit into a spittoon over dinner.

Following these interpretations, Frau Emmy was able to eat relatively normally, and she began to recover her composure. This quick recovery was astonishing given the relative intractability of anorexia to the demand that the patient eat and the lack of success in analyzing away anorexia symptomatology. Interestingly, some of Freud's work presaged current knowledge of some dynamics underlying anorexia. For one, the typical profile of the anorexic is a young girl overly attached to her father and hostile toward her cold mother. And although these dynamics are not the Oedipal conflicts that Freud outlined, sexuality does appear an issue: by refusing to eat, the girl delays sexual maturation and remains her father's little girl. Often, there are oral issues from infancy, such as pickiness—as in the case of Frau Emmy—that we now know may relate to oral sensitivity and food allergies. But the salient issue is body awareness, which is skewed; the typically young girl perceives her body as fat even when she's starving. Freud described the ego as beginning as a bodily ego. When this gets distorted, so does later ego development.

This case yielded much for Freud's evolving theory of psychoanalysis: it opened up a different way of accessing the unconscious—to let the patient free associate; it revealed how the mind cleverly defended the person's conscious self, or ego, from recognizing unpleasant, frightening, or unacceptable thoughts (the elevator fear was more acceptable than Frau Emmy's concern over her daughter's illness); it opened up Freud's eye to the importance of childhood incidents in influencing later behavior; and it let Freud see the importance of tracking each symptom back to its cause to eliminate it.

See **Free Association**.

Fainting Spells

In 1909, while waiting to board a ship to the United States, where Freud was invited to lecture by the American psychologist G. Stanley Hall, Freud, Jung, and Sándor Ferenczi lunched in Bremen. Ceaselessly, Jung spoke of prehistoric remains being dug up in Germany. This got on Freud's nerves; he commented, "Why are you so concerned with these corpses?" Freud suddenly fainted. "Afterwards," Jung states, "[Freud] said to me that he was convinced that all this chatter about corpses meant I had death-wishes toward him."

As Jung and Freud were at that time close intimates, it seems curious that Freud would fear being killed by the jealous son who wished to take his place. In his book *Freud*, Louis Breger suggests that Freud's fear of death came more from his travel phobia, which inhibited him all his life from traveling. Freud was also a man who lived by the clock and needed maximum structure and control to function, which Martha, who arranged everything around his needs, provided him in their household. Now he was suddenly cast off to a new land, the reception of which was quite uncertain. His anxiety about the trip and of losing the comforts of home manifested in New York in physical discomfort: an upset stomach, diarrhea, and urinary problems. Some months after his return home, Freud went to a spa for the "colitis earned in New York."

Freud fainted a second time in Jung's presence. In 1912, at a psychoanalytic gathering in Munich, Jung defended the practice among Egyptian pharaohs of replacing their father's name, etched on public monuments, with their own: "Other pharaohs had replaced the names of their actual or divine fore-fathers on monuments and statues by their own, feeling that they had a right to do so since they were incarnations of the same god. Yet they, I [Jung] pointed out, had inaugurated neither a new style nor a new religion." Freud slid off his chair in a dead faint. The robust Jung carried Freud to a couch in a nearby lounge. Upon awakening, Freud lamented, "How sweet it must be to die."

By this time, there was considerable dissension between the two men, and Freud's antenna was raised high to any hint of a slight from Jung. Apparently, Jung and another Swiss analyst, Franz Rilkin, had not properly acknowledged his work in recent publications, indicating a lack of respect for him as the true father of psychoanalysis, and Freud was worried that Jung, the heir apparent, was happily awaiting his death to assume the father's place. And so he fainted. Freud attributed the incident to "an unruly homosexual feeling" and his early death wish for his infant brother Julius when Freud was one year old. The incident was even more emotionally laden for Freud; years earlier, he had a similar fainting episode in the same hotel when meeting Fliess in Munich.

Family

The Father: Jacob Freud

A wool merchant from Galicia in Poland and living among Catholics, Jacob Freud married Amalia Nathanson, his third wife and Freud's mother, in 1855. He had two sons from his first marriage: Emanuel, born in 1832, and Philipp, born in 1836. After the death of his first wife, the exact date unknown, Jacob may have married a woman named Rebekka, of whom almost nothing is known. Some have suggested that Rebekka may have committed suicide and that Freud's father married his mother *after* she became pregnant with Freud. If so, the family mystery surrounding Jacob Freud's conduct would have made the young Freud feel ashamed and confused. If this woman did exist, Freud never acknowledged her.

A seemingly incurable optimist, Jacob Freud was likable, generous, easygoing, good humored, and proud and highly supportive of his son's prodigious gifts. Although Sigmund had profoundly mixed feelings for his father, whom he considered weak and a failure, Jacob's family adored him and treated him with great respect. His death in 1896 left Freud guilty and angry—feelings that he attempted to understand and cope with in his self-analysis and that he outlined in *The Interpretation of Dreams* (see **Analysis of Self**).

The Mother: Amalia Freud

> *"Unique, without parallel,"* said Freud of the mother-baby bond, the mother *"established unalterably for a whole lifetime as our first and strongest love object . . . the prototype for all later love relations."*
>
> —Sigmund Freud

Amalia Nathanson, Freud's mother, was born in the town of Brody in eastern Galicia. She lived for a time in Odessa, where her older brothers settled. As a child, she moved to Vienna with her parents and her younger brother, where she met Jacob Freud. Attractive, slender, and dark, she had a vibrant, strong personality and ruled the roost in her family.

The firstborn of seven children, Freud was the undisputed favorite of his mother—her golden "Sigi." In turn, he unabashedly adored her and attributed his self-confidence in his greatness to her love. "A man who has been the indisputable favorite of his mother keeps for life the feeling of a conqueror, that confidence of success that often induces real success," Freud lovingly commented.

Yet Freud never admitted it in his writing or perhaps to himself that this adoration was mixed with profound ambivalence. In truth, Freud felt insecure of his mother's love and all his life profoundly feared abandonment. To understand why, we need to look at attachment theory, which was proposed by one of Freud's later followers, the English psychoanalyst John Bowlby. In the 1960s, Bowlby reframed the crucial role of the mother from that of meeting the infant's oral needs to that of meeting the infant's emotional need for attachment to a protective figure. Later, his associate Mary Ainsworth formulated the quality of mother-child attachment into categories of secure-insecure attachment. John Bowlby's theories of attachment, separation, and loss have been the basis for attachment theory for over forty years and have generated enormous research, greatly changed how we view the mother-infant relationship, and spawned a whole field of mother-child therapeutic intervention. In the 1960s, Anna Freud and Max Schur, Freud's orthodox followers, attacked Bowlby's ideas, which were based on evolutionary theory, as "not psychoanalysis."

The nature of the mother–child relationship and the quality of attachment the infant makes to the mother relies on her sensitivity to her infant's needs. When the mother is emotionally available for the child and comforts him in time of need, the child feels protected and secure. Internalizing the good, loving mother, the child learns to love himself, to trust others as benevolent and kind, and to weather setbacks. When the mother is insensitive to her child's needs, the child grows up with shaky self-worth, impaired relationships, and deficient coping skills.

All evidence points to Freud having felt unsure of his mother's love. Inside him lurked a profound insecurity. In a letter to Jung in 1907, Freud almost expressed a self-loathing: "I have always felt that there is something about my personality, my ideas and my manner of speaking, that people find strange and repellent." Rather than trust others as loving and reliable, he felt people at heart were selfish and ready to stab him in the back, as ultimately did those who defied his authority and went their own ways—for example, Adler, Jung, and others.

Secure children feel that should they come in harm's way, their mother will be there with open arms to envelop them and protect them from danger. Comfortable with both closeness and separation, they feel confident that no separation is as strong as the ties that bind. Freud's lifelong fear of death indicates a profound lack of feeling protected from harm. And his travel phobia, which began with his departure from Freiberg when he was three and a half, indicates a lifelong fear of separation and abandonment. At the railway station, the gas jets used for illumination made him think of "souls burning in hell," an association with his lost nanny. Feeling unprotected of danger, the young Freud feared that the train would leave without him, he would be left behind, and he would lose his mother and father just as he had lost his nanny a year before.

Secure children grow up believing that they can depend on people when needed, the world is benign, and they are worthy of support and comfort. Filled with basic trust—the basis of all secure relationships—they later form healthy human connections. Sigmund Freud's relationships were impaired, lacking in intimacy and open communication. He formulated his theory of psycho-analysis in large part from his own pain and unresolved conflicts.

If his mother adored him, why was Freud so insecure? Amalia was likely depressed during Freud's early years and unable to give her infant son the care and attention he needed. When Freud was only eleven months old, Amalia gave birth to a second son, Julius. She named the child after her brother Julius, who had died at age twenty of tuberculosis only a month before Julius's birth. Julius died of an intestinal infection at six or eight months of age, when Sigmund was close to two. Amalia was certainly mourning for her brother when her second son was born, then mourning the baby's loss shortly thereafter. And Freud's nanny, who cared for him dur-ing his mother's pregnancy, had disappeared. In the mind of a two-year-old, mother too could die or abandon him, and he might also get sick and die or disappear. Freud likely felt emotionally neglected throughout his childhood. Before he was ten, his mother had six more babies. Constantly pregnant or caring for his younger siblings, Amalia never could give young Sigmund the time, attention, and care that he needed.

That Freud feared maternal abandonment is evident in a terri-fying dream he had at the age of seven or eight, recorded in *The Interpretation of Dreams*. He had dreamed of his mother with a "peculiarly peaceful, sleeping expression on her features, being car-ried into a room by two or three people with birds' beaks and laid upon a bed." The expression on his mother's face in the dream reminded Freud of his dead grandfather, who he had observed in a coma a few days before his death. Awakening "in tears and scream-ing," he ran into his parents' room and awoke his mother to make sure she was not dead. Thus, the dream appears as a fear of his mother dying, although Freud interpreted it as representing sexual feelings for his mother (see **Analysis of Self**).

Children need their mother for protection. If faced with a withdrawn or depressed mother, children seek to keep her at least minimally involved by behaving to make mother happy: If mother's too sad to care for them, how will they survive? Thus, the young Sigmund, with a mother in turn loving and affectionate and sad and withdrawn, may have adopted a strategy of pleasing his mother to make her happy and thus ensure protection. And what would please her more than a bright, studious, well-behaved, mature child, busy with his activities and destined for greatness to surmount the failure of the kind but ineffective father? Freud may have been the good, well-behaved child also in part for guilt over his baby brother's death, having wished the new rival dead, as many children do upon the birth of a sibling. He wrote to Fliess during his self-analysis: "I greeted my one-year-younger brother, who died after a few months, with adverse wishes and genuine childhood jealousy; and . . . his death left the germ of self-reproaches in me."

Fearing his mother would abandon him if he didn't please her, Freud remained afraid of and compliant to his mother, a formidable and dominating presence, all his life. Although powerful in his marriage, where he dominated his wife, and the all-powerful father of his flock of followers, he would never talk back to his mother, indicating a fear of displeasing her. And he never missed the ritual Sunday family meal with his mother; however, he invariably arrived with an upset stomach, which he attributed to causes other than anxiety over being with his intimidating mother. Whereas Freud painted his beloved mother in idyllic terms, other family members were more open about her difficult nature. Freud's niece Judith Bernays Heller, who spent time living with her older grandparents, did not share Freud's reverence: "My grandmother . . . had a volatile temperament, would scold the maid as well as her daughters, and rush about the house. . . . She was charming and smiling when strangers were about, but I . . . always felt that with familiars she was a tyrant, and a selfish one."

As an adult, Freud interpreted his memories and dreams of his mother and the guilt over his baby brother's death in Oedipal terms. He never openly professed a profound sense of having been abandoned by his mother. But his description of mother "love" in his essay *Femininity*, written when Freud was seventy-five, speaks volumes of his deep ambivalence: "The turning away from the mother is accompanied by hostility; the attachment to the mother ends in hate. A hate of that kind may become very striking and last all through life." Hate for the mother begins with her having given the infant "too little milk," indicating "lack of love." It flares up again with the birth of the next child, preserving "oral frustration" as the mother now needs her milk for the new arrival. Old and embittered, Freud continued to describe almost to a T the unresolved resentment he felt for his mother, which greatly biased his feelings about women:

> In cases in which the two children are so close in age that lactation is prejudiced by the second pregnancy, this reproach acquires a real basis, and . . . a child, even with an age difference of only *11 months*, is not too young to take notice of what is happening. But what the child grudges the unwanted intruder and rival is not only the suckling but all the other signs of maternal care. It feels that it has been dethroned, despoiled, damaged in its rights; it casts a jealous hatred upon the new baby and develops a grievance against the faithless mother . . . *we rarely form a correct idea of the strength of these jealous impulses, of the tenacity with which they persist, and of the magnitude of their influence upon later development.* Especially as this jealousy is constantly receiving fresh nourishment in the later years of childhood and the whole shock is repeated with the birth of each new brother or sister. [emphasis added]

Blinded by his Oedipal script, Freud focused his personal narrative on his love for his mother as a sexual object and his ambivalence for his father as a rival and ignored his *feelings*—the sadness, fear, and anxiety of a child so beset with early loss. Because his mother and father were essentially loving, caring parents, devoted to his welfare, he couldn't openly hate them for any neglect; thus, he repressed the deep unhappiness and insecurity of his childhood and recalled it as "happy." "Deep within me, covered over, there still lives that happy child from Freiberg, the first-born son of a youthful mother, who had received the first indelible impressions from this air, from this soil."

So dangerous was love for Freud that in *Civilization and Its Discontents*, written at the end of his life, he feared that love posed a threat to civilization itself. Love is threatening because it involves giving up control, which leaves us extremely vulnerable: "We are never so defenseless against suffering as when we love, never so helplessly unhappy as when we have lost our loved object or its love." He diminished the idea that the "oceanic" feeling of oneness that the infant feels suckling the mother's breast remains preeminent throughout life. This, he asserted, would give too much power to mothers. Rather he argued that the father was a more powerful figure in childhood: "I cannot think of any need in childhood as strong as the need for a father's protection." This defies Freud's notion that the mother reigns as the "prototype for all later love relations" and perhaps expresses Freud's wish that had his own weak father been more dominant, he may have felt less uncomfortably bound to his controlling, demanding mother and may not have been caught up in his early years in the eternal quest for the father figure in Breuer and Fliess. Freud's confusion about the importance of the mother role reflects his fear of engulfment/ dependency and separation/abandonment that rendered him fearful of human intimacy. Not surprisingly, as the prototype of his mother was deeply ambivalent, so were his relations to his wife and children.

The Wife: Martha Bernays

In April 1882, twenty-year-old Martha Bernays was visiting one of Freud's sisters at his house. Five years Martha's senior, Freud fell instantly in love with this attractive, slender, lively visitor, with marvelously expressive eyes and popularity with the opposite sex. He sent her roses daily and called her "princess." He doggedly pursued her, until Martha, on June 17, 1882, barely two months after they laid eyes on each other, agreed to marry him: "You know . . . how from the moment I first saw you, I was determined—no, I was compelled—to woo you, and how immeasurably happy I have been ever since."

A man of his time, Freud wooed Martha in the ways appropriate to Victorian culture: with kisses and embraces. Martha remained a virgin until their marriage, and it is believed Freud did as well. A poor student living with his parents, Freud could not afford to get married and the engagement was a long four years, during which time he rarely saw Martha because she was living with her mother in Wandsbek, near Hamburg, and he was too poor to visit her often.

Instead, he courted Martha through passionate love letters that he wrote almost daily, spilling out his feelings to her. He longed for her and was preoccupied with the kisses he could not bestow on her; his smoking was compensation for her absence: "Smoking is indispensable if one has nothing to kiss." In the fall of 1885, during his stay in Paris, he bounded up the steps of Notre Dame, imagining if she had been with him: "One climbs up three hundred steps, it is very dark, very lonely, on every step I could have given you a kiss if you had been with me, and you would have reached the top quite out of breath and wild." As he poured his heart out to her, he analyzed his own feelings and hers with every word she wrote. Jealous and possessive, he felt easily slighted by the smallest omission on her part or hint of interest in another man. At times his jealousy was so intense and infused with irrational anger as to appear pathological. Martha must call a cousin by his formal last name. She must not show blatant liking for two of her admirers: one a composer and the other a painter; as artists, Freud feared they had an unfair advantage over a mere scientist. Even more extreme, she must forsake all others, including her mother and her brother Eli, who was shortly to marry Freud's sister Anna. When Martha refused to break with them, Freud was furious, which caused great strains between them.

There were other frictions. Their views on religion caused great tension. Having grown up in a strictly observant Orthodox Jewish family, Martha Bernays was an observant Jew, while to Freud, the atheist, religion was superstitious nonsense. Nor would this be a marriage of equals; a man of his time, Freud firmly believed in the presumed differences between sexes. He demanded that she abandon the religion she had never questioned and made it clear that she would be subservient to him. Defying the Jewish practice of naming children after recently deceased relatives, Freud named all six of his children after important people in his life. Martha apparently had no say in this matter, and not one of the six children bore names related to her or to her family.

Martha put up with Freud's demands because they accorded with her passive, obedient, and conciliatory nature: "I want to be the way you want me to be," she had written him. A typical middle-class, bourgeois *Hausfrau*, her role was to keep Freud's life orderly and comfortable, and this she did well. She "laid out his clothes, chose everything for him down to his handkerchiefs, and even put toothpaste on his toothbrush," noted the historian Paul Roazen. She insisted on punctuality, imbuing the Freud household with its air of dependability—even, as Anna Freud would later complain, of obsessive regularity. When Max Schur, Freud's last physician, sat on Freud's bed to examine him, Martha would object as he would muss it up. Neither Freud's confidante after their engagement nor intellectual partner—she thought her husband's psychoanalytic ideas "a form of pornography"—Martha was exactly what Freud needed to organize his external world so that he could do his inner work to ultimately reorganize the thinking of the Western world.

Following his death, Martha described their life together: "After 53 years of marriage, there was not a single angry word between us, and that I always tried as much as possible to remove the *misère* of everyday life from his path."

"Not a single angry word." How odd for a couple married for fifty-three years. Freud's marriage to Martha had the same quality of avoidant attachment that his relationship with his mother had: lack of closeness, sexual or emotional, and lack of open communication of his thoughts and feelings.

Martha Bernays was a reserved woman, self-controlled, and, according to her son Martin, never rattled. While Freud poured out his feelings in his letters, Martha's were almost cool in contrast, never matching the passion and adoration he bestowed on her during their courtship. "I really think I have always loved you much more than you me." Freud felt that she accepted him "without any great affection" because he "forced" himself upon her, demanding they be engaged after knowing each other less than two months.

Freud chose a woman who would continually make him feel rejected, as this letter reveals:

> Do you remember how you often used to tell me that I had a talent for repeatedly provoking your resistance? How we were always fighting, and you would never give in to me? We were two people who diverged in every detail of life and who were yet determined to love each other. And then, after no hard words had been exchanged between us for a long time, I had to admit to myself that you were indeed my beloved, but so seldom took my side that no one would have realized from your behavior that you were preparing to share my life; and you admitted that I had no influence over you. I found you so fully matured and every corner in you occupied, and you were hard and reserved and I had no power over you. This resistance of yours only made you the more precious to me, but at the same time I was very unhappy.

We see in this letter how Freud, seeking closeness with Martha but at a safe distance, compulsively repeated a balancing act of advance/retreat. Freud bared his soul to Martha; he advanced. Martha felt him uncomfortably close; she coolly withdrew, failing to echo his greatness. Freud got hostile and angry with her; he retreated safely back. She got angry and he feared losing her. He moved back in with apologies and remorse; he reinstated her at arm's length. "My beloved Marty," one such letter began, "I dare to say my beloved although I do occasionally have bad thoughts and write so angrily. If I have offended you again, please put it down on the list with the others and think of my longing, my loneliness, my impatient struggle and the shackles that are imposed on me."

Having deliberately chosen someone with whom he could not be close, Freud was able to fully express the intensity of his passion and longing during their engagement because they were *separated*. Once married, such emotional outpouring frightened him. He had to control his overwhelming feelings lest he be engulfed by his desperate need for love. Martha and Freud became devoted strangers: Martha invested her energy in her home and children; Freud invested his energy in his work and his comrades and looked to idealized men to become his confidants.

In *Civilization and Its Discontents*, Freud wrote that the idea that the oceanic feeling of oneness extends from the mother and baby relationship to that between a man and a woman was infantile and unrealistic; he certainly did not let it happen in his own marriage. Such love was dangerous, Freud asserted, because once you fall into it, the boundaries of your ego could dissolve, as with psychosis. Perhaps his intense jealousy and possessiveness of Martha made him fear at some level that he could go crazy with love. What was Freud's solution to such out-of-control passion that could destroy civilization? Such an intensely pleasurable but dangerous state of love must be tempered and socialized; it must be "sublimated" by way of reason and science. In short, humankind must follow Freud's lead.

The Sister-in-Law: Minna Bernays

In the mid-1890s, when Freud's last child, Anna, was a year old, Freud's sister-in-law, Minna Bernays ("Tante Minna"), moved in with the Freuds. An integral part of the Freud family, she helped care for Freud's six children.

Freud had always felt warmly toward Minna. During his engagement to Martha, he had written Minna intimate and affectionate letters, signed "Your Brother Sigmund," and called her "My Treasure." In those years, she too had been engaged, to Ignaz Schonberg, one of Freud's friends. But Schonberg died young, in 1886, of tuberculosis, and after his death, Minna apparently resigned herself to spinsterhood. She grew heavy and exceedingly plain and looked older than her sister Martha, although she was four years younger.

The living arrangement suited Freud well: Martha was the hausfrau; Minna was witty, intellectual, and able to follow Freud's flights of fancy. In the early years, Freud felt that Minna was his "closest confidante," along with Fliess. She remained close to him; in summer, the two occasionally visited Swiss resorts or Italian cities alone.

The rumor launched by Carl Jung that Freud had an affair with Minna seems unlikely. Freud had low libido or interest in sex (see

Sexuality, Freud's), and, as we've seen, he eschewed intimacy. His relationship with Minna may have helped keep Martha at bay. Perhaps not coincidentally, she moved in with the Freuds around the time that Freud reported to Fliess that he and Martha had become abstinent.

The Children

Only a year after being married, Martha Freud gave birth to their first child, Mathilde, whom Freud named after Josef Breuer's wife, Mathilde. On October 16, 1887, he exuberantly wrote to Frau Bernays and Minna Bernays in Wandsbek: "I am terribly tired and still have to write so many letters, but writing to you comes first. You already know from a telegram that we have a little daughter, Mathilde. She weighs three thousand four hundred grams [some seven and a half pounds], which is very respectable, is terribly ugly, has sucked on her right hand from her first moment, otherwise seems very good-humored and behaves as though she is really at home." Five days later, after being told that little Mathilde "looks strikingly like *me*," he changed his tune—"she has already grown much prettier, sometimes I think already quite pretty."

Mathilde was "altogether feminine" and fell easily into the subservient female role that Freud promoted. She lived an ordinary bourgeois life. In 1910, she married Robert Holitscher, a Viennese businessman twelve years her senior. The couple lived near their parents, and Mathilde saw her parents almost daily. She helped out with the social side of her father's profession, such as assisting psychoanalytic visitors with living arrangements. Childless from surgery, she lived alone following her husband's death and died in London in 1978.

Freud's second child and first son, Jean Martin, named after Jean Charcot, was born in 1889. An imaginative child, Martin constantly entertained his father and wrote little verses at an early age. Freud called him a budding poet. But Martin did not pursue a writing career. Unlike his introspective father, Martin was a thrill seeker who preferred to spend his time in risky physical endeavors such as skiing and mountaineering. Apparently enjoying the adrenaline rush of war, he was rewarded with medals for heroism. After Martin returned from the war in 1919, he married Ernestine Drucker ("Esti") and became a lawyer, helping to oversee the Freud publishing enterprise in 1932. Esti, attractive, artistic, and sophisticated, was "too pretty for our family!" Freud complained—too much the liberated, independent woman. The couple had two children, a boy and a girl. Martin separated from Esti when the family fled Vienna. Esti and her daughter eventually settled in the United States, while Martin remained in London. He lived with a younger woman and ran a small shop, isolated from his family, as Anna disapproved of his private life. He died in Sussex in 1967.

Named after the English general Oliver Cromwell, which fit Freud's military heroic identifications, Oliver, the second son and third child, was born in 1890, fourteen months after Martin. Oliver was very bright and mathematically inclined as a child: as Freud wrote to Fliess from a vacation in the country, "Oli classifies mountains here, just as he does the city railroad and tram lines in Vienna. . . . [He] is again practicing the exact recording of routes, distances, names and places of mountains." He pursued a technical education, and later became a mathematical engineer with the Austrian army during the First World War. He married a Berlin woman named Henny Fuchs in 1923 and had one daughter, Eva. Although he and Henny escaped from France in 1943 and moved to Philadelphia, Eva stayed on under a non-Jewish identity. She died tragically of the effects of a toxic abortion just after the war ended. Oliver died in 1969.

Freud's fourth child and third son, Ernst, named after Freud's beloved teacher Ernst Brücke, was born in 1892. He became an architect but also worked closely with Anna, editing the early collection of his father's letters. He died in 1970. He fathered three boys. His oldest son, Stephen, ran a small store in London, while his other two sons became extremely successful. Lucian Freud, the middle child, is a world-famous contemporary painter. Clement, the youngest, is a television personality and member of Parliament.

Sophie, the fifth child and second daughter, named after the wife of a friend of Freud's, was born a year after Ernst in 1893. The

"Sunday child," she became her mother's favorite. She married Max Halberstadt in 1913, but died of influenza pneumonia in 1920 and left behind her husband and two young children. Freud described her death as "a heavy narcissistic insult" and wore a tiny locket fastened to his watch chain with her photo. In 1923, Sophie's son and Freud's favorite grandson, Heinz ("Heinele") died of tuberculosis, months after Freud's first surgery for cancer. He was "an enchanting little fellow, and I myself was aware of never having loved a human being, certainly never a child, so much." Freud was more depressed than anyone had ever seen him. As Lionel Trilling put it, "Freud believed that the death of little Heinz marked the end of his affectional life." Sophie's surviving son, Ernst, became a psychoanalyst and worked with Anna.

Anna, the last born and the best known of Freud's children, was born on December 3, 1895, and named after Anna Hammerschlag Lichtheim, one of Freud's favorite patients and the daughter of his affectionate and generous old Hebrew teacher Samuel Hammerschlag. Never marrying, Anna appears to have worshipped her father and could only have married a man she felt was comparable to him. She became an important psychoanalytic theorist in her own right, creating the field of child psychoanalysis. Devoted to her father, in the last decade of his life she was his companion, nurse, and admirer: the center of his life. He could never praise her enough. "The most enjoyable thing near me," he wrote Max Eitingon, a close follower, "is Anna's enjoyment in her work and her unchecked achievement" (see **Freud, Anna**).

Freud as Father

In my private life I am a petit bourgeois. . . . I would not like one of my sons to get a divorce or one of my daughters to have a liaison.

—Freud to Marie Bonaparte

The Freud family appeared close and the children fond of their father, who they described largely in warm, loving terms. He and

Martha demanded good behavior and good grades and attempted to treat their children fairly. "I know," Martin Freud recalled, "that we Freud children did things and said things that other people found strange"; theirs was, he thought, a liberal upbringing. "We were never ordered to do this, or not to do that; we were never told not to ask questions. Replies and explanations to all sensible questions were always given by our parents, who treated us as individuals, persons in our own right."

Yet although Freud loved his children and was interested in them, he was an authoritarian, possessive, and demanding father. Believing fully in the Oedipus complex, he discouraged his sons from becoming physicians, much less psychoanalysts, to prevent competition between father and son. Said Martin, "Medicine as a profession for any of his sons was strictly banned by father." He demanded that his daughters assume conventional female roles. When Sophie was young and unsure of finding a man, Freud wrote her, "The more intelligent among young men are sure to know what to look for in a wife—gentleness, cheerfulness, and the talent to make their life easier and more beautiful"—in short, Martha Freud, his wife and her mother.

Freud's relationship with his children appeared to have had the same underlying avoidance as his relationship with his mother and his wife. Uncomfortable with intimacy, he was emotionally reserved with his children and withheld from them the close physical affection that marks intimacy. He was, his nephew Harry remembered, "always on very friendly terms with his children" but not "expansive"; rather, he was "always a bit reserved." Indeed, "it rarely happened that he kissed any of them; I might almost say, really never. And even his mother, whom he loved very much, he only kissed perforce at parting." (Freud never kissed the hand of a woman, a common practice at that time, except a friend's mother at her son's deathbed.) When Anton, the son of Martin and Esti, was three or four months old, Freud criticized Esti for "cuddling him too much." Like many of his generation, he erroneously believed that "too much" physical affection from parents was harmful because it accelerated sexual maturation. Looking, Freud once said, is a civilized substitute for touching.

Yet in 1929, in a letter to Ernest Jones, Freud's ardent English follower and later his biographer, Freud spoke of "a fount of tenderness" within himself on which one could always count. He might not be inclined to parade such feelings, "but in my family they know better." Perhaps his children *consciously* understood this, but underneath Freud's emotional reserve may have affected the happiness of some of his children. Though Sophie and Ernst seemed happy and led productive lives, the other children appeared troubled. Mathilde and Anna were dutiful and compliant, and Anna was profoundly inhibited and inwardly tortured with self-hate. Oliver was obsessive-compulsive and felt alienated from his father. Martin did not love himself nor was he able to love others.

Feminism

The great question . . . which I have not yet been able to answer, despite my thirty years of research into the feminine soul, is "What does a woman want?"

—Sigmund Freud

A man of the repressive Victorian era, Freud felt women were second-class citizens. He reduced women to biologically and morally inferior beings—passive, masochistic, and forever driven by penis envy. He never budged from this stand. Feminists were outraged. While they were fighting for equal rights—at home, at work, at school, in bed—Freud, whose theories were overtaking Western civilization, was espousing their inferiority.

Among the first Freud critics was the French feminist Simone de Beauvoir in *The Second Sex* of 1949. She charged Freud with seeing only men as fully human; women were regarded as mutilated men, as the "other." Social factors, not anatomy, argued de Beauvoir, accounted for male supremacy in culture and public life.

To her and a whole generation thereafter, the idea of women's penis envy was infuriating, to say the least, and was evidence of male narcissism.

In the United States in 1963, in her landmark book *The Feminine Mystique* that launched women's lib, Betty Friedan accused Freud of being limited by the sexist ideas of his Victorian culture and of wishing to maintain women as second-class citizens while ignoring the social injustice to women. Even worse were the American neo-Freudians preaching sexual activity as the road to happiness and belittling feminists as neurotics who were not real women. Wives and mothers were unhappy not because they were neurotic, argued Friedan, but because they lacked equal opportunity, stifling their will.

Feminists continued to attack psychoanalysis on its many sexist fronts, including female sexual inferiority and moral inferiority. Psychoanalysis, argued the feminists, placed women in a sexual straitjacket: To be "normal" meant being passive, masochistic, narcissistic, and morally inferior. Women who lacked these traits were abnormal, masculine, and neurotic. Psychoanalysts further infuriated them by describing woman's work as "masculine protest" and "the masculinity complex."

Another touchy issue was Freud's seduction theory (see **Seduction Hypothesis**). Former members of the analytic community, such as Jeffrey Masson, accused Freud of changing the seduction theory to that of fantasied rather than real abuse (see **Masson, Jeffrey**). Some went so far as blaming Freud for childhood sexual abuse remaining widespread and underreported but at the same time accused therapists of implanting false memories of abuse in women's minds, which supported Freud's theory of fantasied seduction.

Ironically, one of the most distinguished feminists of the time was Bertha Pappenheim—Anna O. The woman whose so-called hysteria launched psychoanalysis was the quintessential example of how stifling female identity breeds psychopathology and how psychoanalytic theory limits an understanding of female identity.

Anna O., as Josef Breuer described her, was a "markedly intelligent [woman with] an astonishingly quick grasp of things and penetrating intuition . . . a powerful intellect [and] great poetic and imaginative gifts." She was very strong willed, "energetic, tenacious and persistent." These traits did not accord with her repressive home environment. The Pappenheims were wealthy Orthodox Jews, and her father expected her to adhere to the strict rules of that religion and become a dutiful Jewish wife. As a result, as Breuer noted, "her excessively regimented lessons offered no outlet for her natural vitality, and a wholly uneventful life gave no real content to her intellectual activities."

Her mother was solemn and emotionally unavailable and Bertha had turned to her father for love, but this left her torn between living a lie with the false identity he imposed on her and following her true interests. To cope, she became a lonely and divided self. Outwardly, she showed a false self to please her father—compliant and dutiful but unemotional; inwardly, she lived a lonely existence in the "private theater" of her imagination, keeping her genuine feelings alive in fantasy. These two different identities emerged as the "good" and "evil" selves of her illness. In her breakdown, the pieces of her personality split apart.

After her father died, Bertha began to express the private the-ater of her imagination in literary compositions. She wrote poetry, fairy tales, plays, a translation and a preface to Mary Wollstone-craft's *Vindication of the Rights of Women*, newspaper articles, and other pieces. Having been disappointed in her mother as a role model, she sought out exemplary women of the past, first Mary Wollstonecraft, the pioneer of the feminist movement, then Gluckel von Hameln, in whose clothes she dressed and had her portrait painted, entitling it "Bertha Pappenheim as Gluckel." Identifying with these remarkable women enabled her to pull together the fragments of her self.

She started a National Association of Jewish Women in Germany, worked with teenagers, unwed mothers, and their babies, and founded a home for abandoned and abused girls in a town near Frankfurt, which she ran for many years. She was devoted not only to girls at risk, the homeless, and tuberculosis sufferers but to com-bating "white slavery" (the procuring of girls from Eastern Europe for prostitution). Although highly disturbed as a young woman,

Bertha Pappenheim overcame her illness and became a major social and intellectual figure in Germany, not because she freed her repressed *sexuality*—in fact, she never married—but because she devoted herself to abused and mistreated girls and women whose rights were denied, as hers had been, thus eventually enabling her to fully use her extraordinary intellectual gifts and free her repressed *self*.

In the 1920s and 1930s, Freud budged slightly in his views on women in response to other analysts, particularly Karen Horney. He alleged ignorance of the "dark continent" of women's sexuality but still considered women as morally weaker than men, a view he defended against "the denials of the feminists, who are anxious to force us to regard the two sexes as completely equal in position and worth." He pronounced, "The feminist demand for equal rights for the sexes does not take us far," because "Anatomy is Destiny"— Freud's paraphrase of Napoleon and the phrase that will forever crucify him in feminist circles. In truth, Freud never understood women, as he admitted in a famous quote: "The great question . . . which I have not yet been able to answer, despite my thirty years of research into the feminine soul, is 'What does a woman want?'" It's no surprise. He was never genuinely intimate with a woman. Feminists believed that Freud privately feared women.

Perhaps he did. Yet it's still unclear why Freud had such demeaning views of women as they belied much of his experience of the opposite sex. Freud's daughter Anna, not his sons, followed in his footsteps. And in his family, it was Freud's father who was passive, submissive, and masochistic; his mother dominated the family *and* her son until the end of her life, and from accounts of family members was quite the shrew.

From its birth, psychoanalysis profited from feminine contributions. Bertha Pappenheim invented the talking cure; Emma Eckstein was the first female analyst trained by Freud. With his support, some women became analysts and part of Freud's inner circle, although he praised them for their masculine minds. Female analysts immigrated to the United States and Latin America after World War II and were instrumental in forming new psychoanalytic societies.

Could there be a rapprochement between Freud and the feminists? Actually, by the 1970s, some feminists began to feel that psychoanalysis had some redeeming qualities. For one, Freud's concept of the unconscious helped in the understanding of how people internalize the rules and values of male-dominated cultures. Academic feminists began extending psychoanalytic approaches to literature and culture, while practicing therapists began to accommodate feminist views.

In 1978, the psychoanalyst Nancy Chodorow in her landmark book *The Reproduction of Mothering and the Sociology of Gender* reinterpreted the Oedipus complex to explain gender differences and to address the psychic consequences of mother-dominated child rearing, especially in isolated middle-class families. Because of their early intense identification with their mothers, girls' sense of self is based on relations and is emotionally rich. Having developed the capacity and desires for maternal nurturance and empathy, they reproduce the psychology of mothering in the next generation. Boys, in contrast, must become different from their mothers, so they become more autonomous and emotionally constrained.

Carol Gilligan extended this hypothesis about women's relational character to moral development, reassessing Freud's infamous judgment that as women are inherently inferior, they develop a weaker conscience (superego) than men.

> I cannot evade the notion . . . that for women the level of what is ethically normal is different from what it is in men . . . they show less sense of justice than men . . . they are less ready to submit to the great exigencies of life . . . they are more often influenced in their judgments by feelings of affection or hostility.

Gilligan argued that although women do develop a different morality from men, it is not inferior but complementary to men's. Women use individual cases rather than abstract rules to construct moral choices. They achieve moral maturity through interdependence by balancing the needs of self and other.

See **Electra Complex; Masson, Jeffrey; Seduction Hypothesis.**

Fliess, Wilhelm
(1858–1928)

A Berlin nose-and-throat specialist, Wilhelm Fliess played a pivotal role in Freud's life as both father figure idealized other and confidant during Freud's self-analysis. Fliess came to Vienna in the fall of 1887 and attended some of Freud's lectures on neurology. The two men quickly developed an extraordinarily close friendship that spanned some thirteen years, meeting frequently in what Freud termed "congresses," and extensively exchanging letters. To his trusted friend, Freud spilled all: his neurotic symptoms, fears, dreams, interpretations, sexual relations with his wife, and medical concerns for which Fliess treated him, including prescribing cocaine.

His letters to Fliess, his "only other," were effusive, increasingly gushing more and more with admiration and love beyond the normal flattery that characterized correspondence with close colleagues: "Esteemed friend and colleague" became "Dear friend," then "Dearest friend," "Dearest Wilhelm," and finally "My beloved friend." He revealed his personal life in intimate detail to Fliess, as if Fliess were *his* analyst. Beginning in late 1893, he confided to Fliess that he was suffering from chest pains and arrhythmia, a troubling heart condition that Fliess attributed to Freud's smoking habit. His wife was not to know. The previous summer, he had disclosed to Fliess that he and Martha were "living in abstinence." He wrote in January 1896, his love and need for Fliess at its peak: "How much I owe you; solace, understanding, stimulation in my loneliness, meaning to my life that I gained through you, and finally even health that no one else could have given back to me." Fliess was the closest Freud came to intimacy with another person.

What piqued Freud's intense interest in this man? Fliess was intelligent, charismatic, and cultivated, his scientific learning wide-ranging and his scientific ambition vast. Many found him fascinating. The novelty of his ideas that were great discoveries to some, quackery to others; his isolation from the medical establishment; his being a Jew—was shared by Freud. "I am pretty much alone here with the clearing up of the neuroses," Freud wrote to Fliess in the spring of 1894. "They pretty much consider me a monomaniac."

Fliess fed Freud ideas and support, firmly grasping his theorizing. A meticulous and perceptive reader of Freud's manuscripts, he helped Freud to better understand human culture: "You have taught me," Freud told him gratefully in June 1896, "that a bit of truth lurks behind every popular lunacy." He helped Freud to see jokes as useful for psychoanalytic scrutiny.

Before Freud openly made infantile sexuality his own idea, Fliess speculated about it in his published writings of the mid-1890s. It was Fliess who first theorized that all human beings are bisexual, a notion Freud made his own and which eventually had caused much contention between the two men. In his *Three Essays*, Freud did take note of Fliess's assertion and spoke of bisexuality as "the decisive factor," adding that "without taking bisexuality into account I think it would scarcely be possible to arrive at an understanding of the sexual manifestations that are actually to be observed in men and women." Actually, the idea that we all begin bisexual probably started with Plato's *The Symposium*, in which Aristophanes relates a fable explaining that originally there were three sexes: men, women, and a hermaphroditic combination of man and woman who had two heads, two arms, two sets of genitals, and so on.

Now considered a crank, Fliess's theories seem quite bizarre. They rest on two notions: the nose is the dominant organ, influencing all of human health and sickness; there exist human male and female biological cycles, twenty-eight days for the female, twenty-three days for the male. Noting an anatomical similarity between the nasal and genital tissues, he expanded this to what he termed the "nasal reflex neurosis." Physical problems such as migraine headaches; pain in the abdomen, arms, and legs; coronary symptoms; asthma; gastrointestinal problems; miscarriages, dysmenorrhea, cramping, and so on; and, of special interest to Freud, sexual disturbances, he attributed to problems with nasal membranes and bones. According to his theory, applying cocaine to the nasal membranes or treating the nose with surgery could cure problems such as sexual difficulties or heart symptoms. Freud tried both: he used cocaine for a while, and Fliess operated on his nose twice. In his theory of periodicity, Fliess extended the notion of male and female cycles to a theory of critical dates. Knowing a person's birthday and other critical dates could predict, for instance, the date of your death, something that Freud initially bought into (see **Occult**).

Around the turn of the twentieth century, Fliess's ideas, now almost wholly discredited, found a sympathetic hearing and even a measure of support from respectable researchers in several countries. His credentials, after all, were impeccable: Fliess was a reputable specialist with a solid practice extending far beyond his home base in Berlin. Besides, the ideas Freud was playing with appeared at the outset as outlandish as Fliess's.

Freud remained convinced of Fliess's ideas for some years, and diligently contributed material to Fliess's collection of probative numbers: the intervals of his migraine headaches, the rhythms of his children's ailments, the dates of his wife's menstrual periods, the length of his father's life. The great rationalist, Freud was not wholly free from superstition, especially number superstition (see **Occult**). Freud once analyzed superstition as a cover for hostile, murderous wishes, and his own superstitions as a suppressed desire for immortality. But his self-analysis did not completely free Freud from this bit of irrationality, and this residue of what he called his "specifically Jewish mysticism" made him susceptible to Fliess's wildest speculations.

Eventually, Fliess's mysticism and numerology appeared incompatible with Freud's thinking. In early August 1900, Freud met Fliess at the Achensee, near Innsbruck, and the two quarreled vehemently, attacking the validity of the other's work. It was the last time they saw one another. Writing to Fliess in the summer of 1901, Freud gratefully acknowledged his debts to him but bluntly stated that they had grown apart and that "you have reached the limits of your perspicacity." Nevertheless, unable to completely let go, Freud continued to correspond occasionally with Fliess for another two years. In the end, Freud made the same turnabout with Fliess as he did with Breuer and ended the relationship with great bitterness; worrying that Fliess would attempt to lure others away from psychoanalysis, he concluded that Fliess is "fundamentally a hard, wicked human being."

Free Association

If you were to enter into psychoanalysis, your analyst would encourage you to speak every thought that comes to mind, without censorship—even if dirty, disgusting, irrelevant, embarrassing, cruel, or criminal. You would *free associate*, and your analyst would listen without judgment.

Free association emerged as the language of psychoanalysis from Freud's dissatisfaction with hypnosis as the port of entry into the psyche. Throughout the late 1880s, Freud continued to experiment with the cathartic method but found increasingly greater problems with its use. To start, not all his patients could be hypnotized and attain the trancelike state needed to relive and release the strangulated emotion of the forgotten trauma. Furthermore, Freud increasingly realized that therapeutic success depended on the nature of the relationship between the physician and the patient. If the doctor–patient relationship was otherwise disturbed, "even the most brilliant results [of hypnotism] were likely to be suddenly wiped away."

Freud needed another therapeutic milieu to open the dam of buried emotions and memories. It came quite serendipitously in May 1889 with a new patient, "Frau Emmy." When Freud continually questioned her, Frau Emmy insisted that Freud just *let her tell him what she had to say* (see **Emmy von N.**), and the method of free association was born. Here's how Freud instructed each of his patients in the new technique:

> You will notice that as you relate things various thoughts will occur to you which you would like to put aside on the ground of certain criticisms and objections. You will be tempted to say to yourself that this or that is irrelevant here, or is quite unimportant, or nonsensical, so that there is no need to say it. You must never give in to these criticisms, but must say it in spite of them—indeed, you must say it precisely because you have an aversion to doing so. . . . Finally, never forget that you have promised to be absolutely honest, and never leave anything out because, for some reason or other, it is unpleasant to tell it.

Free association fit well with Freud's own propensity for following the flow of his thoughts without censorship. In his youth, Freud was impressed with the advice on how to write creatively from the essay "The Art of Becoming an Original Writer in Three Days," by one of his favorite authors, Ludwig Borne:

> Take a few sheets of paper and for three days on end write down, without fabrication or hypocrisy, everything that comes into your head. Write down what you think of yourself, of your wife, of the Turkish War, of Goethe, of Fonk's trial, of the Last Judgement, of your superiors—and when three days have passed you will be quite out of your senses with astonishment at the new and unheard-of-thoughts you have had.

At age fourteen, Freud was given a present of the collected works of Ludwig Borne, and they were the only books of his adolescence to become part of his adult library. Freud acknowledged Borne for providing the seed of the idea that totally revised his therapeutic method.

Freud, Anna
(1895–1982)

Papa always makes it clear that he would like to know me as much more rational and lucid than the girls and women he gets to know during his analytic hours, with all their moods, dissatisfactions and passionate idiosyncrasies. Thus I, too, would really like to be as he sees fit, first out of love for him, and second because I myself know that it is the only chance that one has to be somewhat useful and not a burden and a concern for others.

—Anna Freud, 1925

Freud had longed for an heir to carry on the practice, movement, and theory of psychoanalysis. The man who believed women to be the inferior sex found it not in his three sons, whom he discouraged from entering the field, but in his youngest daughter, Anna, whom he fondly called his "Antigone." Like the daughter of Oedipus, Anna never married but became her father's companion, champion of the cause, and, later, nurse.

Martha was worn out after five close pregnancies, so after the birth of their fifth child, Sophie, the Freuds decided she would be their last. When Martha became pregnant with Anna, she thought her missed periods were a sign of an early and welcomed menopause. When it turned out that Martha was indeed pregnant, Freud had hoped for another son. But he quickly reconciled his dashed hopes, while Martha never could feel affection for Anna, who felt unwanted and "never loved" by her mother—"the tragedy" of her life. Until she was school age, a Catholic nursemaid took care of Anna.

As children desperately need their parents to survive, they will do anything for their parents' love. To please her obsessively clean mother, Anna became obsessive-compulsive about being orderly and clean, as did her brother Oliver, perhaps in part because Martha did not heed her husband's warning about obsessive-compulsive behavior as a consequence of strict toilet training and toilet trained the children as early as possible. Anna was always properly dressed and would become anxious if her clothes were at all disheveled.

While Martha appeared to overtly reject Anna, Freud, who was interested in but emotionally distant from his children, probably more covertly rejected her. Having two emotionally unavailable parents took a deep toll on Anna, who felt miserable as a child— "left out," "a bore" to her family, and herself bored and lonely. She called herself "dumb," "whiny," lacking "diligence," and felt unattractive in contrast to her pretty older sister Sophie, to whom Martha showed her love and whom Freud favored as well.

As a young child, Anna was able to express her jealousy of Sophie and her sadness. She was a naughty child, which amused Freud, who affectionately called her his "Black Devil." But as she matured, she felt increasingly more pressured to fit her father's conception of "normal" femininity, and, burying assertiveness and anger, she became the good, compliant child. That role stuck for life.

By adolescence, the unhappiness and anger of the inhibited "good" child seeped out in other ways: backaches, low energy, and "dumbness." At age eighteen, she wrote her father, to whom she increasingly turned for love—she signed her letters to "Papa" with "hugs and kisses"—of a mysterious feeling, not quite an illness, that rendered her exhausted and stupid.

Feeling empty, unloved, insignificant, and self-hateful—feelings she couldn't freely express to Papa, the creator of "talk therapy"— the adolescent Anna poured her heart out in a poem. "For one hour, one day, I do so wish to be rid of my self." She wished to be like the drayman, whose shoulder rubs sore from the strap, or the porter, "his neck bent, burdened; Someone other, who has no need to cover up—As I have been doing for so long." The lowest man's work gave meaning to his life and he did not have to hide his pain, while she had nothing and had to suffer in silence. Daydreams and masturbation assuaged her loneliness.

In 1913, Sophie got married while eighteen-year-old Anna was on a tour in Italy. Freud felt it unnecessary for her to return for the wedding. Anna felt left out and told her father so. Ignoring her feelings, Freud interpreted her complaints as jealousy of her sister's new husband—a disguised Oedipus complex as the brother-in-law was really the father who had won the mother's love. Anna said she did not feel this interpretation applied to her—a familiar tune that Freud's female patients echoed. Freud said she was being "overzealous, restless and unsatisfied because you have run away like a child from many things of which a grown-up girl would not be afraid." She would get past her moodiness when she accepted her "normal feminine" place. This Anna did by becoming compliant to his wishes, trading her identity for his approval by ultimately becoming a guinea pig for his psychoanalysis, both as a victim of his insensitive Oedipal interpretations of her behavior and, at age twenty-three, by going into analysis with her father, a man ill able to understand her feelings and from whom she had to hide her true self.

By now, Anna knew she wanted to become a psychoanalyst and started attending the psychoanalytic societies. In 1922, she wrote a paper, *Beating Fantasies and Daydreams*, which she presented as if it were about a patient she was treating. In fact, it was based on her own analysis by her father, the existence of which both Freud and Anna hid. In this paper, Anna described a young woman patient obsessed with two fantasies. In the first, a grown-up is beating a boy or boys. The feeling is highly sensual and ends with masturbation. Anna dated the fantasy to her fifth or sixth year. This fantasy is "ugly" and creates "violent self-reproaches, pangs of conscience, and temporary depressed moods." In the other fantasy—her "nice fantasy"—she spins tales largely in the Middle Ages where a knight threatens an innocent young boy but at the last moment spares the boy and grants him favors. These nice fantasies were nonsexual and thus guilt-free.

Both fantasies, she noted, have a similar theme. They involve a strong and a weak person, a dangerous situation with mounting tension, and a pleasurable resolution. She interpreted these fantasies in typical psychoanalytic fashion: the girl/Anna was motivated by incestuous feelings for her father—"in early childhood all the sexual drives were concentrated on a first love object, the father." Because Anna repressed her feelings, her Oedipus complex reemerged "in the language of the anal-sadistic organization as an act of beating." The nice stories represented healthy sublimation, as tender friendship replaced her sensual love. Freud added his own interpretation: The masturbation and the daydreaming were the primary causes of Anna's troubles. To become normal, she must give up her neurotic fantasies and masturbation.

Deeply attached to her father and committed to devoting her life to *his* work, *his* happiness, *his* well-being, Anna never married. She seemed interested in several men, but all met with her father's disapproval. At eighteen, she visited London, where the thirty-five-year-old Ernest Jones wooed her. Freud strongly discouraged involvement. When Anna was twenty-five, Hans Lampl, a friend of the family, showed an interest in her. Freud felt him unsuitable and Anna agreed. Freud wanted Anna for himself. In 1922, when Anna was twenty-seven and Freud sixty-six, he wrote to Lou

Andreas-Salomé, a surrogate mother to Anna: "I too very much miss Daughter-Anna. . . . I have long felt sorry for her for still being at home with us old folks . . . but on the other hand, if she really were to go away, I should feel myself as deprived as I do now, and as I should do if I had to give up smoking!" He could no more give up his dependence on her to satisfy his narcissistic needs than he could give up the cigars that ultimately killed him. At the same time, like a good father, he worried about her devotion to him and his science. "My Anna is very good and competent," he proudly told Arnold Zweig in the late spring of 1936, but worried how she "almost wholly sublimates her sexuality!"

Seeking a loving mother, Anna sought closeness with many women, several of whom were older, married, and mothers, and all were tied to her father. Lou Andreas-Salomé, who was her mother's age, especially lent a sympathetic ear and could share her feelings. In 1924, she wrote Frau Lou: "In the last week my 'nice stores' all of a sudden surfaced again and rampaged for days as they have not for a long while. Now they are asleep again, but I was impressed by how unchangeable and forceful and alluring such a daydream is, even if it has been . . . pulled apart, analyzed, published, and in every way mishandled and mistreated." Freud and Lou wrote often about their shared "Daughter-Anna." Ironically, Lou, the seeker of personal freedom above all else and who engaged in the free love that many falsely thought Freud had promoted, encouraged Anna's desire to stay at home and dedicate herself to her father and his work.

After Freud was diagnosed with cancer of the jaw and mouth and forced to wear a prosthesis, he withdrew from public life, and Anna became his intermediary with analysts and others, totally devoting herself to his care. She became his nurse following his surgeries and even helped him change his prosthesis.

And she brilliantly carried on his legacy. Fittingly, as the child of psychoanalysis, she took psychoanalytic inquiry into the realm of childhood disturbance. In 1927, when Anna was forty-two, she published her first book, *An Introduction to the Technique of Child Analysis*. In it, she broadened psychoanalysis from its focus on adults to the treatment and understanding of children, thereby making her own important contribution to her father's life work.

In 1936, three years before her father's death, Anna published *The Ego and the Mechanisms of Defense,* in which she greatly extended the ego's use of defense mechanisms to cope with conflict and anxiety, without diminishing the power of the id. This book opened the way for the ego's empowerment and the subsequent development of the school of "ego psychology." Based largely on her clinical work with children and adolescents, Anna extended her father's psychosexual sequence to include developmental lines in childhood from complete dependency, passivity, and irrationality to rational independence and active mastery of the environment. The book was a landmark for not only launching ego psychology but because it gave Anna her own voice/ego, enabling her to become more expressive of self without diminishing her father's work. Anna Freud continued to contribute greatly to her father's science and in her own right became a highly influential and famous psychoanalyst.

See **Family, the Children**.

Freud the Person

Freud has emerged as a person stranger and less explicable by his own theories than he himself realized.

—Charles Rycroft

Bearded, stern, and seemingly austere, from his photos Freud appeared a reserved introvert. Not so, according to the man who, comparing Freud's outgoing nature to the psychologist Alfred Adler's reserved character, devised the notion of introvert/extrovert: Carl Jung. To Jung, Freud was an extrovert. He was friendly, direct, charming, earnest, and kind. Freud's friend Ludwig Binswanger remarked on how Freud never omitted sending cordial greetings to his wife or asking about her. Anna Freud and her brother Martin described their father as, in general, "even tempered, optimistic, and even gay." He rarely showed anger at anyone in spite of the infamous rifts with colleagues over the years. The familiar somber expression may have come from Freud's dislike of being photographed. When caught off-guard by his sons' cameras, reveling in awesome mountain scenery or savoring a succulent mushroom, he looked much less formidable.

This giant of men was only about five feet seven inches tall, slight of build, and later somewhat stooped. Yet greatness and dignity emanated from him, and he stood out in a crowd with his authoritative presence, well-groomed appearance, and probing eyes. Freud had mesmerizing X-ray eyes, and many who knew him commented on how keen and penetrating they were and how they missed very little. Joan Riviere, a British analyst, spoke of the "critical exploring gaze of his keenly piercing eyes," and Hanns Sachs of his "deep-set and piercing eyes." Mark Brunswick, a patient of Freud's in the 1920s, described his eyes as "almost melodramatic."

Ever looking the part of the successful professor, Freud was fastidious about his appearance. To him, clothes were basic to self-respect, and he insisted that his children be well dressed. He once commented: "The good opinion of my tailor matters to me as much as that of my professor." When he was poor, often he would not go out because of the holes in his coat and occasionally borrowed a friend's coat. He used any extra funds to enhance his appearance. Preparing for an evening at the Charcots' in Paris in 1886, he wrote Martha: "My appearance was immaculate except that I had replaced the unfortunate ready-made white tie with one of the beautiful black ones from Hamburg. This was my tail coat's first appearance; I had bought myself a new shirt and white gloves, as the washable pair are no longer very nice; I had my hair set and my rather wild beard trimmed in the French style; altogether I spent fourteen francs on the evening. As a result I looked very fine and made a favorable impression on myself."

Highly intelligent and witty, Freud had a great sense of humor and abounded in jokes, mainly Jewish stories, and, with his sharp memory, quoted easily apt passages from poets and novelists. As his writing was literary, his lecturing was equally poetic and riveting; his German precise and deliberate, his gestures sparing, his face open and expressive, and his voice always well modulated, he delivered his speech slowly, clearly, and energetically without notes, infusing his presentation with humor and informality and enthralling his audience. He was fond of using the Socratic method and would frequently ask his audience questions or invite criticism, to which he retorted wittily and persuasively. The American radical Emma Goldman, who had heard him speak in the late 1890s, remarked: "His simplicity and earnestness and the brilliance of his mind combined to give one the feeling of being let out of a dark cellar into broad daylight. For the first time I grasped the full significance of sex repression and its effect on human thought and action. He helped me to understand myself, my own needs, and I also realized that only people of depraved minds could impugn the motives or find 'impure' so great and fine a personality as Freud."

This was Freud's persona: assured, authoritative, witty, kind, intense, tenacious. But who was Freud beneath the mask? If we go by Freud's famous statement made to his disciple Erik Erikson—"The mature person should be able to love and to work"—Freud was mature and healthy. In fact, his love life was highly conflicted and unsatisfying. And although his work was enormously gratifying and brought him the fame he had long desired, he often dwelled on the sour grapes: on those who left his flock to start their own kingdoms; on how late in coming were the celebrations in his honor; on the recognition he did not receive, like the Nobel Prize. And in spite of Freud being the master psychic detective, his theories could not adequately explain the true Freud. Those of some of his disciples offer greater insight into his psyche.

To Alfred Adler, Freud's bitter enemy, Freud, a poor Jewish boy living among gentiles, was beset with inferiority feelings. To compensate for feeling inferior, Freud sought power.

Attachment theory, as first proposed by the British psychoanalyst John Bowlby and later expounded by his associate Mary Ainsworth, reveals Freud's relationships with his mother, father, wife, children, and colleagues as insecure and wanting. At heart, Freud's early relationship with his mother left him fearful of separation and abandonment, and he avoided human intimacy. Some part of him remained a frightened child who sought protection from surrogate parents. His first crush was on a woman his mother's age. Later, he idealized strong, charismatic men: Ernst Brücke, Jean Charcot, Josef Breuer, and last, Wilhelm Fliess, the person with whom Freud came closest to emotional intimacy but whom he kept at arm's length by communicating through letters and rarely seeing him. After the disappointment with Fliess, Freud never again attached himself to a father figure. So vulnerable was he to the hurt of disappointed love that he kept an emotional distance, as if he didn't need anyone, exhibiting grandiosity: "I'm so great, I can do everything myself." But this independence was pseudomaturity—compulsive self-reliance, as John Bowlby called it—fueled, in his childhood, by the inability to use his mother as a secure base from which to explore and by the need to shut her out, as if to say, "It's not that you won't relieve my discomfort, it's that I don't need anyone."

Freud's need to idealize Fliess, his unhappiness when his *alter* was unavailable, and his dependence on Fliess's acceptance and support for self-worth would be analyzed in the 1970s by the psychoanalyst Heinz Kohut, whose theories have helped give rise to the currently popular *self-psychology* of modern psychoanalysis as problems with *narcissism*. As hysteria was the common affliction of the early part of the twentieth century, the narcissistic personality, whose central disturbance involves feelings of emptiness and depression, is the psychological affliction of today's age of anxiety.

To feel whole and loved, Kohut identified two basic trends in the narcissistic personality: the need to idealize a significant other and the need to be idealized. Freud needed Fliess as an idealized other and as a mirror to Freud's greatness. When Freud lost the connection to Fliess, he felt lost and empty. For instance, Freud admonished Fliess for not quickly answering his letters: "Remember that I regularly develop the gloomiest expectation when your letters fail to arrive." But Fliess would be Freud's last idealized father figure. From here on, Freud was the patriarch—*he* was to be idealized. When his sons— Adler, Jung, Rank, and so on—deidealized the father and followed their own thoughts, Freud took it personally—he felt narcissistically wounded, as Kohutians would say—and he was unforgiving.

Freud started out his career firmly believing that all neurotic behavior had a neurological cause and only later changed his thinking to the psyche as the origin of human misery. Today neuroscience proposes that our individual biochemistry greatly influences the path of our psyche. Freud appears to have had a sensitive constitution, suggesting that his biochemistry could have led him to overreact to stress at times and become easily anxious. He was beset with migraines and lifelong digestive upsets, both of which are induced by stress, and palpitations that were diagnosed as harmless, but they nevertheless worried him. He appeared to have been sensitive to noise; upon entering a restaurant with a band playing, he would have a "pained expression on his face" and "quickly his hands would go over his ears to drown the sound."

Freud's proneness to apathy and depression may have had underlying physical causes. His slight stoop and lack of exercise other than walking suggest poor musculature and some problems getting his body moving. Further, his addiction to nicotine, especially to help him work, and his use of cocaine—both stimulants— suggest some need to self-medicate to get his arousal up to be alert and interested in the world. His low libido and aversion to human closeness indicate some problems with body awareness, which likely contributed to his fear of closeness. Freud himself said that the ego is "first of all a bodily ego."

Freudian Slip

See **Psychopathology of Everyday Life**.

Goethe Prize for Literature

A gifted writer, Freud won the coveted Goethe Prize for literature in 1930. He received a stipend of $2,500, of which he gave $250 to his aging friend Lou Andreas-Salomé.

Why *literature*? Adam Phillips, the editor of a new translation of Freud's work, asserts that Freud should be read like "any great novelist." Take his case of Dora, which has been compared to the twentieth-century novels of Marcel Proust, Henry James, and James Joyce, and to the plays of Henrik Ibsen. Rather than moving only in chronological sequence, Freud moves back and forth, presenting multiple analytic perspectives by using modern techniques such as theoretical digressions, dramatic flashbacks, and warnings to the reader. At the same time, the case flows smoothly with an inherent inner logic.

That his writing reads like literature was not an accomplishment that always sat well with Freud. In 1895, reporting on Elisabeth von R., he found it a bit odd "that the case histories I write read like novellas, and that they, so to speak, lack the serious stamp of scientific method."

Freud had mixed feelings about receiving the Goethe Prize. He was pleased with the recognition and connection with Goethe, who was one of his idols; yet, like his university professorship, it was late in coming and a small token of his accomplishments, unlike the prestigious Nobel Prize, which he had long coveted but never received.

Goldwyn, Samuel
(1882–1974)

On his way to Europe, the mega–Hollywood producer Samuel Goldwyn told a *New York Times* reporter that he intended on visiting sixty-nine-year-old Freud, "the greatest love specialist in the world," to offer Freud a lavish fee of $100,000 to write the consummate love story. "Love and laughter are the two ideas uppermost in Samuel Goldwyn's mind in producing pictures," the reporter observed, and added that Goldwyn intended to "prevail upon the expert in psychoanalysis to commercialize his study and write a story for the screen, or come to America and help in a 'drive' on the hearts of the nation. . . . Scenario writers, directors and actors," Goldwyn thought, "can learn much by a really deep study of everyday life. How much more forceful will be their creations if they know how to express genuine emotional motivation and suppressed desires?"

On January 24, 1925, the *New York Times* tersely reported: FREUD REBUFFS GOLDWYN/VIENNESE PSYCHOANALYST IS NOT INTERESTED IN MOTION PICTURE OFFER. In fact, according to a Viennese boulevard paper, *Die Stunde*, which claimed to interview Freud, Freud denied Goldwyn's request for an interview with a one-sentence letter: "I do not intend to see Mr. Goldwyn."

Hartmann, Heinz
(1894–1970)

Called the father of ego psychology, Heinz Hartmann moved beyond Freud's conflict theory and explored the strengths of the ego, independent of the id. He argued that the ego and the id derive their energy from a common instinctual source and each regulates and influences the other. In so doing, Hartmann freed the ego to assume control of higher-level activities, such as perception, thinking, and intelligence, which Freud basically ignored. Further, argued Hartmann, much of human behavior and experience does *not* involve conflict and tension reduction; rather the ego can exist in a *conflict-free* sphere where its primary role is to adapt to the environment. Such revision of the ego's role radicalized psychoanalytic doctrine and thrust it out of its negative, deterministic dirge where the individual was just a victim of id impulses.

Homosexuality

Freud disagreed with the accepted views of homosexuality, which he termed "inversion," in the repressive Victorian era as being degenerate or innate. He argued that many homosexuals are highly intelligent, cultured, and distinguished, whatever their sexual behavior. In *Three Essays on the Theory of Sexuality* of 1905, he liberally noted how the high civilization of ancient Greece valued homosexuality in its many forms and practices. Yet, declared Freud, it would be better to live a "normal" heterosexual life, and, although he was open at times about his "homosexual libido," as in the Fliess and Jung affairs, for the most part he professed his longing for a man's love as a dangerous inner force.

Not knowing at that time that homosexuality exists on a continuum of occasional same-sex acts to exclusively homosexual sexual orientation, Freud lumped all homosexuality into one category, then argued that the existence of both heterosexual and homosexual orientation in one person pointed to acquired rather than genetic roots. He noted that while homosexuality persisted throughout life in some, in others it could go into temporary remission or be a detour in the path of "normal" development. Further, it often appears following a long period of apparently heterosexual activity and may fluctuate between being overt or covert. Although many homosexuals assert that they could never remember any attachment to the opposite sex from their earliest years, Freud asserted they may only be repressing their positive heterosexual feelings. In addition, Freud pointed out that many homosexuals feel both homosexual and heterosexual arousal, and only at puberty might homosexual attachment overtake heterosexual adjustment.

At the same time, Freud believed that all human beings are capable of homosexuality, which does suggest innate roots, and may experience same-sex attraction unconsciously. It manifests when some early experience—for example, castration anxiety—drives libido in a same-sex direction. In his study of Leonardo da Vinci, he described male homosexuality as emotions from a repressed attachment to the mother highlighted by having identified with her. The absence of a father and growing up in a feminine environment, or the presence of a weak father dominated by the mother, furthers feminine identification and homosexuality; some homosexuals may flee women to remain faithful to their mothers. Similarly, having a cruel father may disrupt male identification.

Having believed that homosexuality was acquired, Freud believed that it could be "cured." To this end, he initially tried hypnotic suggestion to unearth the unconscious material "causing" homosexuality, but this method failed. By 1910, though, he felt that psychoanalysis could cure homosexuality and other perversions. But by 1920, he expressed caution of a complete cure following publication of "Psychogenesis of a Case of Homosexuality in a Woman."

In this famous case, an eighteen-year-old girl who had attempted suicide was brought to Freud by her parents to cure her homosexuality. She had become linked with an older "society lady" or "cocotte"—apparently a bisexual prostitute—and openly paraded the relationship, mortifying her parents. Her father happened upon the two women in the street one day and looked angrily at the daughter. She thereby threw herself over an embankment onto a railroad track and just escaped permanent injury. While Freud believed her suicide attempt was serious, he viewed it as a manipulation to get her way with both her parents and the society lady. Ignoring how her suicide attempt revealed profound suffering, he found her not particularly anxious or symptomatic; his interest in her was as "a case of homosexuality in a woman," noted Louis Breger.

Freud interpreted her homosexuality as a search for mother love: "The analysis revealed beyond all shadow of doubt that the lady-love was a substitute for—her mother." In support, he pointed out her attraction to older women and an earlier attraction to a mother with children. Her own mother "treated her children in quite different ways, being decidedly harsh towards her daughter and over-indulgent to her three sons." The mother, "still quite youthful herself, saw in her rapidly developing daughter an inconvenient competitor; she favoured her sons at her expense, limited her independence as much as possible, and kept an especially strict watch against any close relation between the girl and her father." In contrast, the father was "an earnest, worthy man, at bottom very tender-hearted, but he had to some extent estranged his children by the sternness he had adopted towards them." Learning of his daughter's homosexual tendencies, "he flew into a rage and tried to suppress them by threats [viewing her] as vicious, as degenerate, or as mentally afflicted. . . . [Her] homosexuality aroused the deep bitterness in him, and he was determined to combat it with all the means in his power." Freud ignored the fact that the father's insensitive, angry glance had precipitated her suicide attempt.

Unlike the girl's parents, Freud initially was compassionate and tried to help her understand her discontent. He saw her as making a "positive transference" in the analysis, following the girl's description of a series of dreams that predicted her being cured of her homosexuality through the analysis, and "express[ing] her joy over the prospects in life that would then be opened before her, confessed her longing for a man's love and for children."

But then he switched gears, perhaps as a result of an unconscious negative countertransference. "Warned through some slight impression or other, I told her one day that I did not believe these dreams, that I regarded them as false and hypocritical, and that she intended to deceive me just as she habitually deceived her father. I was right; after I had made this clear, this kind of dream ceased."

Freud's rationale for his disbelief was that sometimes dreams "lie," contradicting his own theory that dreams, unlike conscious thoughts, reveal the unconscious and thus are always true. Freud concluded that, despised as a female, the girl adopted a male role to seek love and affection from a mother figure. Ever trotting down the Oedipal path, he played on her sense of injustice that girls were not granted the same freedom as boys by concluding that "she is in fact a feminist," a result of her "pronounced envy for the penis." Penis envy and the Oedipus complex filled her with revenge for her father for having given her mother yet another baby, her younger brother. The suicide attempt was a symbolic expression of the wish to have a child by her father: "falling" over the embankment was an enactment of the German word *niederkommen*, which means both "to fall" and "to be delivered of child."

The girl rejected his interpretations, which he analyzed as her "Russian defense," referring to General Kutuzov's attempt to out-maneuver Napoleon: "The resistance . . . withdraws to a certain boundary line, beyond which it proves to be unconquerable. The resistance very often pursues similar tactics . . . Russian tactics, as they might be called." He concluded that his failure resulted from her wish to hold onto her homosexuality, that she was transferring her anger at her father and her "repudiation of men" onto him, and he abruptly ended the analysis.

Although initially Freud felt that a traumatic experience could lead a person, especially a woman, into homosexual activity, this case and others led him to conclude that it was especially diffi-cult to analyze an individual at "peace" with a perversion they find "natural." Success is more likely with those who are neurotic and who rebel against and view their sexual behavior as path-ological.

In summary, Freud believed that homosexuality is caused by early accidental fixating experiences, including seductions, fol-lowed by a traumatic Oedipal period (castration anxiety). By plac-ing the origin of homosexuality in childhood events, Freud helped dispel some of the prejudice of his age regarding homosexuality as a perversion. But he inadvertently reinforced the false notion that homosexuality is something learned and therefore can be *un*learned. Even today, some psychotherapists try to analyze away one's sexual orientation, and clergy, who view it as "God's curse," exorcise it away as demonic possession, although such efforts are by and large unsuccessful, as Freud found in his own failed attempts. In fact, research points to a strong biological component for homo-sexuality. Often found in families, homosexuality can be genetic, or it can be congenital, as a result of stress the mother incurred during pregnancy. In other words, many homosexuals are born with a pre-disposition to choose a same-sex partner, and viewing it as a choice further propagates homophobia. Certainly this was not Freud's intention. That homosexuality may be to a large extent biological would have accorded with his basic theory that we are all born bisexual but have markedly different tendencies toward becoming primarily heterosexual or homosexual.

Horney, Karen
(1885–1952)

The view that women are infantile and emotional creatures, and as such, incapable of responsibility and independence is the work of the masculine tendency to lower women's self-respect.

—Karen Horney, *Feminine Psychology*, 1932

In 1922, Karen Horney bravely stood up at the International Congress of Psychoanalysts in Berlin, with Freud in the chair, and proposed her revised version of *penis envy*. Horney conceded that it exists—but within normal female development. Penis envy does not create femininity but expresses it; nor does this envy necessarily lead women to the "repudiation of their womanhood." Quite the contrary, "we can see that penis envy by no means precludes a deep and wholly womanly love attachment to the father." Cautiously presenting her case, she only *speculated* that penis envy was "masculine narcissism," which had led psychoanalysts to accept the view that half the human race is discontented with their sex—a conclusion about women that "is decidedly unsatisfying, not only to feminine narcissism but also to biological science": one small step for psychoanalytic revision; one large step for feminism.

Born in Hamburg, Karen Horney decided at age thirteen to become a physician. She was one of the first women in Germany admitted to medical school and received her medical education at the universities of Freiburg, Gottingen, and Berlin. In 1909, she married Oskar Horney, a social scientist she had met while they were both students at Freiburg, and separated from him in 1926.

In 1910, she began analysis with Karl Abraham, the first psychoanalyst to practice in Germany, and underwent a second analysis with Hanns Sachs in the early 1920s. She was one of the six founding members of the Berlin Psychoanalytical Institute. In 1932, Franz Alexander invited her to become associate director of the newly formed Chicago Psychoanalytic Institute, and she immigrated to the United States. She moved to New York in 1934 and became a member of the New York Psychoanalytic Institute. In 1941, she became founding editor of the *American Journal of Psychoanalysis*, organized the American Institute for Psychoanalysis, and served as its dean until her death in 1952.

An important early feminist and neo-Freudian psychoanalyst, Horney believed that childhood anxiety, caused by the child's sense of helplessness, sets off the desire for love and security. In countering Freud's assumptions that women have weak superegos and suffer penis envy, Horney later described men as equally capable of "womb envy."

Horney's thought went through three phases. In the 1920s and early 1930s, she wrote a series of essays in which she tried to modify Freud's ideas about feminine psychology while staying within the framework of classical theory. In *The Neurotic Personality of Our Time* (1937) and *New Ways in Psychoanalysis* (1939), she tried to redefine psychoanalysis by replacing Freud's biological orientation with an emphasis on culture and interpersonal relationships. In *Our Inner Conflicts* (1945) and *Neurosis and Human Growth* (1950), she developed her mature theory in which individuals cope with the anxiety produced by feeling unsafe, unloved, and unvalued by disowning their spontaneous feelings and developing elaborate strategies of defense. She ranks as one of Freud's most influential intellectual daughters.

Hysteria

Hysteria comes from the ancient Greek word *hystera*, meaning "uterus." The cause was thought to be a wandering womb. By traveling to various parts of the body, the wayward womb caused symptoms such as temporary paralysis of limbs or sense organ dysfunction (e.g., temporary blindness).

Particularly common in repressive Victorian times, hysteria manifested in bizarre bodily symptoms that defied satisfactory explanation, although they had been recognized for millennia.

Patients would demonstrate paralysis, loss of speech, blindness, inability to swallow, and so on. The symptoms had no apparent physical cause. One day a patient was paralyzed. The next day she would get up and walk. The cause of hysteria was unknown. Doctors would accuse these suffering women of faking their symptoms, of maligning. Hysterics were condemned as witches or thought to be possessed of the devil. There was no cure and the disease was a death sentence; patients would be locked up in institutions for years.

Studies on Hysteria by Josef Breuer and Sigmund Freud was a revelation. By disclosing this illness as psychological—as a result of "reminiscences"—and often curable through the cathartic method, Breuer and Freud brought hysteria out of the dark ages.

See **Anna O. (Case); Breuer, Josef; Seduction Hypothesis.**

Instincts

Beyond the basic animal instincts to seek food and avoid pain, Freud identified two sources of psychic energy, which he termed *drives*: libido (also termed *love* or *eros*) and aggression (also termed *death wish* or *thanatos*). These *unconscious* drives shape our behavior without involving our waking minds; they surface, heavily disguised, only in our dreams. At first, Freud used terms such as *instinct* and *drives* indiscriminately. But in later translation *instinct* replaced *drives*.

Motivating most behavior, the instincts, which reside in the id, supply the psychic energy to get the mental apparatus running. They seek an external object to reduce tension. For example, an infant's hunger drive is directed toward the object of food; when sexually aroused, we seek someone sexually appealing. The object of an instinct, however, varies and changes as we develop. For instance, the sexual drive changes from oral to anal to phallic to genital. Further, people's object choices depend greatly on their personal histories. As in dreams, we may displace one satisfying object to another. Prisoners, for example, confined with members of their own sex, often resort to masturbation or to homosexuality as substitutes for heterosexual partners, only to return to exclusive heterosexual activity upon release. Conversely, a single object can satisfy several instincts simultaneously. Thumb sucking may partially alleviate the infant's hunger, soothe teething discomfort, and feel pleasurably stimulating.

Interpretation of Dreams, The

Dreams are the royal road to the unconscious mind.

—Sigmund Freud, *The Interpretation of Dreams*

I read *The Interpretation of Dreams* when I was in my twenties. I dreamed much and lucidly. I still recall one particular dream. My brother had lost his job and I feared losing mine. In my dream, my brother and I were on a lake *in the same boat*. This visual image of a thought appeared to me compelling evidence that dreams, as Freud proposed, vividly symbolize unconscious processes.

Freud considered his dream book his magnum opus, his "most significant work," and felt immensely proud of his accomplishment, and rightly so. Not only was he the first to break the dream code but this pioneering work heralded the idea that changed the history of Western civilization: unconscious forces shape our mental and emotional lives. Further, he unlocked the key to treating and understanding neurosis; dream interpretation became a cornerstone of psychoanalytic therapy. And yet, far from breaking new ground, initially this monumental achievement went largely unnoticed. In its first six years, only 351 copies were sold. But eventually it caught the public's attention and has never let go.

The dream book contains the seeds of concepts that would comprise the canon of psychoanalytic theory: the Oedipus complex, the distinction between primary and secondary process thinking, the infantile origins of adult functioning, and much more. In 1931, in his preface to the third English edition, Freud described the magnitude of his "dream book" in his life: "It contains, even according to my present-day judgment, the most valuable of all the discoveries it has been my good fortune to make. Insight such as this falls to one's lot but once in a lifetime." You may disagree with many of his ideas, but this book unquestionably placed Freud as one of the world's most original and important thinkers.

Wish Fulfillment

As Freud sat listening to his early patients ruminate, a memory of a recent dream would often emerge. This intrigued Freud. Although he now had, after formulating his seduction hypothesis, the discovery of the unconscious mind under his belt, he lacked the tools to penetrate it. At first he looked only at the narrative of the dream. But then he discovered that not all dreams follow a haphazard plan; sometimes he could piece together an obvious message. An example would be my boat dream whose meaning is immediately apparent.

Then his little daughter, Anna, had her famous "stwawbewwie" dream:

> My youngest daughter, then nineteen months old, had an attack of vomiting one morning and had consequently been without food all day. During the night after this day of starvation she was heard calling out excitedly in her sleep: "Anna Freud, stwawbewwies, wild stwawbewwies, omblet, pudden!" . . . The menu included pretty well everything that must have seemed to her to make up a desirable meal.

Freud now played with the idea of dreams as wish fulfillment. But what of scary, violent dreams, like being chased by monsters, falling from mountains, stabbing one's spouse? Do we *wish* these events? Freud hit upon the answer to this conundrum.

Although little Anna's dream seems a straightforward, undisguised dream-as-a-wish, the adult dream, Freud discovered, is more deceptive and complex. In this hallucinatory state, dreams are twisted to be as we would desire them. The importance of the dream, said Freud, was to *preserve the state of sleep*. Were we to consciously become aware of what was lurking in the depths of our unruly unconscious, we would become alarmed and awake. The solution? The dreamer seeks circuitous paths to wish fulfillment so that the most threatening and anxiety-provoking aspects of the dream are disguised to become acceptable to the dreamer. Once we interpret the meaning of a dream, the seemingly horrific aspects appear in a different light. How ingenious.

Consider this dream by a young female patient of Freud's as she described it to him:

> As you will remember, my sister has only one boy left now—Karl; she lost his elder brother, Otto, while I was still living with her. Otto was my favorite; I more or less brought him up. I'm fond of the little one too, but of course, not nearly so fond as I was of the one who died. Last night, then, I dreamt that I *saw Karl lying before me dead. He was lying in his little coffin with his hands folded and with candles all round—in fact just like little Otto, whose death was such a blow to me.*

If dreams represent wish fulfillment, this dream appears to wish that little Karl had died instead of little Otto. To Freud this didn't fit; this patient was not cruel. As the girl revealed her story and as she followed Freud's direction to tell him whatever popped into her head, the dream began to take shape.

An orphan, this patient had been raised by an elder sister. A male lecturer, nicknamed "the professor," was a frequent visitor to the sister's home and had caught the patient's fancy. Marriage plans were made, then disrupted between the girl and the professor, and he stopped visiting. Secretly, although hurt, Freud's patient longed to see her paramour. She couldn't forget him, and whenever he lectured publicly, she hid in the back of the audience. She sought to see him from a distance in other ways. At Otto's funeral, she felt momentary happiness when the professor showed up to express his condolences.

Here lay the key to her dream. If little Karl were to die, she might again see her beloved professor without initiating any actual meeting. Thus, her wish was not for Karl's death but to be able to see the professor again.

Freud's insight into dreams as wish fulfillment and the fruit that discovery would bear was set in stone with his famous dream "Irma's Injection" (see **Irma's Injection**). Irma was a young woman who was Freud's patient and also a family friend. The night before the dream, Freud asked Otto Rie, the Freud family's pediatrician, who had recently stayed with Irma and her family, how Irma was doing. Rie replied in what, to Freud, seemed a rebuke: "Better, but not quite well." In defense, Freud wrote out Irma's case history in detail and sent it to Josef Breuer, from whom he was now estranged but whose judgment he still valued. That night he had the momentous dream.

The Freuds are in a large hall receiving many guests, among them "Irma." Addressing her with the familiar *du*, Freud takes her aside to admonish her for ignoring his "solution" and tells her that if she still has pains, "it is really your fault." She replies, "If you only knew what pains I've got now in my throat and stomach." Taken aback, Freud peers down her throat and sees a white patch and some grayish scabs formed like the turbinal bones of the nose. In the fear that he has missed some organic ailment, he calls over Breuer, who, clean-shaven and limping, looks very different from his bearded self. Otto, also present, begins tapping her chest, saying, "She has a dull area low down on the left," pointing to signs of disease on her shoulder, to which Breuer says, "There's no doubt it's an infection, but no matter, dysentery will supervene and the toxins will be eliminated." Earlier in the dream, Otto has thoughtlessly given Irma an injection. "A propyl preparation, pro-pyls . . . ," Freud stutters, "propionic acid . . . trimethylamin," and "probably with a syringe that was not clean." The dream closes with Freud thinking that "injections of that sort ought not to be made so thoughtlessly, and it was also probable that the syringe had not been clean."

Freud quizzically pondered every aspect of the Irma dream. To start, Irma had been on his mind after the conversation with Rie the evening before the dream. This led to his discovery that dreams have as their impetus the "day's residues." But what of the seemingly nonsensical features of the dream? What was the meaning of his odd conversation with Irma and what he saw upon looking down her throat? Why was Breuer disguised, and why did both Breuer and Rie appear incompetent? And what was the meaning of the remark about dysentery, the dirty syringes, and the injection of propionic acid with its formula? None of these images clearly expressed a wish.

After exhaustively analyzing the dream image by image, speech by speech, he made numerous associations. The syringe is unclean, unlike *his* clean syringes, so he is not at fault for Irma's pain. The scabs in the turbinal bones refer to his own predilection for cocaine, which he was using at the time to cure his own anxiety and depression. The chemical trimethylamin was, his friend Fliess once told him, associated with sexual chemistry—this enabled Freud to keep Fliess's theories viable (see **Irma's Injection**)—but Freud interpreted it at the moment as advancing his own controversial ideas about the sexual etiology of neurosis, which he assumed to be at the heart of Irma's troubles.

Added up, these interpretations revolved around his proficiency as a healer. The dream was "a plea" for his innocence; he was not guilty of medical mismanagement; compared to the other doctors, *he* was conscientious. As the dream demonstrated, he was not to be blamed for Irma's continuing pains; it was the fault of others: Irma should have accepted his interpretation; Rie should not have given her injections with a dirty needle; Breuer was medically incompetent; Rie and Breuer should have supported him. Freud concluded that the dream "was the fulfillment of a wish and its motive was a wish," which became, in the next chapter, the innovative principle that "all dreams are wish fulfillments." He felt he had unlocked the key to interpreting *all* dreams and excitedly wrote to Fliess: "Do you suppose that someday one will read on a marble tablet on this house [where he dreamed the dream]:

Here, on July 24, 1895
The secret of the dream revealed itself
to Dr. Sigm. Freud"

Dream Work

Freud discovered much more. Like a surreal play, a dream is cleverly transformed into assorted and often nonsensical pictorial scenes, with people who may be playing themselves but look like a different character, who may act like themselves or like a character totally unlike them. Such disguises are necessary to hide wishes and desires that would appear perverse and unethical while awake. Deciding what the dreamer should be aware of while dreaming or remembering goes to the preconscious *censorship system*, the border guard between the unconscious and conscious mind. Morally unacceptable wishes—sleeping with your mother—will be distorted in the dream. In the Irma dream, Rie and Breuer are the bad doctors, the disguised bad guys presented as the incompetent doctors, as Freud would have found it catastrophic if it were he or Fliess, who as it turns out it was (see **Irma's Injection**).

Interpreting the meaning of the dream requires translating the mental drama, or what we remember, which Freud termed the *manifest* content, into its psychical meaning—the "perverse," unacceptable impulses that like "masked criminals" are far more common in mental life than clear-cut, undisguised urges, which he termed the *latent* content. Unearthing the latent content requires digging deep into the narrative to discover the *dream work* that orchestrated the dream. Through clever tricks such as *condensation, displacement*, and *visual imaging*, the dream work converts strivings, wishes, and needs into the disguised images of the manifest content.

Freud observed that while we can generally describe our dreams in a few words, interpreting the manifest content can spin a long tale. The manifest content must be compressed, Freud thought, into a *condensation* of the actual dream—a composite photograph of a single person made from the characteristics of several. It may "look like A perhaps, but may be dressed like B, may do something that we remember C doing, and at the same time we may know that he is D." In the Irma dream, Irma was a composite of two other figures. Her chief features were like Anna Lichtheim, daughter of Freud's religion teacher Samuel Hammerschlag, a young widow, and one of Freud's favorite patients. But Anna Lichtheim closely resembled another of Freud's patients, Emma Eckstein, who was the subject of Fliess's botched nasal surgery and whom the latent dream story is really about.

Displacement replaces a latent dream element in consciousness by a more remote idea or a shift of emotional accent from one thought to another to leave the dreamer feeling that the dream was strangely connected, or of having made "much ado about nothing." In the dream, Freud was not the bad guy; Freud displaced incompetency onto Rie, who should not have given Irma injections with a dirty needle, and Breuer, who was medically incompetent (Freud was on the outs with Breuer).

Dreams use all sorts of puns and other wordplays. An example is one that Freud did not use in the dream book but that others have "pointed out"; the unclean "syringe" with which Otto Rie injects Irma is, in German, *spritze*—"squirter"—the colloquial word for penis, as "prick" is in English. Emma became ill by having a dirty prick squirt in her. Freud alludes to his wife in this association but omits that she was at that time five months pregnant with their last child, Anna, a pregnancy that she did not want. And Anna was named after Anna Lichtheim. Freud's dirty penis had caused this unwanted swelling in Martha just as Fliess had intruded into Emma Eckstein's nose with disastrous consequences, both real incidents that filled Freud with guilt that he attempts to disavow in the dream. Another example comes from one of my own dreams that I had while reading the dream book. I dreamed of a "Mr. Hodgepodge"—a compilation of different men in my life. On rereading the dream book, I was astounded to read Freud describe how wordplay may represent a "hodgepodge" of ideas. That I had unconsciously retained that page in the book, which apparently served as the impetus for my dream, convinced me at the time that, as Freud had posited, the mind does indeed retain everything it learns, although much remains unconscious.

Dream as Archaic

Freud viewed the dream as archaic, an infantile view of the world before language—a regression to our early years. The world of the infant is one of sensory impressions and memory images of such impressions; words are attached to mental images later in development. Thus, a dream's latent content may contain a wish that dates from childhood: "To our surprise, we find the child and child's impulses still living on in the dream." For instance, flying dreams symbolize the joyful infantile feeling of being thrown in the air.

Rarely do adults retain more than a few incidents of memories of the first five or six years of life. Yet Freud discovered these memories to not be forgotten but merely inaccessible or latent. When triggered by a current, similar incident, these early unconscious childhood memories may emerge during dreams. Something in the dreamer's current waking life—an incident, a thwarted desire, a disturbing emotional happening—somehow connects to the stored memories of the unconscious and together these initiate a dream.

Dream Symbolism

The aspect of Freud's dream interpretation that has most penetrated into the public domain is his use of symbols. Although Freud felt that the dreamer's free association to the dream holds the key to interpretation, he became convinced that some symbols were universal and could be reliably interpreted: the king is the father; the queen is the mother; the prince or princess is the dreamer. And of course there are the shared sex symbols: elongated objects represent the penis; receptive objects the vagina. In chapter 6 of *The Interpretation of Dreams*, Freud elaborated on the well-known Freudian phallic symbols in dreams:

> All elongated objects, such as sticks, tree trunks and umbrellas . . . may stand for the male organ, as well as all long sharp weapons such as knives, daggers and pikes. . . . Boxes, cases, chest, cupboards and ovens represent the uterus, and also hollow objects, ships, and vessels of all kinds. . . . Steps, ladders or staircases . . . walking up or down them, are representations of the sexual act.

Could anyone dream of a snake burrowing into a hole and not think sex? Climbing stairs or ladders, which entails increasing breathlessness and rhythmic movements to get to the top, represents sexual intercourse. Although Freud's universal interpretations are compelling, we can imagine other scenarios. For instance, *climbing to the top* may indicate how hard it is to get ahead, and *heavy breathing* may connote our struggle to the top.

Irma's Injection

In 1895, two months after the publication of *Studies on Hysteria*, Freud dreamed his groundbreaking dream, Irma's Injection. The longest analysis of dreams in *The Interpretation of Dreams*—sixteen pages—it was the driving force for his theory that dreams are wish fulfillments. Freud's initial interpretation of the dream, as expounded in the dream book, was concern for his professional competence. Yet, although this dream and others reveal something of the workings of Freud's unconscious mind, they were only "extinctions . . . shirkings . . . partial revealments of the truth." Only in his shared intimacies with his close friend Wilhelm Fliess did he explore his deepest self. In fact, after careful and exhaustive analysis by later authors, ultimately the dream was not about Freud's professional competence but about *Fliess's*, whom he would apparently go to any length to protect.

So blinded was Freud by his idealization of Fliess that he, the master picklock of dream symbolism, appears to have misinterpreted his own momentous dream: Irma was really Emma Eckstein, one of Freud's patients and the victim of a botched nasal surgery by Fliess. Looking down Irma's throat, the turbinal bone-like structure that Freud viewed was like the bones Fliess operated on. The injection of trimethylamin was a substance that Freud and Fliess had discussed subsequent to the dream in relation to "sexual processes."

In addition to hysterical anxiety symptoms, Emma Eckstein suffered severely from nasal pains and bloody secretions. While Freud thought her nosebleeds psychogenic, he had asked Fliess to examine her, lest he mistake her diagnosis. In the Irma dream he worried precisely about making such a faulty diagnosis. Accordingly, Fliess came to Vienna and operated on Emma Eckstein's nose. Following the operation, she was in great pain and hemorrhaging. Alarmed, Freud called in Viennese surgeons, and on March 8, 1895, he related to Fliess what had happened.

His old school friend Ignaz Rosanes, a reputable specialist, had met Freud at Emma Eckstein's apartment. She was bleeding from the nose and mouth, and the "fetid odor was very bad." Rosanes "cleaned the surroundings of the opening, pulled out adhesive blood clots, and suddenly pulled at something like a thread." He kept pulling and "a good half meter of gauze had been taken out of the cavity. The next moment a flood of blood followed, the patient turned white, with bulging eyes and without pulse." Rosanes quickly packed the cavity with fresh gauze, and the bleeding stopped. Grasping what had happened, Freud felt sick and "fled" to the next room to drink a bottle of water and a little glass of cognac. As he returned to her side, "a little tottery," Emma Eckstein greeted him with the "superior" remark: "So this is the strong sex." Freud protested that it had not been the blood that unmanned him but rather "the pressure of emotions." Freud felt greatly conflicted. He could not reconcile that Fliess, his *other*, could be so careless and capable of an almost fatal malpractice.

A few hours after he had dreamed his momentous dream, Freud sent an unusually brief message to his friend in Berlin. He wondered why Fliess had not written lately and whether Fliess still cared about Freud's work, asked after Fliess's own ideas, his health, and his wife, and mused on whether the two were destined to be friends only in times of misfortune. There was no mention of "Irma."

When Freud finally wrote Fliess of what had happened to Emma Eckstein, he said that she was perfectly normal and her nosebleeds had been caused not by hysteria but by "a piece of iodoform gauze that had got torn off as you were pulling it out and was left in for two weeks." But then he assumed blame himself: he should not have urged Fliess to perform an operation in a foreign city where he could not follow up. "You did it as well as one can." The accident with the gauze was one "that happens to the luckiest and most circumspect of surgeons."

Emma Eckstein remained a victim long after the botched surgery. Her face was disfigured by a cavity in her cheek. Yet later Freud blamed the whole disaster on Emma. A year later, he reported to Fliess "a quite surprising solution of Eckstein's hemorrhages will please you very much." Freud thought he could prove that Fliess, who had claimed that "her bleeding was hysterical, happened from *longing*," had been right all along. He added: "Your nose has once again smelled right." Emma Eckstein's bleedings were "wish-bleedings," to bolster her belief that her various ailments were real, not imaginary. Freud's need for Fliess was such that he distorted the whole incident so that Fliess could remain untarnished. Though he picked apart every aspect of the dream, Freud missed this association.

Jokes and Their Relation to the Unconscious

"Take my wife, *please!*" said comedian Henny Youngman, which never failed to get a laugh. What do people find funny about marital discord? Many people experience it. But were you to announce at a dinner party your lack of sex in your marriage, for instance, you might find the door locked when you got home. Jokes, like dreams and slips of the tongue, Freud discovered, are a socially acceptable way to express repressed sexual and aggressive tendencies. So before you accept your spouse's statement, "Oh, I was only joking," remind him or her that, according to Freud, jokes reveal unconscious motivation and are to be taken very seriously!

In June 1897, Freud told his friend Fliess that he was starting a collection of "profound Jewish stories" and other jokes. He brought these stories together into a book, *Jokes and Their Relation to the*

Unconscious, published in 1905, along with his book *Three Essays on the Theory of Sexuality*. In fact, starting in the early 1900s, he wrote the two books simultaneously, working on one or the other according to his mood.

Like dreams, jokes use the same techniques of condensation, indirect representation, and displacement. But unlike dreams, which are unintelligible, asocial, and cloaked in mystery and disguise as to motivation, joking is highly social, quickly understood, and explicitly exposes the underlying thought in blatant defiance of accepted modes of conscious expression. The energy directed to censoring forbidden impulses or wishes gets discharged in laughter. What renders the joke so intensely pleasurable is this circumventing of the censor and expressing our inhibited thoughts.

As in *Psychopathology in Everyday Life*, the examples of jokes that Freud analyzed covered a wide array of motives: sexual, need for power and grandeur, coming to grips with life's absurdities. As we would expect, the themes often related to some of his own pressing issues. For instance, Freud's embarrassing indebtedness to friends in his earlier years engendered some "schnorrer" or beggar jokes, such as the following marvelous example of denial:

A. borrowed a copper kettle from B. and after he had returned it was sued by B. because the kettle now had a big hole in it which made it unusable. His defense was: "First, I never borrowed a kettle from B. at all; secondly, the kettle had a hole in it already when I got it from him; and thirdly, I gave him back the kettle undamaged."

In another joke that Freud told to Fliess just prior to the publication of *The Interpretation of Dreams*, he expressed apparent hostility toward his wife of now thirteen years:

Uncle Jonas meets his nephew who has heard of his engagement and congratulates him. "And what is your fiancée like, uncle?" he asks. "Well, that's a matter of taste, but personally I don't like her."

Although Freud appeared to not take his joke book as "seriously" as his other work, his work on humor opened up other vistas, such as literature and art, a field now called applied psychoanalysis.

Jones, Ernest
(1879–1958)

Freud's official biographer, Ernest Jones, discovered Freud in 1905, following the publication of the case history of Dora. A physician working in Toronto, Jones spent some time with Carl Jung at Burgholzli in Switzerland learning more about psychoanalysis. In the spring of 1908, he sought out Freud at the Salzburg Congress of Psychoanalysts after hearing Freud give his memorable talk on the Rat Man. Upon being introduced to Jones, Freud remarked that he knew from the shape of Jones's head that he could not be English but must be Welsh. Jones was astounded—many from Central Europe did not even know Wales existed—and from that moment attached himself to Freud. Thus began a long and close relationship between the two. As Jones conducted most of his vast correspondence with Freud in English, he greatly helped Freud polish up his English.

Initially, Jones had his doubts about psychoanalysis. But once he committed to the sacred psychoanalytic text, he became one of its most energetic advocates and the token gentile in Freud's intimate circle. On Jones's fiftieth birthday, Freud honored him by telling him, "I have always numbered you among my inmost family." From 1912 on, Freud analyzed Jones's mistress Loe Kann, a morphine addict. Ignoring the sacred rule of confidentiality, he routinely reported to Jones on her progress.

Jones began lecturing on psychoanalysis in Canada and the United States. In 1911, he helped to found the American Psychoanalytic Association and, upon returning to London in 1913, the London Psycho-Analytic Society.

Judaism

Freud was an avowed atheist. He did not practice any Jewish rituals in his home, and on the first Friday night of his marriage, he
forbade his deeply religious wife to light the Sabbath candles, as is
Jewish custom, although this deeply upset her. He celebrated
Christmas with a Christmas tree and gifts to his children. He
rebelliously ignored the Jewish tradition of naming children after
recently deceased relatives—Freud himself was named after his
paternal grandfather—a tradition even the most nonreligious
Jewish families followed. He named all six of his children after
living people who were important in his life. All three sons had
been named after powerful men who had been Freud's idols and
mentors, while his three daughters were named after women from
the families who supported him financially during his years of
poverty.

Freud grew up surrounded by gentiles as well as Jews, starting
with his devoutly Catholic nanny who fed him pious stories and
dragged him to church. "Then," Freud's mother told him, "when
you got home, you would preach and tell us what God Almighty
does." His upbringing was religious but not orthodox. Jacob Freud
had emancipated himself from the Hasidic practices of his ancestors; he married Amalia Nathanson in a Reform ceremony. In time,
he discarded most religious observances, mainly celebrating Purim
and Passover as family festivals. His father, Freud recalled in 1930,
"allowed me to grow up in complete ignorance of everything that
concerned Judaism." Yet, although striving for assimilation, Jacob
Freud was never ashamed of and never sought to deny his essential
Jewishness. He continued to read the Bible at home, in Hebrew,
and "spoke the holy language," Freud believed, "as well as German
or better," creating for the young Freud an enduring fascination
with "biblical history" (the Old Testament) before he had "barely
acquired the art of reading."

Freud felt profoundly ambivalent toward his Jewish heritage. As
a scientist, he wished to assimilate into European society and to be
unlike his obedient and religious father (see **Analysis of Self**). But
in response to the anti-Semitism rampant in Europe at the time, he

began to identify himself *as a Jew*. While studying in Paris with Charcot in 1886, Freud announced during a political discussion in Charcot's home that he was "neither Austrian nor German," but a "*Juif.*" In 1926, Freud told an interviewer, George Sylvester Viereck, "My language is German. My culture, my attainments are German. I considered myself German intellectually, until I noticed the growth of anti-Semitic prejudice in Germany and German Austria. Since that time, I prefer to call myself a Jew."

Freud also wished to prove to the world that a Jew could achieve greatness and later felt proud that psychoanalysis owed something to his being Jewish. "To profess belief in this new theory," Freud wrote, "called for a certain degree of readiness to accept a position of solitary opposition—a position with which no one is more familiar than a Jew."

He felt comfortable that his early adherents to psychoanalysis were all Jews. "May I say that it is kindred Jewish traits that attract me in you." Writing within the family, as Jew to Jew, Freud bluntly warned his close follower Karl Abraham against "racial predilections" in his followers and to not "neglect the Aryans, who are fundamentally alien to me." Worried that the world would perceive psychoanalysis as a "Jewish science," further alienating the mainstream, he relied on his non-Jewish adherents: "Our Aryan comrades are, after all, quite indispensable to us; otherwise, psychoanalysis would fall victim to anti-Semitism." He favored Jung as his heir apparent in part because Jung could save "psychoanalysis from the danger of becoming a Jewish national concern." Thankfully, Freud lived to see psychoanalysis universally embraced by people of all races and religions.

Jung, Carl Gustav
(1875–1961)

See **Dissenters**.

Katharina (Case)

"Are you a doctor?" Freud heard a young girl ask who had noticed that he had signed his name as "Dr." in the guest book of the mountain inn where he was staying while on vacation in the Austrian Alps. "The truth is my nerves are bad." Freud looked up to see "Katharina," an eighteen-year-old country girl, his third case reported in *Studies on Hysteria* and whose hysteria he interpreted in a single meeting. Katharina proceeded to confide to him nervous symptoms of shortness of breath, dizziness, a choking feeling, a crushing feeling in her chest, and a frightening image of an angry male face.

She had discovered her drunken father on top of her older sister. Witnessing this seduction reminded her of when he tried to force himself on her two years earlier, when she was fourteen, terrifying her. This is when her symptoms had begun, and they represented the classic signs of fear as well as being specific to the incident; for instance, the crushing feeling signified her father's body pressing on her. She told her mother of his incestuous behavior. The couple quarreled angrily, divorced, and the father turned his "senseless rage against her"—thus, the image of the angry male face. Freud listened sympathetically. Imagine the young girl's relief to be able to relay her forbidden trauma to a receptive listener. Her mood brightened, leading Freud to believe that she was cured, but he didn't know how. At this time, Freud was operating on the simple idea that hysteria comes from a repressed memory of a traumatic event, and when you make it conscious, you are cured.

Leopold, Nathan, and Loeb, Richard

In the summer of 1924, the United States was abuzz with the sensational murder trial of the infamous young killers defended by the formidable attorney Clarence Darrow. Colonel Robert

McCormick, the publisher of the *Chicago Tribune*, sent Freud a telegram offering him $25,000 "or anything he name come Chicago psychoanalyze" to analyze the infamous two from wealthy families, who killed a friend for the thrill of committing a perfect crime. McCormick even offered to charter a steamer to bring the sixty-eight-year-old analyst to the United States. Freud declined.

Libido

When men hit fifty and women go through menopause, some will complain of lack of *libido*, or sex drive. Freud used the term *libido* more broadly—as psychic energy, encompassing sexuality but also including the desire for pleasure through stimulation and achievement. In other words, libido is our life force, driving us not only to the bedroom but to the refrigerator, the mall, yoga, and a painting class. It is that nebulous, unmeasurable energy called *chi* by the Chinese, *prana* by the Hindus, and *orgonne energy* by Freud's contemporary Wilhelm Reich.

Little Hans (Case)

In Freud's famous case study, a five-year-old boy known as Little Hans was intensely fearful of horses. Afraid that a horse might bite him or fall down in the street and "make a row," he refused to venture outside. Although he only saw Little Hans once, Freud learned the details of the case through letters from his father, with whom he consulted and who carried out the child's treatment.

Hans described black things around the horses' mouths and things in front of the eyes, leading Freud to speculate that the horse represented the boy's father, who wore glasses and had a mustache. Freud interpreted the child's fears as representing a severe Oedipus complex and castration anxiety. Horses, with their large "widdlers," were like the father, whom Little Hans both loved and feared as the one who would castrate him.

Over the years, this case is cited as evidence of the Oedipal complex. In fact, the case weakly supports Freud's sexual theory. Although it's easy to see how a small child intimidated by his very large father would displace his fears onto the big horse with such big teeth, as he can avoid a horse but not his father, nothing in the boy's fears hints at castration and the Oedipal complex.

Further, Hans was more frightened of his mother than his father, for it was *she* who threatened him with castration. The boy liked to touch his penis, which he called "widdler," and wished his mother to touch it too. She warned him not to and even threatened to have it cut off. She also threatened him with abandonment: "Mummy told me she won't come back." Indeed, the parents divorced shortly after the incidents reported in the case, which Freud omitted in his report. Shortly before the boy's phobia appeared, he had a tonsillectomy: not only was something cut out of his body but very large people — like large horses — loomed over the little child and, ignoring the child's terror and screaming, knocked the child unconscious. The mother had also given birth to Hans's younger sister, further threatening his tenuous tie to his mother. Hans likely felt intense rivalry. Hans's horse phobia may also have represented a fear that his mother might hurt him. He had seen his mother hitting his baby sister and associated the baby's screams with his fear of horses "making a row," and the mother warned him that he would be whipped with a carpet beater if he misbehaved. Given the tonsillectomy, castration threats, and beatings, Hans's phobia appears more a fear of real physical harm and of abandonment than a fear of his father castrating him.

Little Hans's real name was Herbert Graf, the son of music critic Max Graf, who was in Freud's early inner circle but became disenchanted with psychoanalysis, and of his wife, one of Freud's patients. Herbert later became the stage director of the New York Metropolitan Opera.

Lucy R. (Case)

Miss Lucy, an English governess employed by a wealthy widower, was the second case Freud reported in *Studies on Hysteria* (1895). Her symptoms were unusual but relatively mild: she could not rid herself of the odor of "burnt pudding" and felt depressed.

Rather than dismissing her odd smell hallucination, Freud followed the path that led to its origin by encouraging Miss Lucy to speak freely of whatever came to mind. Having followed his treatment of Emmy von N. and Elisabeth von R., this case, which was fairly straightforward, was ideal material for Freud to further explore the efficacy of the newly found technique of free association as the psychoanalytic tool for unraveling the mysteries of a patient's symptoms. Encouraging Miss Lucy to "let her criticism rest" and allow her thoughts to wander freely, he faced what would become a standard complaint: Miss Lucy protested that blurting out trivial, irrational, repetitious, irrelevant, or obscene thoughts was difficult. Freud aided her through suggestion and the pressure technique, in which he placed his hand on the patient's forehead or took her head between his hands and told the patient that she would think of something significant relating to her symptom when he released the pressure of his hand. During the 1890s, Freud had not yet assumed the passive listening that he would later call "evenly suspended" or "evenly hovering" attention, but was actively involved with his patients, rapidly interpreting his patients' confessions while probing to deeper levels of meaning.

Eventually, Miss Lucy revealed that she was secretly in love with her employer, and, encouraged by some remarks he made, hoped that he would return her affection. Her sentiments created conflict with the other servants who thought she was desiring above her position. Later discovering that her love was not reciprocated, she decided to quit her position but was distraught over losing contact with his two daughters, whom she loved. It was during an incident involving the possibility of losing her connection to the children that she smelled burnt pudding. Connecting her symptoms to these events, Freud managed to dispel her bizarre smell sensation after working with her for nine weeks. Today we would consider this an unusually short psychoanalysis.

Masochism and Sadism

Originally, Freud spoke of masochism—passive seeking of physical or mental suffering to seek sexual arousal and gratification—as a type of perversion. He described sadism—inflicting physical or mental suffering to seek sexual arousal and gratification—as its paired opposite. In *Three Essays on the Theory of Sexuality*, he plainly equated femininity with "passivity," which he connected to "masochism," and concluded that women are biologically predisposed to masochism, while masculinity was equated with "activity" and "sadism."

Freud believed the roots of sadism to exist in the normal male, in that

> the sexuality of most male human beings contains an element of aggressiveness—a desire to subjugate; the biological significance of it seems to lie in the need for overcoming the resistance of the sexual object by means other than the process of wooing. Thus sadism would correspond to an aggressive component of the sexual instinct which has become independent and exaggerated and, by displacement, has usurped the leading position.

Masson, Jeffrey
(1940–)

In 1984, the former psychoanalyst Jeffrey Masson published *The Assault on Truth: Freud's Suppression of the Seduction Theory*. He charged that Freud abandoned the seduction hypothesis, denying the actual sexual abuse toward women and children in turn-of-the-century Vienna. Further, Freud did so willfully, in part to protect the professional image of his close friend Wilhelm Fliess. Masson's charges were far ranging:

> By shifting the emphasis from an actual world of sadness, misery, and cruelty to an internal stage on which actors per-formed invented dramas for an invisible audience of their own creation Freud began a trend away from the real world that, it seems to me, is at the root of the present-day sterility of psychoanalysis and psychiatry throughout the world.

Working from the unedited Freud and Fliess letters, Masson argued that Freud ignored Emma Eckstein's repeated nose bleeding as a result of a surgical operation that Fliess performed and botched, and instead interpreted it as a neurotic symptom resulting from fantasy (see **Irma's Injection**). Freud's denial of Emma's symptoms as physical and real, Masson declared, spurred his later rejection of sexual abuse as real in favor of sexual fantasy. Further, Masson suggested that Fliess may have molested his own son, and that Freud, wishing to protect his friend, felt further motivated to ignore the reality of his patients' seductions and change his theory of the origin of hysteria.

Although Freud did pervert the truth in the case of Emma Eckstein and was willing to go to extremes to defend his "other," most believe Masson's accusations were unfounded; Freud always believed seduction to be more widespread than previously imagined and enormously damaging to the child. But Freud also stood firm that children can confuse reality with fantasied desire of sex. And Freud's new theory of sexual desire was even more politically incorrect than the seduction hypothesis. It took great courage to introduce such ideas into the ethos of the time: nineteenth-century Viennese physicians could more readily accept some men as villains than their children as sexual beings.

Masson's accusation in this highly visible controversy has had horrendous consequences. Convinced that almost anyone traumatized was sexually abused as a child, some psychotherapists convince clients into believing that they were abused but have "repressed" the memory. Sometimes these forced "memories" emerge but are questionable; research has shown early memories often to be false. Further, some innocent parents and child care workers have been falsely accused of childhood sexual abuse, as social workers and child therapists pull out preposterous false memories from children of not only sexual abuse but satanic rituals and other bizarre tales.

In an article titled "On the Abuses of Freud," Jeffrey Prager countered Masson's accusations by imagining the consequences of Freud *not* having changed the seduction theory:

> Masson [expresses] nostalgia for a pre- (or early) Freudian world . . . a world where things are precisely as they appear, always reflecting a hard, obdurate reality that can be easily and readily perceived. No interpreting self, no unconscious one. What happens happens, and there is no mystery as to how one processes, interprets, and gives meaning to those occurrences.

See **Irma's Injection; Seduction Hypothesis.**

Money

Having come from poverty, Freud had a "constant fear of it" and wished not just fame but fortune and the social status it conferred. This was a long time coming.

As a student and during his tenure at the General Hospital of Vienna, Freud was constantly strapped for funds. Lack of finances to start a household was what led to his long engagement to Martha Bernays. Repeatedly forced to accept gifts and loans from his friends, Freud resented the dependence that this indebtedness engendered and viewed himself as a "schnorrer," or beggar.

To defend against his helpless position, Freud invented "schnorrer phantasies" in which he imagined coming into a fortune. For instance, he fantasied that he stopped a runaway horse, saving from ruin some great person riding in the carriage. In return, the grateful person naturally lavished Freud with a generous gift of money.

Freud's need for money to enhance his status at times interfered with the supreme rationality in which he prided himself. For instance, in 1884, planning to visit Martha in Wandsbek, Freud asked his friend Josef Breuer, who frequently lent Freud money, for an extra fifty gulden for his trip. Breuer refused Freud, declaring that he would squander it on frivolous extravagances that he couldn't afford. Offended, Freud asked Breuer not to interfere with his "adventurous style." Breuer, who was extraordinarily generous to the younger Freud, did give him the fifty gulden and explained that he merely wished to caution Freud about his spending, not to actually restrict it.

Although never rich, Freud did later earn enough money to run his household comfortably. And although he did not squander it, he liked to spend it, for instance, on his many antiquities. He liberally provided his children with money, enjoyed giving gifts, and generously contributed to help needy friends such as Lou Andreas-Salomé.

Freud was even known to tactfully help out patients. Around 1905, Freud, almost fifty, met with the young Swiss poet Bruno Goetz, who was suffering from unexplainable headaches. Prior to their meeting, Freud had been sent some of the young man's poems. After listening to the young man's life story, including intimate sexual details such as occasional flirtations with sailors, Freud announced that Goetz did not need psychoanalysis and asked the poet when he had last eaten steak. Goetz responded that he had not had steak for at least four weeks. Freud gave him some advice on diet and an envelope: "You must not be offended with me, but I am a grown doctor and you are still a young student. Accept this envelope from me and permit me to play your father just this once. A small honorarium for the pleasure you have given me with your verses and the story of your youth. Adieu, and call on me again some time. True, my time is heavily occupied, but half an hour or a whole one should turn up. *Auf Wiedersehen!*" When Goetz later opened the envelope, he found two hundred kronen in it. "I was," he recalled, "in so agitated a state I had to weep out loud."

Moses and Monotheism

Freud identified deeply with Moses. In 1909, Freud wrote to Carl Jung in connection with his succession as head of the psychoanalytic movement. "If I am Moses then you are Joshua and will take possession of the promised land of psychiatry, which I shall only be able to glimpse from afar."

In 1901, Freud visited Rome and spent hours viewing the statue of Moses sculpted for the tomb of Pope Julius II by Michelangelo. "No other piece of statuary has ever made a bigger impression on me than this," wrote Freud. But it wasn't until 1913, when he wrote the essay "The Moses of Michaelangelo," that he revealed his true fascination and deep identification with the biblical giant. Freud reinterpreted the statue as being not of the biblical Moses who leapt to his feet to smash the holy Tablets but of a Moses "who desired to act, to spring up and take vengeance and forget the Tablets; but . . . [who] has overcome the temptation. . . . Nor will he throw away the Tablets so that they will break on the stones, for it is on their special account that he has controlled his anger; it was to preserve them that he kept his passion in check. . . . He remembered his mission and for its sake renounced an indulgence of his feelings."

The essay is intensely personal. During the writing, Freud and Jung were at the height of conflict. In the same month, Freud wrote "The History of the Psycho-Analytical Movement," his attempt to dissociate the work of Jung and his followers from mainstream psychoanalysis. Perhaps, like Moses, Freud needed to control his need for vengeance at Jung's defection.

But Freud's obsession with Moses stretches beyond his conflict with Jung. Moses haunted him his whole life, Freud told Lou Andreas-Salomé in 1935. In *Moses and Monotheism: Three Essays,* Freud wrote that Moses "tormented me like an unlaid ghost." Moses, it appears, symbolized Freud's own internal conflict and his deep ambivalence about his Jewish roots. On a conscious level, he was proud of his Jewish heritage and of Moses the great leader. On an unconscious level, he rebelled against that heritage and identified with the idolatrous mob—the unruly id.

In *Moses and Monotheism*, Freud advances four hypotheses. First, Moses is not, as the Hollywood movie portrays, a son of a Jewish mother but the son of an Egyptian mother, denying the Jewish people kinship with Moses. Second, the monotheism that Moses gave to the Jewish people had *Egyptian* roots, from the worship of Aten, founded by Akhenaten, who ascended the throne around 1375 B.C.E., denying the Jewish people as the proud originators of monotheism. To further the blow, the rite of circumcision was originally an Egyptian custom. Third, the Jews killed the Egyptian Moses in the desert, and the strict monotheism he taught was submerged under the Semitic worship of the volcano god Yahweh (propagated by a second, Midianite, Moses). Fourth, the murder of Moses was a reenactment of the primal parricide that Freud had described in *Totem and Taboo*, which the Jews repressed, thus creating enormous guilt in their people.

> A growing sense of guilt had taken hold of the Jewish people. . . . Till at last one of these Jewish people found . . . the occasion for detaching a new . . . religion from Judaism. Paul, a Roman Jew from Tarsus, seized upon this sense of guilt and traced it back correctly to its original source. He called this the "original sin"; it was a crime against God and could only be atoned for by death.

The anti-Semitism that the Jews have experienced throughout the centuries, Freud claimed, is, in part, a result of their refusal to acknowledge and atone for this primal murder of the father.

> The poor Jewish people, who with their habitual stubbornness continued to disavow the father's murder, atoned heavily for it in the course of time. They were constantly met with the reproach "You killed God!"

Freud, old, ill, and bitter, knew that *Moses and Monotheism*, begun in 1934, would create hostility in the Jewish community at a time of rising Nazi power and anti-Semitism in Germany. Jewish leaders pleaded with Freud not to write the book. Freud plunged ahead undeterred—even as he himself was forced into exile in England. Once Freud got hold of an idea, it possessed him as the ultimate truth.

> To deprive a people of the man whom they take pride in as the greatest of their sons is not a thing to be gladly or carelessly undertaken, least of all by someone who is himself one of them. But we cannot allow any such reflection to induce us to put the truth aside in favour of what are supposed to be national interests.

Mussolini

Until the late 1930s, when Mussolini, now aligned with Hitler, introduced anti-Semitic legislation, fascist Italy was not caught up in the sweep of Jew hatred. In 1933, Freud had one indirect contact with Mussolini. The Italian analyst Edoardo Weiss brought a very sick patient to see Freud. The patient's father, who accompanied them, was a close friend of Mussolini's. After the consultation, the father asked Freud for a present for Mussolini and asked him to write a dedication. Said Weiss: "I was in a very embarrassing position, for I knew that under these circumstances, Freud could not deny the request. The work he chose, perhaps with a definite intention, was 'Why War?' a brief published correspondence with Albert Einstein, in which Freud had confessed to pacifist sentiments. The dedication was 'with the devoted greeting of an old man, who recognizes the cultural hero in the ruler,'" an illusion, Weiss noted, to Mussolini's "*large-scale archeological excavations,*" in which "*Freud was very much interested.*"

Narcissism

In an ancient Greek myth, the beautiful boy Narcissus falls so deeply in love with his own reflection in a pool of water that he plunges into the pool and drowns. Freud used this image to describe self-love. In the earliest stages of life, libidinal energy in the ego produces narcissism, or self-love. From this self-love emerges object libido—love interest in the other. Thus, Freud conceptualized libido, the energy of the sexual or pleasure instincts, as separate from the ego instincts, which are governed by the reality principle.

But he noted that in some psychotic patients the distinction between the two instincts blurs and this separation ceases. The schizophrenic may withdraw interest in the external world and behave as if reality no longer exists; only his own ideas, feelings, or urges matter, as if the person overvalues their own ideas, his own body, his own person: "The libido that has been withdrawn from the external world has been directed to the ego [in the schizophrenic] and thus gives rise to an attitude which may be called narcissism."

In a sense, it was Freud's own narcissism—hubris—that made him lose scientific credibility. He described the Oedipus complex as needing to be mastered by "every new arrival on this planet," dismissing individual experience or cultural differences. The recognition of the universality of the Oedipus complex and the central role it plays in neurosis "has become the shibboleth that distinguishes the adherents of psychoanalysis from its opponents." An Old Testament term, *shibboleth* is the criterion or test to distinguish religious believers from heretics. Those who questioned this dogma were expelled from Freud's court. And one by one, they left. And still Freud refused to budge from this position.

Nazism

In May 1933, the Propaganda Ministry organized book burnings in Berlin and other German cities; Freud's books were thrown on the pyre along with those of other Jews, such as Einstein, Marx, Kafka, Schnitzler, and Stefan Zweig, as well as non-Jews whose views were deemed dangerous by the Nazis, such as Thomas and Heinrich Mann, Emile Zola, and Havelock Ellis. Freud sardonically noted to

Ernest Jones, "What progress we are making. In the Middle Ages they would have burnt me, nowadays they are content with burning my books."

As a Jew, Freud finally found it necessary to leave Vienna and emigrated to London in 1938.

Neurosis

To be neurotic is to be guilty, sometimes for breathing. That psychoanalysis has been called by some "the Jewish disease" fits well with the conception of the Jewish mother as creating neurotic guilt-ridden children. She would, however, be mortified to learn that underlying that guilt, at least in her sons, may be repressed sexual desires *for her*.

To Freud, the cause of neurosis was an incomplete repression of unacceptable sexual wishes that left the person unprotected from unconscious guilt, consequently causing distress. The buried wishes seek expression, which they find in neurotic symptoms. In an attempt to hopefully avoid guilt, the incompletely repressed wish is disguised to bypass the censor that originally repressed it.

Repression supposedly reaches its peak in the Oedipus complex, where the male confronts "castration anxiety" and the female "penis envy." In a footnote added to the *Three Essays* in 1920, Freud wrote, "It has justly been said that the Oedipus complex is the nuclear complex of the neuroses, and constitutes the essential part of their content. It represents the peak of infantile sexuality of adults. Every new arrival on this planet is faced by the task of mastering the Oedipus complex; anyone who fails to do so falls a victim to neurosis."

Freud's views of the origin of neurosis as sexual emanated not only from material uncovered in his neurotic patients but appeared directly related to his own unsatisfied Oedipal longings for his mother's love and his own sexual inhibitions (see **Sexuality, Freud's**). He would never waver from his stand that *all* neuroses had a sexual etiology. If a patient denied his interpretations, he shouted "resistance," which he was certain he could, in every case, topple.

> We must not be led astray by initial denials. If we keep firmly to what we have inferred, we shall in the end conquer every resistance by emphasizing the unshakable nature of our convictions. . . . If one proceeds in this manner with one's patients, one also gains the conviction that, so far as the theory of sexual aetiology of neurasthenia is concerned, there are no negative cases. In my mind, at least, the conviction has become so certain that where an interrogation has shown a negative result, I have turned this to account too for diagnostic purposes.

As far as Freud was concerned, that psychoanalysis successfully relieved neurotic symptoms in many cases justified that he was correct. As the unconscious is an elusive entity, no one could prove Freud wrong. Such a lack of scientific inquiry and circular thinking has led the psychiatric community to by and large dismiss Freud's sexuality theory.

Freud used the term *neurotic* to delineate those conditions that reflect anxiety and its defenses such as conversion, repression, and displacement: hysteria, phobias, obsessive-compulsive disorder. Today the term *neurotic* is rarely used to delinate psychopathology. The *Diagnostic and Statistical Manual of Mental Disorders* (DSM-IV) of the American Psychiatric Association places anxiety disorders in separate categories: panic, phobias, post-traumatic stress disorder (PTSD), obsessive-compulsive disorder, and generalized anxiety. In jargon, "neurotic" is used loosely to describe anyone who behaves excessively—who's finicky, overworries, overworks, obsesses, complains, avoids, or otherwise behaves irrationally or compulsively—for example, spending a paycheck on something one neither needs nor can afford—or who sabotages what he or she wants—for example, going on a job interview and announcing that you're two months pregnant! There aren't enough psychotherapists around to treat all those folks!

Obsession and Compulsion

A nineteen-year-old woman enacts bedtime rituals that take hours and that make her and her parents miserable. She would give anything to give them up, yet she feels desperately compelled to perform them perfectly. The pillows must be arranged precisely so that they don't touch the headboard, for example.

In typical Freudian fashion, Freud interpreted the symptoms in this classical case of obsessive-compulsive disorder (OCD) as Oedipal strivings. The headboard represented man and the pillow woman. The ritual represented the command that mother and father must not touch each other. As a young child, before the patient developed these rituals, she had insisted that the door between her room and her parents' room be left open, presumably to soothe her anxieties, but in actuality to monitor and prevent her parents from having sex. To Freud, this was clear evidence that, from early childhood, she had been erotically attached to her father and angry and jealous of her mother.

In his clinical work with obsessive-compulsive patients, Freud observed that obsessive-compulsives, who he believed were fixated in the anal stage of development, were "especially *orderly, parsimonious,* and *obstinate*"—three traits sometimes called the three p's: pedantry, parsimony, and persistence. While hysterical types repress ideas whose emotions have been converted into a bodily symptom, obsessional types detach the emotion from the original repressed idea and reattach it to different ideas, which then become obsessional.

Today many in the psychiatric community believe OCD to have a biochemical cause. A part of the brain called the caudate nucleus, which controls instinctive, repetitive behavior such as grooming and nesting, is implicated. Antidepressant medications that raise serotonin levels in the brain appear to normalize this activity. OCD, which may be more medical than psychological, can result from head injuries, brain tumors, strep throat, or encephalitis. Freud's original hunch that psychopathology was neurological in origin has gained support in many cases of OCD.

Obsessive-compulsive behavior was no stranger to Freud. Freud characterized his son Oliver as an obsessive-compulsive type. Oliver was very bright, and Freud initially harbored high hopes for him. But as a young man his orderliness and interest in classifying assumed obsessive-compulsive proportions. Freud wrote to Max Eitingon of Oliver: "It is particularly hard for me to be objective in this case, for he was my pride and my secret hope for a long time, until his anal-masochistic organization appeared . . . clearly I suffered very much with my feelings of helplessness." In analysis with Franz Alexander in Berlin in the early 1920s, Oliver seemed to find some relief. Freud's daughter Anna was obsessively neat and clean, as was his wife. Freud too had his own obsessions, which he readily admitted. In a letter to Carl Jung in September 1907, Freud characterized the differences in their personalities: "If a healthy man like you regards himself as an hysterical type, I can only claim for myself the 'obsessional' type, each specimen of which vegetates in a sealed-off world of his own."

Occult

Freud, the Jewish scientist, was superstitious, believed in numerology, and was, in turn, fascinated by and deeply skeptical of the occult, illustrated in this joke from *Jokes and the Unconscious*:

> Frederick the Great heard of a preacher in Silesia who had the reputation of being in contact with spirits. He sent for the man and received him with the question "You can conjure up spirits?" The reply was: "At your Majesty's command, But they don't come!"

"At your Majesty's command" suggests the occult abilities of the preacher. "But they don't come" denies the abilities of the miraculous and the occult.

In *The Psychopathology of Everyday Life*, Freud wrote of several incidents of his superstitious behavior. For instance, when studying with Charcot in Paris, he would hear disembodied voices: "I quite often heard my name called by an unmistakable and beloved voice; I noted down the exact moment of the hallucination and made anxious enquiries of those at home about what had happened at that time. Nothing had happened." Freud was enough of a believer to fear his auditory hallucinations as an omen of real danger. And although nothing came of them, he continued to entertain beliefs of the occult.

Freud feared his death would bring an end to his theories. His superstitious belief in sinister omens reinforced this fear especially as related to some of the more extreme aspects of Wilhelm Fliess's "theory of periodicity." Fliess believed in the concept of male and female biological periods of twenty-three and twenty-eight days, respectively, which he later extended to the cosmos to predict dates such as death. According to his "necrological bookkeeping," Freud prophesied his own death at various dates throughout his life—in 1918, for example, when he was sixty-two. But in 1910 he wrote to a friend, "Let us anyhow not that I determined some time ago to die only in 1916 or 1917." After the death of his father, Freud was convinced that he would die between the ages of sixty-one and sixty-two. He wrote to Carl Jung of his trip to Athens with his brother Alexander:

It was really uncanny how often the number 61 or 60 in connection with a 1 or 2 kept cropping up in all sorts of numbered objects, especially those connected with transportation. . . . It depressed me, but I had hopes of breathing easy when we got to the hotel in Athens and were assigned rooms on the first floor. Here, I was sure, there could be no No. 61. I was right, but I was given 31 (which with fatalistic license could be regarded as half of 61 or 62), and this younger, more agile number proved to be an even more persistent persecutor than the first. From the time of our trip home until very recently, 31, often with a 2 in its vicinity, clung to me faithfully.

Freud at different times in his life feared the numbers forty-one, forty-two, fifty-one, sixty-one, and eighty-one and one-half. The number seven seemed to draw him, and many of his works have this many chapters.

"Fascinated, as well as repelled" by telepathy, as his daughter Anna wrote, Freud performed some telepathic experiments on her because he was open to "the possibility of two unconscious minds communicating with each other without the help of a conscious bridge." Freud also wrote an essay, "Psycho-Analysis and Telepathy," which he read to some in his inner circle, and a year later "Dreams and Telepathy."

Freud's most dramatic occult experience occurred when Jung visited him in March 1909. As the two men were discussing occult phenomena late into the night, Jung suddenly felt as if his diaphragm were made of iron and was glowing red hot. Suddenly, they heard a loud explosion in the bookcase. Both men were alarmed. Jung told Freud that it was an example of a "catalytic exteriorization phenomenon." "Sheer bosh," countered Freud. But Jung then predicted that another explosion would take place at any moment and indeed it did. Freud "stared aghast" at Jung. Jung later believed that the incident had aroused Freud's increasing distrust of him.

Yet in spite of some flirting with the occult, the rational scientist in Freud denied any basis for a belief in spirits or spiritual phenomena. He warned that any acceptance of the occult proposes the existence of religion, which to Freud was mere illusion.

Oedipus Complex

A single idea of general value dawned on me. I have found, in my own case too, the phenomena of being in love with my mother and jealous of my father, and I now consider it a universal event in early childhood.

—Freud to Wilhelm Fliess

Imagine that somewhere between the ages of three and six, little boys lust after their mothers, hate their fathers, and fear that the fathers will cut off their penises. If your spouse argues that this is hogwash, that *he* had no such feelings, Freud would have argued that Oedipal strivings are universal; your spouse cannot remember such feelings because he is *repressing* them.

The story of Sophocles's *Oedipus Rex* is familiar. Oedipus, the son of Laius and Jocasta, king and queen of Thebes, is left on a mountain to perish following the oracle's warning to his father that he will grow up to kill his father and marry his mother. A shepherd saves him and takes him to another city where he is adopted by the king and queen. Oedipus learns of the prophecy and flees the city, believing it is his adopted father who is in danger. In his journey, he meets Laius, quarrels with him, and kills him. Oedipus saves Thebes from a terrible curse and marries Jocasta, the widowed queen. He learns that he has killed his real father and married his mother. Horrified, he blinds himself and flees Thebes to become a wandering, homeless beggar.

Why has the play had such lasting power? Because, surmised Freud from the tales told by his patients and his self-analysis, we all identify unconsciously with the story: in a vague, unspeakable, and strange way, all little boys wish to kill their father and marry their mother, and all little girls wish to get rid of their mother and marry their father. So catastrophic are these fantasies that they must remain buried deep in the unconscious, but they create intense conflict throughout life.

How did Freud make sense out of this deeply unconscious fantasy vis-à-vis the child's development? His thinking went something like this. At around age three or four, the child senses that his mother's attention and soothing care are not exclusively his. They must be shared with troublesome siblings and especially with father, whom the young boy resents and wants out of the way; unconsciously, he desires to kill his father even if he loves him. Perceiving his father as powerful and all-knowing, the young boy feels certain that his father knows his forbidden thoughts and will take revenge by castrating him, as he perceives little girls are castrated. Castration by the father becomes the overwhelming fear for the young boy's budding ego, and the child ultimately deals with this fear by erecting defense mechanisms, notably by repressing his thoughts. Freud believed the male conscience developed out of resolving the Oedipal rivalry with this father.

Freud discovered his own unconscious wish to murder his father in his intensive self-analysis that he began in 1897, shortly after his father died (see **Analysis of Self**), along with quasi-erotic feelings for his mother. These revelations, along with the sexual material coming from his patients, put him on a sexual bandwagon, leading him down a narrow, myopic path that possessed him, and he could never let it go; until the end he argued that all sons wish to marry their mother and feel profound emotional ambivalence for the father. Member after member left his Psychoanalytic Society; the world of psychiatry ignored his theories as unscientific hogwash and ostracized him; newspapers, magazines, and books derided psychoanalysis as obscene and made him a laughingstock; patients denied Oedipal feelings as central to their problems and some quit treatment. Freud dismissed all dissension as repression and refused to ever modify his position that the Oedipal complex was a universal pattern and the origin of all angst. Freud, said Carl Jung, treated the brain like "an appendage to the genital glands."

Penis Envy

See **Electra Complex**.

Primal Scene

In Freud's day, the average middle-class child did not have her own room but often shared the parents' bedroom, at least as a young child. At some point most young children would witness their parents having sexual intercourse. Witnessing "the primal scene," Freud felt, constituted a trauma for the young child. Scientific evidence does not support Freud's view unless the sexual act includes violence or other aberrant parental actions.

Project for a Scientific Psychology

In the early spring of 1895, Freud embarked on a wildly ambitious "project for a scientific psychology." Filled with grandiose plans, he wanted to "investigate what form the theory of mental functioning assumes if one introduces the quantitative point of view, a sort of economics of nerve forces; and, second, to extract from psychopathology a gain for normal psychology." He wished to outline how the mental machinery works: how it receives, masters, and discharges excitations.

Working on his "Psychology for Neurologists," as he had described it to Fliess in April, "tormented" him. "I have devoted every free minute in the past weeks, spent the night hours from eleven to two with such fantasizing, translating, and guessing," he wrote in May. Overworked, he barely had interest in his practice.

By November, he could no longer understand "the mental state in which I hatched the Psychology." His ideas were moving too quickly in a different direction from the physiology and biology of the mind to the domains of the unconscious as manifested in slips, jokes, symptoms, defenses, and, of course, dreams.

Although he never finished the project and ignored it in his autobiographical reports, he never abandoned his ambition to found a scientific psychology. In his *Outline of Psychoanalysis* written during the last year of his life, Freud argued that the emphasis on the unconscious in psychoanalysis enabled it "to take its place as a natural science like any other." He speculated that in the future, psychoanalysts might "exercise a direct influence, by means of particular chemical substances, on the amounts of energy and their distribution in the mental apparatus." The formulation echoed his 1895 project to predict the later use of psychotropic medication to treat mental illness.

Psychoanalysis, the Theory

All psychology is psychoanalysis; what is left is the physiology of the senses.

—Sigmund Freud

Freud first used the term *psychoanalysis* in 1896. The theory of psychoanalysis proposes that problems arise from unconscious desires and unresolved childhood conflicts. It rests on the hotly contested tenets of determinism, conflict, and the unconscious.

According to the psychoanalytic tradition, behavior, whether overt, such as moving your arm, or covert, such as thinking about lunch, is *determined* by prior mental events—both from the outside world and our inner psychic life—of which we have no control. Our lives are shaped by two primary instincts: (1) sexuality and all other life instincts driven by libido and (2) aggression and all other death instincts. A psychoanalysis alters undesirable behavior by identifying and eliminating its psychic determinants.

To Freud, *conflict* is inevitable. Behavior is not only dictated by forces—many instinctual, over which we have little control—but these forces constantly conflict with each other and with the outside world: we seek to love and to kill; to live and to die. It is this warring within that often prevents libidinal and aggressive urges from being channeled into useful expressions and which makes us anxious and, many, neurotic.

Not only are we motivated by forces over which we have little control and which are in perpetual conflict, rendering us anxious, miserable, and discontented, but also we do not even know what these forces and conflicts are! The major determinants of our personality, the intrapsychic mysteries of the mind, are *unconscious*—outside of our awareness.

Psychoanalysis, the Therapy

Where id was, there ego shall be.

—Sigmund Freud

A woman walks into her analyst's office, takes off her shoes, and lies down on his couch. The analyst sits unseen behind her. She speaks whatever comes into her mind, and this often includes last night's dream. The analyst interprets her meanderings as they relate to her childhood and her relationship with him and significant others, along with any resistance that emerges—for instance, her forgetting, again, to pay him. The woman gains insight into her unconscious conflicts and desires, and her neurotic symptoms start to fade away.

To Freud, the goal of psychoanalysis was for the ego to dominate the unreasonable, instinct-driven id: for reason to dominate passion; sublimation to dominate the sexual drives; and reality to dominate fantasy. To reach this goal, the analyst interprets the patient's free associations, transference, and dreams to reveal the repressed wishes underlying her neurotic symptoms. In this way, the patient is able to work through her uncomfortable feelings and memories and reach a catharsis, or working through.

Psychoanalysis, as Freud outlined it, had set rules. It took place for a set fee over a fixed series of hours—originally six but then changed to five (today an analysis is typically four hours a week). Whereas today a psychoanalysis can be quite long term—three or more years—Freud's analyses were often weeks or months. Initially, he took on a patient for one or two weeks; if a patient discontinued treatment at this time, she would not yet feel "having failed."

Lying on a couch out of the analyst's sight to avoid distracting the patient from freely expressing his thought, in contrast to other forms of therapy where the patient and therapist generally sit facing each other, the analysand is instructed to communicate everything that pops into his mind and the analyst listens with "evenly hovering attention." As the analysand begins to resist revealing all, the analyst interprets the resistance, as well as the analysand transference to the analyst. For instance, if an analysand chatters about how his boss only tells him when something is wrong and his wife burned his toast that morning, the analyst might say, "You're talking a lot today about people disappointing you. Have I disappointed you in some way?" The focus on the analysis then switches to the analyst–analysand relationship rather than the day's meanderings, the latter of which can become tedious. Some people in other forms of psychotherapy will quit when their sob stories begin to sound like a broken record. Unlike other forms of psychotherapy popular today, the psychoanalyst does not advise a person about what to do. Her role is primarily to interpret thoughts and feelings to enable the person to gain insight into his inner life.

To be successfully psychoanalyzed, Freud outlined certain qualifications: the patient "must be capable of a psychically normal condition" and "a certain measure of intelligence and ethical development"; those with "deep-rooted malformation of character traits of an actually degenerate constitution" may exhibit resistance that cannot be overcome in an analysis. Psychoanalysis works best with the transference neuroses: "phobias, hysteria, obsessional neurosis." Freud said little about character neuroses, or what today may be termed *personality disorders*. Those over fifty may not benefit from psychoanalysis. Today, a successful psychoanalysis requires that a person be motivated to persevere with such an intense, costly, and lengthy treatment, be able to form a relationship with the analyst and ultimately detach from him, have the capacity for introspection and insight, and have the ego strength to accept the sometimes painful hidden thoughts and emotions that surface.

To maximize transference feelings onto the analyst, Freud urged psychoanalysts to assume a personal detachment. The analyst should act like "a surgeon who puts aside all his feelings, even his human sympathy, and concentrates his mental forces on the single aim of performing the operation as skillfully as possible." The analyst "should be opaque to his patients and, like a mirror, should show them nothing but what is shown to him." He must be "neutral," "anonymous," and "abstinent." Normal conversation, answering questions, and revealing personal things can contaminate the treatment. At the extreme, this becomes the caricatured bearded Freudian who refrains from even saying hello or good-bye. But Freud also urged the analyst to create a supportive environment by being "benevolent" or "compassionate" and refrain from moralizing or teaching—to be warmly nonjudgmental.

The significance of the therapy Freud created is ill appreciated. Listening without interruption and often silently to analytic patients for weeks, even years, is new in the history of human relations and something each of us profoundly desires. In no other relationship—not with mother, father, sister, or spouse—do we find nonjudgmental listening without interruption with personal interjections such as "You think you have problems, let me tell you mine." The only other relationship in which we find such focused attention is that of mother and infant.

Freud as Analyst

What was Freud like as an analyst? The reviews are mixed. Freud's approach to his patients varied, and he often defied his own set of rules, even long after he had written the psychoanalytic manual. At times he was stoic, at times intrusive; at times empathic, at times critical; at times the silent, neutral strict *Freudian;* at times, paternal, friendly, and advice-giving.

Freud-as-analyst emerged both in his case studies and in reports from some who were analyzed by him. Many patients noted that Freud was at his best when interpreting their dreams (see **Dora**). Abram Kardiner, who had lost his mother when he was three, felt that Freud's interpretation of a dream so hit the mark that it sent shivers through him. Kardiner had had a phobia of masks and wax figures but was clueless as to why. From a dream, Freud postulated that "the first mask you saw was your dead mother's face." Later checking with his older sister, Kardiner discovered that when his mother died, he had been left alone with her body for a terrifying day. Kardiner described Freud's interpretation as the most convincing and brilliant of his analysis.

But Kardiner also felt that Freud fixated on his favored interpretations, particularly unconscious homosexuality in men and the Oedipus complex. In his own case, Freud's emphasis on these put him "on a wild-goose chase for years for a problem that did not exist." And although Kardiner found his analysis with Freud extremely valuable and himself made a successful career as a psychoanalyst and a researcher in New York, he further felt that Freud did not work through his issues: "He thought that once you had uncovered the Oedipus complex and understood your unconscious homosexuality, that once you knew the origins and the sources of these reactions, something would happen that would enable you to translate these insights into your current life and thereby alter it."

At other times, Freud surprisingly took off his psychoanalytic hat altogether. For instance, in 1910, Bruno Walter, the conductor of the Vienna Opera, sought Freud out because of a "professional cramp" in his right arm that he feared was an incipient paralysis that could endanger his career. Expecting a long psychoanalytic treatment, he was surprised when Freud instructed him to travel to Italy for a few weeks, forget about his arm, and just use his eyes. When Walter returned, with his arm hardly better, Freud told him to start conducting again. Freud's treatment of Walter seems contradictory to analytic treatment.

Contemporary Psychoanalysis

Freud died greatly doubting the value of the therapy he labored so long to develop and disappointed in the ability of psychoanalysis to alleviate life's problems. He can rest in peace. Though transformed from how he practiced it, psychoanalysis remains viable today.

Over the years, the basic structure of a psychoanalysis has remained the same: the analysand lies on a couch out of the analyst's view; the therapy is typically three to four sessions a week for sometimes years; the analysand is encouraged to speak freely of whatever pops in her head; childhood issues, dream interpretation, and the transference remain central. But the original focus on unearthing the repressed sexual impulses that created one's neurotic symptoms has shifted to a focus on early feelings—for example, of fear of abandonment and loss; of feeling unworthy, unappreciated, and unvalidated. And the heart of treatment rests less on unearthing unconscious conflicts than on the patient–analyst relationship analyzed through the transference.

Nor is the analyst encouraged to be stoic and reticent to best encourage the transference. Today's psychoanalyst is more relaxed and friendly and allows herself much more self-disclosure. Similar to Carl Rogers's humanistic client-centered therapy, followers of Heinz Kohut's self-psychology, a popular modern-day form of psychoanalysis, use empathic listening to fill in for the mother's lack of empathic mirroring of the young child's grandiosity.

Further, in addition to full-term psychoanalysis by a psychoanalytically trained psychiatrist, a person can see psychoanalytically trained social workers, psychologists, or lay psychoanalysts for short-term depth psychology.

Psychopathology of Everyday Life, The

He that has eyes to see and ears to hear may convince himself that no mortal can keep a secret. If his lips are silent, he chatters with his finger-tips; betrayal oozes out of him at every pore. And thus the task of making conscious the most hidden recesses of the mind is one which it is quite possible to accomplish.

—Sigmund Freud

A man, excited about his sexy date, tells her, "I'll pick you up at sex," instead of at six. Guilty about having an extramarital affair, the husband "accidentally" leaves a note from his lover hanging out of his trouser pocket.

Most of us can recall having made a "Freudian slip." Freud found these mistakes of everyday life—"parapraxes" such as slips of the tongue, mistakes in reading and writing, forgetting someone's name, and everyday failed actions—anything but accidental. Like dreams, they were a superb window into the unconscious mind. To misspell a familiar name, forget a favorite poem, mysteriously mislay an object, or fail to send one's wife the usual bouquet of flowers on her birthday were all clues for the psychoanalytic detective to decode. Freud gave the example of a financially strapped patient who, not wanting any large pills, said, "Please do not give me any bills, because I cannot swallow them."

Freud began to collect his own slips and mistakes during his self-analysis, analyzing them as if they were symptoms or dreams. He also interpreted the errors of his patients, and upon completion of *The Interpretation of Dreams*, he began to gather all this material together into a book: *The Psychopathology of Everyday Life*. The book is filled with examples of parapraxes. For instance, a young woman is unable to recall the name of an English novel, although she remembered the story and could even visualize the book's cover. Upon analysis, the title came to her—*Ben Hur*, words that were too close to the German *bin Hure*—"I am a whore"—an expression that she "like any other girl did not care to use, especially in the company of young men."

As parapraxes were a clear and convincing way to introduce newcomers to the idea of an unconscious, Freud opened his *Introductory Lectures* with a long description of the phenomenon. He found one of his favorite stories in his favorite newspaper, the *Neue Freie Presse*. The president of the lower house of the Austrian parliament, anticipating a stormy session, opened it by declaring that the session "was now closed."

The Psychopathology of Everyday Life ranks as Freud's most widely read work; it enjoyed no fewer than eleven editions and translations into twelve languages in his lifetime.

Psychosexual Stages of Development

See **Childhood Sexuality**.

Publications

A gifted writer, Freud filled twenty-four volumes on psychoanalysis (*The Standard Edition*, edited by James Strachey), including wide-ranging essays and monographs on theory and clinical practice as well as special papers addressing religious, cultural, and artistic questions. A new translation of Freud's work has been published, edited by the British psychoanalyst Adam Phillips.

Rank, Otto

See **Dissenters**.

Rat Man (Case)

The year was 1908. Freud's work had attracted followers both at home and abroad, and in April the first meeting of the International Congress of the Psychoanalytic Society was held in Salzburg, a city halfway between Vienna and Zurich and the second most prominent center of psychoanalysis, with Jung at the helm. Freud needed a case that would awe his audience. And he had one. Speaking for more than three hours, without notes as usual, he presented his case of "The Man with the Rats." That summer he wrote up the case and published it, in 1909, as *Notes Upon a Case of Obsessional Neurosis*.

The Rat Man was twenty-nine-year-old Ernst Lanzer, who suffered from severe obsessional neurosis. He was obsessed with rats, as well as other tormenting obsessive-compulsive symptoms, which began when he was on military training maneuvers. He overheard a captain, "obviously fond of cruelty," describe an Asiatic punishment involving strapping a pot filled with hungry rats to the buttocks of the victim. Thereafter, Ernst became tormented by a fantasy of rats nibbling at the backside of his girlfriend and similarly of rats feeding on his father's anus. Compulsive rituals, obsessive ideas, and fantasies to ward off these frightening thoughts took hold of his life.

Ernst feared that his thoughts could harm and kill others, particularly the woman he loved and his already dead father, as well as his fear of slashing his own throat. From Ernst's free-associative ramblings, Freud deduced that Ernst's neurosis emanated from an attraction to both men and women and ambivalent feelings for his father. Consciously Ernst saw his father as admirable and loving. But beneath the surface he harbored hate, which emerged symbolically in his fantasy of the rat nibbles, and was accompanied by intense fear and guilt. This guilt was also mixed up with his sexuality, because his father had interfered with his childhood sexual play. To undo these terrifying thoughts, he had to enact various private word games and prayers, which Freud used to illustrate the role of magical thinking in obsessive-compulsive neurosis.

In the course of the analysis, Freud uncovered an entire glossary of rats. They stood for the father himself, who was a gambler (in German, *Spielratte*; literally, "gambling rat"); for money; for penises; for filthy creatures that spread disease, especially syphilis, with its sexual connotations for children—Ernst had three older sisters, several of whom were involved in his childhood sexual games; and, finally, for the patient himself, who recovered the memory at a key point in the analysis of how he had been severely punished by his father for biting a nurse, for acting like a nasty little rat.

As a child, the patient had seen a rat near his father's grave and fantasized that it had been nibbling at the corpse. Freud demonstrated how the symptoms provided a temporary escape from conflict by preventing him from finishing his education, and marrying a socially acceptable woman, thereby ending his current relationship with his beloved mistress.

Freud asserted that the treatment "led to the complete restoration of the patient's personality, and to the removal of his inhibitions." It appears that Freud may have exaggerated the success of the case to impress his foreign visitors. Freud omitted some important information about Ernst's life. His mother was never mentioned in the published report, although she was in Freud's notes, giving the reader the impression that the father was the central figure in the life of this deeply disturbed man. In fact, the mother was a powerful force in Ernst's life; he had to get her permission to see Freud, and, although he was at the time a twenty-nine-year-old attorney, she controlled his money.

Religion

Freud considered himself a "godless" Jew, believing that the core of religion comes from the helplessness of the child and the deification of the father: God was a projection of the all-powerful father of childhood. The religious feeling of something "boundless," "oceanic," must emanate from a survival of very early ego-feeling originating in early infancy before the infant has separated from the mother.

In his essay *The Future of an Illusion,* written in 1926, Freud argued that ordinary people could only be induced to perform the work of civilization by strong leaders, and he described religion, implying Catholicism, as a system that kept the masses in check with its rules and fear of a god who rewarded and punished. Religion was a group neurosis that paralleled the neurosis of the individual: both substituted wishful fantasies or illusions for reality, both relied on magical rituals—prayers, supplications, obsessions, and compulsions. Freud explained, "One might venture to regard obsessional neurosis as a pathological counterpart of the formation of a religion, and to describe that neurosis as an individual religiosity and religion as a universal obsessional neurosis."

At the same time, from the age of around seven on, the Bible strongly impressed Freud: "My deep engrossment in the Bible (almost as soon as I had learnt the art of reading) had, as I recognized much later, an enduring effect upon the direction of my interest."

Repetition Compulsion

My friend Amy has a habit of getting involved with married men. They promise to get divorced and never do. Every time Amy begins a new relationship with someone else's spouse, her friends spend endless hours on the phone trying to discourage her from repeating the same mistake. What unconscious forces keep pulling Amy into bed with Mr. Unavailable? Amy is locked into what Freud called the "repetition compulsion." She keeps repeating the same unhappy situation over and over. If Amy looked closely at her choice of lovers, she would see that they are eerily similar to her father: cold, unresponsive, angry men whom Amy is forever appeasing and trying to please.

Freud noticed that his patients would often manipulate the analyst into repeating the parental relationship: in the transference, the analyst becomes like the patient's father. It's as if by repeating the same painful situation of childhood, the person is trying to gain mastery over it. Yet it was still surprising to Freud that people seemed to be needlessly inviting "unpleasure." Freud had long believed that Eros, the life force, drives behavior. The repetition compulsion defied this belief. This inconsistency led Freud to his discovery of a second driving force more powerful than the life force: Thanatos, or the death instinct.

See *Beyond the Pleasure Principle*.

Rolland, Romain

See *Civilization and Its Discontents*.

Schnitzler, Arthur
(1862–1931)

A contemporary of Freud, Arthur Schnitzler was the quintessential Renaissance man: physician, psychologist, novelist, and playwright. He caught Freud's eye for his penetrating psychological studies of sexuality in contemporary Viennese society. In his novel *The Road to the Open*, a Jewish physician says to his son who is protesting against the prevailing bigotry: "Personality and accomplishments will always prevail in the end. What harm can come to you? That you'll get your professorship a few years later than somebody else." He could have been speaking directly to Freud.

Seduction Hypothesis

Were Freud's early neurotic female patients seduced by their fathers, as they often reported, or were their seduction stories part of a universal Oedipal fantasy? If the first was true, as some assert— for example, Jeffrey Masson and some feminists—then Freud is to be damned for covering up the real problem of sexual abuse in Victorian families of the time. If the second is true, as others believe, then Freud is to be lauded as opening up explorations into fantasy and imagination, unconscious dynamics, and the psychosexuality of children.

In Freud's day, sexual feelings were a man's prerogative. Unless depraved, women were pure of such base urges. In his early treatment of hysteria, Freud was struck by the powerful sexual feelings of his respectable, middle-class, largely Jewish female patients. Although jolted by this finding, Freud courageously probed deeper. As he did, he discovered something even more shocking: the tale told by all of his eighteen cases was seduction by an adult, often the father. As he urged his patients to free associate, Freud discovered that their physical symptoms were invariably the result of erotic impulses from childhood. Could the origin of hysteria lay in the sexual abuse of children and the basis of neuroses be an erotic conflict? It seemed a reasonable deduction.

Defying the conventional wisdom of Victorian times, the Jewish Viennese physician followed his patients' stories, and in a paper on the "neuropsychoses of defense," written early in 1896, on the basis of thirteen cases he asserted that the traumas causing hysteria "must belong to early childhood (the time before puberty), and their content must consist of an actual irritation of the genitals (proceedings resembling coitus)." The childhood episodes that analysis uncovered, Freud added, were "grave," on occasion "downright loathsome." The villains were above all "nursemaids, governesses, and other servants," as well as teachers and "innocent" brothers. He did not outright implicate the father. The *seduction hypothesis* was born.

Yet, he wrote to his confidant Wilhelm Fliess in 1897, it seemed improbable that sexual abuse of children could be so common as to pervade the lives of nearly all his neurotic patients. Further, revealing the seduction did not seem to cure his patients of their neurotic symptoms; something else must be at work. Perhaps neurotics merely *fantasized* these early seductions, the thought of which initially left Freud with "helpless bewilderment." Much later, Freud wrote that when the seduction theory, which had been "almost fatal to the young science," had broken down "under its own improbability," his first response had been "a stage of complete perplexity."

> If the reader feels inclined to shake his head at my credibility, I cannot altogether blame him. . . . When, however, I was at last obliged to recognize that these scenes were only phantasies which my patients had made up or which I myself forced on them, I was for a time completely at a loss."

Perhaps he should have given up at that point and resumed his respectable but dull career as a physician. But Freud's mind wouldn't rest. If the first theory didn't match, then what would? And then it hit him. "If hysterics trace back their symptoms to fictitious traumas," he wrote, "this new fact signifies that they create such scenes of fantasy, and psychical reality requires to be taken into account alongside actual reality." History was made. There are two aspects of the mind: objective external reality and subjective internal reality; both are equally *real* and guide the person's behavior accordingly.

This idea was earth-shattering. If Freud's hunch was correct, then rather than passive victims of real sexual abuse, most hysterics were active participants in their own neuroses, spinning imaginary tales of seduction and intrigue. Children, Freud pondered, must be inherently sexual beings, with strong sexual longings for parents; the seduction fantasies were part of the universal Oedipal/Electra conflict, as every little girl *wishes* to replace the mother in her father's bed. These early sexual experiences were later repressed to defend against associated guilt and anxiety. Freud now began to read his patients' free associations as coded messages—distorted, censored, meaningfully disguised: psychoanalytic theory was born.

Freud's ideas concerning sexuality upset the whole Victorian apple cart of forbidden fruit. And if that wasn't enough, his discovery of the unconscious mind defied what religions had preached for thousands of years about the devil as the perpetrator of evil deeds. Since the birth of organized religion, human beings believed that they were essentially two entities: a physical and mortal body, and a nonphysical and indestructible soul or spirit. The purpose of life was to test the soul's ability not to yield to the temptations of the body. All one needed was willpower. A wicked man chose to be wicked. But there was hope. With spirituality, the most wayward could take responsibility and regain control of their affairs, summed up in the saying: "I am the captain of my fate and master of my soul."

Then here comes that pervert, the Jew Freud, to announce that some aspect of our mind is not subject to our will; it has hidden primal wishes, of which our conscious mind is not only unaware but which proceed independently down their own irrational path. Phobias and compulsions were not the devil's work but that of unconscious forces of which the conscious mind had no control. The hysterics lying on Freud's couch were not spiritually bereft but suffering from conflicts between their conscious, rational, and willful self and powerful, irrational, and primal unconscious forces. Such heresy! Little wonder Freud's theories took so long to take hold.

See also **Childhood Sexuality; Feminism; Masson, Jeffrey.**

Sexuality, Freud's

The man reputed to have shattered Victorian sexual morality, warning that inhibiting sexual behavior leads to neurotic conflict, and of ushering in the sexual revolution, from the flappers of the Roaring Twenties to the "free love" of the hippies of the sixties, was . . . a prude. As an adolescent, Freud warned his friends against the evils of premarital sex and reprimanded his sisters for reading books too sexually lurid. With the exception of a brief adolescent crush on an older woman, Freud had little contact with women until he met and instantly fell in love with petite, nonintimidating, and compliant Martha Bernays.

Freud wrote Martha passionate love letters throughout their four-year engagement but restricted sexual contact to kisses and embraces and remained a virgin until his wedding night at age thirty. Once married, the couple's passion waned, and a mere eight years later, their sexual life appears to have come to a halt. Following the birth of their sixth child in 1894, thirty-eight-year-old Freud confided to his friend Wilhelm Fliess—to whom he seemed far more emotionally attached than to his wife—that Martha Freud was enjoying a "revival" since "for the present, for a year, she does not have to expect a child," and that he and Martha "are living in abstinence." In 1900, he noted that he was done "begetting children." Apparently, though, he continued to have occasional sex with his wife. In July 1915, he wrote of a dream about his wife: "Martha comes toward me, I am supposed to write something down for her—write into a notebook, I take out my pencil. . . . It becomes very indistinct." Interpreting the dream, Freud described the dream's residues, including its "sexual meaning": the dream "has to do with successful coitus Wednesday morning." He was then fifty-nine. Having to note "successful coitus" intimates that he was at times impotent. This same year, Freud revealed to James Jackson Putnam that he had "made very little use" of the sexual freedom he was advocating.

Apparently faithful to Martha, Freud appeared to abhor extramarital affairs—perhaps they were unbefitting his lofty status or perhaps he wasn't attracted to other women, although he would have had ample opportunities to meet many women enamored of such a great man, including patients. Jung had no problem bedding at least two of his. Even Lou Andreas-Salomé, the femme fatale who stole and broke the hearts of many of Freud's contemporaries, was only an intimate intellectually speaking. Freud said that he "was very fond of her . . . strange to say without a trace of sexual attraction." Low libido, sexual inhibition—Freud seemed hardly the candidate to overturn Victorian sexual morality.

Freud was uncomfortable even discussing sex and never spoke to his children about sexual matters. When the subject of the difference between a bull and a steer came up, Freud commented to his son Martin, "You must be told these things," but said no more. He "warned" his sixteen-year-old son Oliver against masturbation, who became "quite upset for some time." The experience alienated the two. Freud spoke of the "injuriousness of masturbation," calling it "a vehicle of pathogenic effects" in the neuroses.

Freud's long, forced sexual inhibition before marriage and abstinence during marriage sheds some light on his theories about the
sexual etiology of most mental ailments revealed in his writings.
Civilized Sexual Morality and Modern Nervous Illness, written in
1908, speaks volumes of his marriage to Martha. Freud assumed
that all "civilized" people remain virgins until marriage. After marriage, sexual intercourse is greatly restricted, as there are "very few
procreative acts. As a consequence . . . satisfying sexual intercourse
in marriage takes place only for a few years; and we must subtract
from this . . . the intervals of abstention necessitated by regard for
the wife's health," meaning during and after pregnancy. After
abstaining for three to five years, "the marriage becomes a failure in
so far as it has promised the satisfaction of sexual needs." All con-
traceptive devices "impair sexual enjoyment," while *coitus interruptus* produces "hysteria or an anxiety neurosis in both the man and
woman." Not only does the fear of pregnancy end physical affection but "it usually puts a stop as well to the mental sympathy
between them, which should have been the succession to their
original passionate love." Marriage is doomed to "spiritual disillu-
sionment and bodily deprivation," and couples are no better off
than before marriage, "except for being the poorer by the loss of an
illusion, and they must once more have recourse to their fortitude
in mastering and deflecting their sexual instinct."

But Freud also felt proud of his abstinence. In his paper on civilized sexual morality published in 1908, he observed that modern
civilization makes extraordinary demands on the capacity for sexual restraint, especially in those claiming a modicum of cultivation;
it asks people to refrain from intercourse until they are married,
then to confine their sexual activity to a single partner. Most
humans, Freud was convinced, find such fidelity impossible to obey,
or obey it at a steep emotional cost. "Only a minority succeeds in
mastery through sublimation, through the deflection of sexual
instinctual forces to higher cultural aims, and then only intermit-
tently." Most others "become neurotic or suffer damage in other
ways." Before marriage, Freud felt it normal to inhibit his sexual
desire; after marriage, he felt it normal to abstain from sex with his
wife, who was too busy with pregnancies, home, and children, and

to sublimate his libido into "higher cultural aims" by becoming engrossed in his work and male colleagues: psychoanalysis consumed his libido and blinded him to the power of the sex drive.

If Freud was himself uncomfortable with sex, why did he stick to his sexuality theory, in spite of the legitimate problems raised by those closest to him? Why did he seem on the one hand obsessed with sex and on the other afraid of it? In his insightful book *Freud*, Louis Breger suggested that Freud's intense conflict between longing for closeness and fear of engulfment drove "his conception of sexuality as the most powerful—the most dangerous and disruptive—of drives. In short, his dread of giving in to his infantile yearnings was transformed, in his theories, into the image of a menacing sexual instinct."

Like his lifelong addiction to smoking and early addiction to cocaine, Breger suggested that sexuality for Freud "had the lure of an addictive substance. It was always tempting; because giving in to it could take one over, it had to be controlled, mastered, sublimated, and channeled into socially acceptable activities." In "Sexuality in the Aetiology of the Neuroses" (1898), Freud himself noted a connection between addiction and sexuality, and appears to clearly describe his own experience:

> Left to himself, the masturbator is accustomed, whenever something happens that depresses him, to return to his convenient form of satisfaction. . . . For sexual need, when once it has been aroused and has been satisfied for any length of time, can no longer be silenced; it can only de displaced along another path. . . . Not everyone who has occasion to take morphia, cocaine, chloral-hydrate . . . acquires in this way an 'addiction' to them. Closer inquiry shows that these narcotics are meant to serve—directly or indirectly—as a substitute for a lack of sexual satisfaction.

Shell Shock

Newspapers carried daily reports of the carnage of World War I. Freud encountered the "war neurosis" or "shell shock," or what today we call post-traumatic stress disorder, though he never saw shell-shocked victims. The psychiatric community was called to duty along with medical doctors. But the military did not know what to do for these men, whose symptoms strikingly resembled hysteria: tremors and uncontrollable shaking, paralysis of all sorts, blindness, deafness, hallucinations, tics, obsessive-compulsiveness, recurring nightmares, hypervigilance, and hypersensitivity to stimulation. As with hysteria, no medical condition could explain these symptoms.

At a loss, military doctors put the afflicted in hospitals and shocked them with painful electric currents, hoping to return them to the front. Some did return to war, but many relapsed, others died, and some committed suicide. The military needed a better solution to the problem than torture. Having read Freud's books, some English, French, and German physicians thought psycho-analysis might be helpful and began applying psychoanalytic theory and technique. The English physician W. H. R. Rivers, in charge of a hospital outside Edinburgh, recognized that the symptoms of the shell-shocked patients under his care were a result of unconscious emotional conflicts, and he encouraged them to openly express their feelings. In his words: "The great merit of Freud is that he had provided us with a theory of the mechanism by which this experi-ence, not readily and directly accessible to consciousness, produces its effects, while he and his followers have devised clinical methods by which these hidden factors in the causation of disease may be brought to light."

Three Essays on the Theory of Sexuality

It is astonishing that the human race could have for so long clung to the belief that children were asexual beings.

—Sigmund Freud, *Introductory Lectures*

No sooner did Freud finish his masterpiece *The Interpretation of Dreams*, which alone would have secured him a position in history as an original, iconoclastic thinker, than he was hot on the trail (no pun intended) to debunk the myth long held by Western civilization that childhood was a time of innocence: sexuality, argued Freud, begins not at adolescence but *at birth*. Further, women are also sexual beings, contrary to their puritanical role in Victorian society, and sexual drives and emotions play a vital role in "normal" life, an assertion that jarred the moral and religious ethos of his time.

Three Essays on the Theory of Sexuality, published in 1905, was a monumental contribution to the understanding of sexuality. Freud approached sexuality as progressing developmentally through stages—oral, anal, phallic, latency, and genital—and demonstrated how early sexual experience undergoes transformations that pervade adult life in various forms. He emphasized the infant's early bodily and physical sensations and experiences of pleasure and pain. In so doing, he recognized that the body speaks its own language. In fact, the ego starts as a bodily ego.

Fixation at any stage can produce neurosis and affect our choice of a love object, our sexual preferences, and the meaning of many habits and practices. Adult orality, such as kissing, drinking, and smoking, has roots in the sensual-sexual nature of nursing and suckling. Conflicts around toilet training foreshadow compliance and disobedience. Adult sexual choice and action—whom we fall in love with, whether opposite sex or same-sex partners; what turns us on, the sight of our partner's genitals or his feet; whether we are oversexed or laissez-faire about hopping into bed—are laid down by early "prototypes," by the images, emotional predispositions, and expectations first encountered in our earliest relationships. In Freud's words:

> It often happens that a young man falls in love seriously for the first time with a mature woman, or a girl with an elderly man in a position of authority; this is clearly an echo of the phase of development that we have been discussing, since these figures are able to re-animate pictures of their mother

or father. . . . Every object-choice whatever is based . . . on these prototypes. In view of the importance of a child's relations to his parents in determining his later choice of a sexual object . . . any disturbance of those relations will produce the gravest effects upon his adult sexual life. Jealousy in a lover is never without an infantile root or at least an infantile reinforcement.

Three Essays begins with homosexuality, then covers a wide variety of sexual preferences and practices, from bisexuality and fetishism to sadism and masochism. The second essay begins with infantile amnesia: we remember nothing of our first two to three years of life—not when we started to walk, talk, our "birth trauma," or our early sexual experiences. Freud then outlined the stages of psychosexual development, from the sensual pleasure of suckling at the breast and masturbating to the Oedipal conflict of early childhood, which disappears briefly during latency. The last essay discusses puberty and adolescence, when sexuality reemerges in full force with the exploding hormones of adolescence.

Topographical Model

The conscious mind is only the tip of the iceberg.

—Sigmund Freud

Early in his career, Freud pictured the regions of the mind as three adjacent compartments: conscious, preconscious, and unconscious. Mental thought of which we are currently aware is *conscious*: the sentence you are now reading. Mental thought of which we are unaware but is easily retrievable without being threatening is *preconscious*: what color blouse you wore yesterday. Mental thought of which we are unaware and is exceedingly hard to access because it is threatening is *unconscious*: how you wanted your baby sister to die.

The master of metaphor, Freud portrayed the unconscious as being like an iceberg, mostly hidden. Our conscious awareness is the part that floats above the surface. To understand the interplay between conscious and unconscious processes, he used another metaphor, that of two adjoining rooms.

Imagine a large entrance hall filled with mental images—the *unconscious*—all attempting to enter an adjoining small drawing room—*consciousness*. Standing in the doorway dividing the two rooms is a guard in charge of examining each impulse or thought and deciding if it should be let in; those that would create fear, guilt, shame, or other uncomfortable emotions are turned away. For instance, if you ask your friend why he didn't smile at the news of his wife's promotion, he might not know: his fear that she might surpass his accomplishments would be unacceptable to his conscious mind. Were his fear to sneak past the threshold, the watchman would push it back into the entrance hall—and *repress* it. Once the impulses make their way into the drawing room, they are in the *preconscious* until they catch the eye of consciousness. In the preconscious, mental events can be called to consciousness at will, like the name of the high school you attended or the first boy you kissed. *Resistance* to the analyst's attempt to lift repression and free the patient is governed by the same watchman.

No matter how great the effort, repressed memories that are unacceptable to the conscious ego cannot be recalled. A good example is hysterical symptoms. Anna O.'s false pregnancy and psycho-childbirth was a cover for her unacceptable desire to have Breuer's child.

To illustrate the concept of the unconscious and repression, in one of his lectures Freud relayed the story of a patient who felt compelled to hurry into a nearby room, stand by a certain table, summon the parlor maid, and, as she came, dismiss her. The table-cloth contained a red stain that the maid could readily see. She would compulsively repeat this sequence, clueless as to the meaning of the ritual. And then it hit her. On her wedding night, her husband, from whom she was now separated, was impotent. Throughout the night, he had repeatedly rushed into her room, attempted intercourse, and failed. To hide his shame, he poured red ink on the bed the next morning, to fool the maid into thinking his bride had been deflowered. But in his hurry he unknowingly poured the ink into a spot where no hymenal blood would have flowed. By summoning the maid and making certain she saw the red stain, the woman was unconsciously saving her husband, whom she greatly respected and admired, from humiliation. Until Freud questioned her, the meaning of her bizarre behavior was a mystery—it was *unconscious*.

In the unconscious entrance room, tension reduction is urgently sought and disregards reality: satisfaction must be had whatever the cost. Freud termed this process *primary process thinking*, which comes from the emotional, limbic brain. This is the thought process of the young child where wishes become realities. If you wished your baby brother dead, you're as guilty as if you killed him. If he did die later—as happened to Freud—the guilt is profound, although Freud was not responsible for his brother's death. Likewise, no contradictions exist in primary processing thinking. You can scream at your spouse to leave you alone, then yell, "Don't leave me!" as he bolts out the door. The same dynamics govern dreams, where thinking is also the same as acting, impossible situations exist, and opposites coexist without contradiction and govern neurotic symptoms. But primary process thinking is not all bad. On the contrary, it operates on the *pleasure principle*. Freud believed that when the infant cries for the breast and the mother does not immediately come, the infant hallucinates the breast to satisfy the urge to suckle, a phenomenon we now know isn't possible until around eighteen months of age when the infant's brain is mature enough to imagine something not present. Primary process thinking is also the source for our creativity, playfulness, and use of metaphor, story, and myth.

Totem and Taboo

In *Totem and Taboo*, published in 1913, Freud speculated that the origin of social institutions such as government and religion lie in a prehistoric real-life enactment of the Oedipal complex. He outlined a scenario where, long ago, people lived in primal hordes governed by an autocratic father. Ruled by uncontrolled instinctual urges, the patriarch kept the women for his own sexual pleasure and prohibited the younger men, his sons, from sharing in his delights. Jealous of the father, the young men of the primal horde overthrew him and killed and devoured his flesh in a totem meal— symbolically assuming his identity. Collectively possessing his power and his women, they established new fraternal social clans that, to assuage their guilt, had strict taboos to inhibit sex and aggression, especially incest, the most heinous of crimes. For having slept with his mother, although unknowingly, Oedipus was doomed to blindness and wandering. Thus, the Oedipus complex has evolutionary roots.

Transference

Transference . . . was one of Freud's most central and profoundly creative discoveries. It is a powerful concept, speaking to the essence of the unconscious—the past hidden within the present—and of continuity—the present in continuum with the past.

—E. A. Schwaber, *The Transference in Psychotheraphy*

Paul, a stock broker, complained to his analyst how his wife did not appreciate him. He also had described his mother as having been too busy with her work as an interior decorator when he grew up to give him much attention. One day he walked into the analytic session and excitedly told the analyst about having had the highest sales commission the previous day. The analyst said, "You must feel pretty accomplished." Paul retorted angrily, "You don't much care, do you?" Paul had felt that the analyst's response was too matter-of-fact, too unemotional. He had displaced his feelings for his mother and wife onto the analyst. In psychoanalysis this phenomenon is called the *transference*, the central feature of an analysis.

We perceive other people through the representational models of our significant others: if our mother was loving and trustworthy, we tend to see people as benign; if she was cold or unpredictable, we tend to see people as untrustworthy and fear they will hurt and disappoint us. The more intense the relationship, the more we imbue the person with qualities that belonged to important people in our lives and experience the broad range of emotions connected with these early relationships. A psychoanalysis, which may involve therapy three, four, or five days a week for perhaps years, is by its nature intense and emotion laden. Thus, in little time the analyst becomes, sometimes subtly and often blatantly, father, mother, lover, friend, rival, scoundrel, or superman. Using the transference, the analyst interprets the thoughts in context of the psychic meaning, and attempts to take the information neither personally nor critically.

A good example of the centrality of the transference in a psychoanalysis is the case of the Rat Man. Rat Man Ernst openly expressed his conflicted feelings toward Freud. At one point, Ernst, frightened that Freud would beat him for his evil thoughts, got off the couch, but Freud, unlike Ernst's punitive father, accepted this reaction. Had Freud chastised Ernst for his evil thoughts, he would have been guilty of *countertransference*—the analyst's emotional reaction to a patient.

The concept of the *transference* was one of Freud's most brilliant insights. His first intimation that the therapeutic relationship can stir powerful feelings in patient *and* doctor, of which they may not be entirely aware, and that unconscious forces could distort the patient's vision of the therapist, was the case of Anna O., the famous patient of Josef Breuer. She had experienced a false pregnancy, as if he, Breuer, had impregnated her. Breuer, mortified, ended the therapy and took his wife on a second honeymoon—the countertransference.

Both transference and countertransference can be negative when hostility predominates, as in the above examples, or positive, as when the patient feels friendly and affectionate toward the analyst. As with Anna O., often a patient will feel a romantic inter-est in the analyst—positive transference—who, flattered, returns the feelings—positive countertransference, as probably happened to Breuer, who saw Anna O. daily, often in her bedroom, for two years. The analyst must become aware of her emotional response as countertransference and abstain or the analysis will by its nature be terminated. For this reason, all psychoanalysts must themselves be analyzed.

In 1915, Freud mentioned the "rule of abstinence" in his tech-nique paper "Observations on Transference Love." Women patients, Freud said, always fall in love with their doctor. The ana-lyst must recognize that the woman's love is the resistance, not a result of the analyst's personal charms, and has to be analyzed—something perhaps Jung didn't realize, who had affairs with two of his patients. The doctor must deny the patient's cravings while allowing the patient to persist to bring into consciousness deeply hidden erotic desires. Only then may she know and bring under her control the infantile roots of her love and the fantasies wound around it.

Freud discovered two unconscious forces at work in the trans-ference. The first is the *template* formed by our earliest relationships in which we try to fit later relationships. If you experienced your father as cold and critical, in an analysis you will unconsciously see the analyst in the same way. The second force was that of the *rep-etition compulsion*. Unknowingly, you may have chosen an analyst who is reserved and even stoic, and you may act in a way to annoy the analyst, to cause him or her to behave critically toward you. The attitudes and expectations from your earliest relationships are "transferred" from parent to therapist. Today, we also call the trans-ference a *self-fulfilling prophecy*. Because you expect the man to reject you, you do not smile back when he smiles at you. Consequently, he does reject you.

Interestingly, Freud was often accused of not using transference well in his own interpretations, which tended not to focus on his relationship with the patient. Speaking of his own analysis with Freud, Abram Kardiner wrote: "The man who had invented the concept of transference did not recognize it when it occurred here.

He overlooked one thing. *Yet, I was afraid of my father in childhood, but the one whom I feared now was Freud himself.* He could make or break me, which my father no longer could. By his statement, he pushed the entire reaction into the past, thereby making the analysis a historical reconstruction."

In Freud's early case of Dora, he admitted that he had failed to "master the transference in time"; indeed, he had "forgotten to take the precaution of paying attention to the first signs of the transference." At this time, Freud was only beginning to understand the emotional bond between analysand and analyst, and he had failed to observe what he perceived, probably falsely, as Dora's "infatuation" with him, unconsciously relating to him as father, lover, enemy. But, worse, he had failed to recognize his transference onto Dora—the countertransference had escaped his analytical self-observation. Consistent with the patriarchal sex roles of his time, Freud was domineering and too quickly dismissed her protests of innocence and betrayal, and he showed too little sympathy for Dora's plight as a young girl unwittingly trapped in an intrigue.

Unconscious

See **Topographic Model.**

Vaginal and Clitoral Orgasm

Before accepting their castrated state, Freud declared in *Three Essays on the Theory of Sexuality* (1905), the sexuality of little girls was "of a wholly masculine character," and their clitoris, which they assumed was a small "atrophied" penis, was their "leading sexual zone." As such, little girls' masturbatory pleasure was less than little boys', causing girls to feel deficient, inferior, and envious of boys and forever struggling to renounce their wish to be a boy. Freud would have been surprised to learn that all human embryos start out *female*; the penis grows from the clitoris to produce a male appendage.

These misconceptions led to Freud's notion of penis envy as the foundation for female development. As it is futile to compete with the superior sex, girls replace their wish for a penis with a wish for a child. They transfer their affections from their mothers to their fathers, and with their discovery of the vagina at puberty, girls become feminine by transferring their "erotogenic susceptibility to stimulation . . . from the clitoris to the vaginal orifice." If the girl does not forsake clitoral masturbation, she will never accept her lack of a penis and will become neurotic. This thinking led Freud, who had very little knowledge of the feminine sexual response, to declare that only vaginal orgasms were "normal."

Vasectomy

Considering the possibility that a poor flow of libidinal energy may have promoted his cancer, on November 17, 1923, Freud underwent an operation on his testicles that was supposed to rejuvenate his energy supply and battle his debilitating cancer. Known today as a vasectomy, the operation ligates the vas deferens, the duct that conveys sperm from the testicle to the seminal vesicle. Afterward, Freud said he felt at times younger and stronger.

Vienna Psychoanalytic Society

In the fall of 1902, "a number of younger physicians gathered around me with the declared intention of learning," wrote Freud, "practicing, and disseminating psychoanalysis. A colleague who had experienced the beneficial effects of analytic therapy on himself gave the impetus." The Wednesday Psychological Society was born and launched with a discussion of the psychological impact of smoking.

The colleague to whom Freud referred was Wilhelm Stekel, an inventive and productive Viennese physician who had been in brief but successful analytic therapy with Freud to alleviate symptoms of psychological impotence. In addition to Stekel, Freud invited three other Viennese physicians: Max Kahane, who introduced Stekel to Freud; Rudolf Reitler, who became the world's second analyst, after Freud, but died young; and Alfred Adler, a Socialist physician who later developed his own psychology and became one of Freud's most bitter enemies (see **Dissenters**). This small group formed the core of what became the Vienna Psychoanalytic Society in 1908.

In those early years, Freud was the undisputed god and there was little friction among the members. Stekel described himself in his autobiography as "the apostle of Freud who was my Christ!" Stekel recalled the first sessions of the Wednesday-night group as "inspiring." There was "complete harmony among the five, no dissonances; we were like pioneers in a newly discovered land, and Freud was the leader. A spark seemed to jump from one mind to the other, and every evening was like a revelation."

New members were soon added by unanimous consent and initially only a few dropped out. In 1902, the musicologist Max Graf, the father of the boy who would become Freud's famous case "Little Hans," and the bookseller and publisher Hugo Heller joined. In 1903, Paul Federn, a Viennese general practitioner, joined and remained faithful to Freud until the end. By 1906, the year Freud turned fifty, there were twenty members, mostly Jewish, about a dozen of whom were regulars and who would reliably engage in animated, aggressive talk. Many were physicians who wished to apply Freud's ideas in their practices; others were intellectuals from art, music, literature, and publishing. In October of that year, the fifth year since its inception, Otto Rank, the group's first employed secretary, began to record the proceedings of each meeting. Rank's notes recorded discussion of case histories, psychoanalysis of literary works and public figures, reviews of new psychiatric literature, and previews of forthcoming publications by members.

Between 1908 and 1911, new members included Sándor Ferenczi from Budapest, the jurist Victor Tausk, and the witty lawyer Hanns Sachs. A stream of visitors from outside of Vienna trooped to make Freud's acquaintance and attend the Wednesday-night sessions, among them the German physician Max Eitingon and Karl Abraham, a German psychiatrist raised in an Orthodox Jewish family. After having been introduced to psychoanalysis by Carl Jung and his mentor Eugen Bleuler during psychiatric training in Zurich, thirty-year-old Karl Abraham met Freud in 1907 and immediately became a devout member of Freud's inner circle. Calm, methodical, intelligent, and cheerful, Abraham was a bastion of common sense and stability in this often volatile group. Freud called him an incurable optimist. The most loyal of Freud's original inner circle, Abraham became Freud's right-hand man in the history of the psychoanalytic movement and made a number of original contributions to psychoanalytic thinking.

The Swiss psychiatrists and advanced medical students working in Zurich and elsewhere in Switzerland came as early as 1907 and included Ludwig Binswanger and Carl Jung. Determined to spread his gospel abroad and to attract a gentile following, lest psychoanalysis be branded a Jewish science, Freud quickly began courting Jung, whom he hoped to make his heir apparent. The two enjoyed an intimate and intense friendship until 1911, when Jung, who by then had grave doubts about Freud's insistence on sexuality as central to the neuroses, broke away to eventually form his own religion of the psyche. The following year, other visitors important for the future of psychoanalysis stopped by to meet Freud and his Viennese group: A. A. Brill, Freud's American apostle and translator who formed the New York Psychoanalytic Society; Ernest Jones, who became Freud's most influential British supporter, formed the American Psychoanalytic Society, and became Freud's official biographer; and the pioneer of psychoanalysis in Italy, Edoardo Weiss.

Initially, the group met at Freud's apartment. Gatherings would begin with one of the members presenting a paper, followed by a brief coffee break and socializing. Then the discussion ensued, with cigars and cigarettes smoking up the heated atmosphere. Freud spoke last and decisively. The atmosphere in the room, as Max Graf described it, was as if in a holy place: "Freud himself was its new prophet who made the heretofore prevailing methods of psychological investigation appear superficial. . . . Freud's pupils— he was always addressed as 'The Professor'—were his apostles." Louis Breger commented: "If they were looking for the strong father they never had—as Jung and Rank so clearly were—or for the love they had missed—as was the case with Ferenczi—or for a new identity, heroic model, calling, or vocation—as was true for most of them—Freud and the fledgling movement held out enormous promise." Their ties were further intensified as they continually analyzed each other, interpreting symptoms, dreams, and slips of the tongue. Freud participated in this but also held himself aloof, letting it be known that his unconscious conflicts had been "resolved" in his self-analysis. He analyzed them much more than they him. For his followers, he was the strong, omnipotent, wise father figure.

Freud's group was unlike any other community. Unable to find answers to life's mysteries in religion, psychoanalysis became its own religion, satisfying a quest for deeper meaning in life. As the Society became increasingly defined as an embattled in-group, the members came to feel like comrades in arms in a crusade for a noble cause, men who shared special knowledge and their own private language. Karl Furtmüller, who joined the Vienna Society in 1909, described it as "a sort of catacomb of romanticism, a small and daring group, persecuted now but bound to conquer the world." The excitement produced by Freud's early discoveries gave the participants a sense that they possessed mysterious secrets that set them apart and above others in their society: only they understood the unconscious meaning of neurosis and dreams; only they could trace all sorts of personal traits to their hidden roots.

Many initially attracted to Freud came not only looking for ways to help their own clients and patients but also to find ways to unload their own psychic baggage, to gain self-understanding and the hope for healing. Herman Nunberg, editor of the minutes of the Vienna Psychoanalytic Society, noted that "at the meetings of the Society they discussed not only the problems of others, but also their own difficulties; they revealed their inner conflicts, confessed their masturbation, their fantasies and reminiscences concerning their parents, friends, wives, and children." Like the psychological confessionals in the 1970s with groups such as EST, this group of serious, educated men engaged in their own form of scientific self-exhibition. One by one the members got up and confessed their most intimate sexual problems. In October 1907, Maximilian Steiner, a dermatologist and specialist in venereal diseases, revealed how psychosomatic symptoms that he suffered while living in sexual abstinence disappeared upon starting an affair with the wife of an impotent friend. In early 1908, Rudolf von Urbantschitsch, director of a sanatorium, admitted to early masturbation and a penchant for sadomasochism. In his closing comments, Freud told Urbantschitsch that he had offered the group a kind of "present."

As happens during anyone's reign, sparks of dissent eventually began to fly and new factions to form, some of whom broke away altogether to form their own empires. As the membership increased, meetings grew acerbic, as disciples sparred for position near their god, flaunting their originality, and at times bopping each other on the head with hostile remarks under the guise of analytic frankness.

At the beginning, Freud's authority reigned supreme. But soon members began to resent Freud's word as gospel and some started to drop out. Max Graf was one: "Good-hearted and considerate though he was in private life, Freud was hard and relentless in the presentation of his ideas. . . . I was unable and unwilling to submit to Freud's 'do or don't'—with which he confronted me—and nothing was left for me but to withdraw from his circle." Years later, Helene Deutsch, initially one of Freud's most loyal followers, voiced the same resentment of Freud's obstinate refusal to openly embrace change from his psychoanalytic scripture: "[His] pupils were to be above all passive understanding listeners . . . projection objects through whom he reviewed—sometimes to correct or to retract them—his own ideas."

By 1908, the provocative and threatening nature of psychoanalytic inquiry, which crassly invaded the most intimate and intensely guarded areas of the fragile psyche, was generating an atmosphere of discomfort and irritability. To complicate matters, none of the early crusaders had actually been analyzed, although many could have used it. And this included Freud, whose self-analysis by its nature was not truly psychoanalysis—to whom could Freud transfer feelings?

Except Otto Rank—who was later banished—Freud felt increasingly disappointed in the Viennese faction of the Society, who he felt would not amount to anything, and as years went by invested his hopes abroad, with foreigners and, as with Jung, with the gentiles, as most of the Viennese group were fellow Jews. Four of these foreigners, Max Eitingon and Karl Abraham in Berlin, Ernest Jones in London, and Sándor Ferenczi in Budapest, were to carry the flag of psychoanalysis through years of arduous service to the cause—editing, debating, organizing, raising money, training candidates, making interesting, sometimes problematic clinical and theoretical contributions of their own. In sharp contrast to the dramatic collaboration and no less dramatic collision that marked Freud's relations with Jung, the association of these four men with Freud was highly profitable to both sides if at times somewhat tense. Abraham, the first German to practice psychoanalysis, founded the Berlin Psychoanalytic Society in 1908. For some years, he was the only practicing psychoanalyst in the German capital. In time, Abraham became a sought-after therapist and the leading training analyst of the second generation of analytic candidates. Although never himself analyzed, Abraham analyzed many prominent psychoanalysts, including Helene Deutsch, Karen Horney, Melanie Klein, and Theodor Reik.

In 1910, the second International Congress was held in Nuremberg, Germany. By now, Jung was unquestionably Freud's favorite, and the conference opened with the proposal that they form an international association housed in Zurich and run by Jung, its president for life. Squabbles broke out in the Viennese group because they believed that Freud had devalued them, preferring Jung and the Swiss.

While Freud had set up the congresses as a forum to discuss his ideas, he was open to the contributions of others—up to a point. If they went too far in defying the sacred psychoanalytic text, they got excommunicated. The first to go was Alfred Adler, who in 1910 became the first president of the Viennese Psychoanalytic Society.

By 1911, Adler openly criticized Freud's basic tenets as ignoring the role of the family and society. In his mind, feelings of inferiority were central in forming the personality; sexuality was secondary. Adler left the society to form his own psychology. Freud never forgave him.

The split with Adler and signs of Jung starting to disagree with the father led Jones, with the support of Ferenczi and Rank, to propose in 1912 the formation of a secret group to protect Freud and the movement—the Committee. The Committee remained active until 1936, keeping each other informed of theoretical and political developments. It eventually controlled membership in the international psychoanalytic journals and influenced the translations of Freud's work into English. The group constituted the core of Freud's most dutiful followers: Jones, Abraham, and Eitingon. Hanns Sachs also joined in 1909 and became a loyal follower till the end, worshipping Freud. In *Freud: Master and Friend*, Sachs wrote that Freud was different from other men, even other geniuses, and revealed in Freud a certain distance from his followers:

> I simply could not believe that he was made of the same clay as others. Some special substance had been infused in him and gave the finished product of a higher grade of perfection. This meant a gulf between us which I did not try to cross. Although he called me his friend, I did not feel I was; fundamentally he remained as remote as when I first met him in the lecture hall.

By 1912, Jung's loyalty was greatly suspect, as he appeared to be drifting away from the sexuality theory, and Abraham and other members of the Committee were busily writing each other about the apparent infidel. Freud and Jung finally exchanged verbal blows, and by 1914 Jung was forced to resign as the president of the International Psychoanalytic Association and the editor of the *Jahrbuch*. Those who had dared to defy Freud's theory that central to neurotic behavior was an unresolved Oedipal conflict were forced to leave: Adler, Jung, and in 1924, Rank. All three went on to develop their own theories and make their own contributions to psychology. Jung's theories especially became highly popular, and his following continues to grow.

In 1925, Freud's *Autobiographical Study* addressed his feelings regarding the excommunications of the infidels:

> The secession of former pupils has often been brought up against me as a sign of my intolerance or has been regarded as evidence of some special fatality that hangs over me. It is a sufficient answer to point out that, in contrast to those who have left me, like Jung, Adler, Stekel, and a few besides, there are a great number of men like Abraham, Eitingon, Ferenczi, Rank . . . who have worked with me for some fifteen years in loyal collaboration and for the most part uninterrupted friendship.

If his sexuality theory, which was the fabric that held psychoanalysis together, was wrong, then Freud was wrong and psychoanalysis would die, proving his father right when he yelled after the young Freud urinated in his parents' bedroom that "the boy would come to nothing." The ones who stayed were those who mirrored Freud's grandiosity.

Fortunately, psychoanalysis did not die with the end of the sexuality theory, which died gradually after Freud's death. The strength of psychoanalysis, after all, did not rest with libido but with the notion that human behavior is not all that it appears to be, and only depth psychology can probe and root out its unconscious origins. Today, psychoanalytic communities are in place and thriving throughout the world, including many major cities—New York, Los Angeles, Chicago, and many more—in the United States.

Wolf Man (Case)

Between 1911 and 1914, Freud treated the young Russian aristocrat Sergei Pankejeff, known as "the Wolf Man" because of a childhood dream of wolves. The case history was published in 1918 in *From the History of an Infantile Neurosis*. As he did in all his case studies,

Freud tried to locate the cause of the Wolf Man's neurosis in infantile sexual events, and also tried to show that later experiences and adult traumas were of little significance. Sergei was an extremely disturbed young man at the time of his analysis, suffering from a variety of hypochondriacal and depressive symptoms, with a shaky hold on reality, including an unclear sense of who he was, along with obsessions, compulsions, and the inability to function effectively in almost all areas of his life.

In his analysis, Sergei reported the memory of a frightening dream that he recalled from the age of four in which his bedroom window opened to reveal six or seven wolves sitting in a tree, staring silently at him. He awoke in terror, afraid they were going to eat him. Freud reconstructed the events of Sergei's infancy, focusing on the wolf dream. Presumably at the age of one and a half, Freud asserted, he had witnessed his parents having sexual intercourse, with the father penetrating the mother from behind. It was here that Freud elaborated his theory of the traumatic effect of exposure to the "primal scene," tracing almost all of Sergei's symptoms and life problems to the "scene" and related infantile sexual events. Freud's interpretation seemed unlikely, asserted Louis Breger in *Freud: Darkness in the Midst of Vision*. Sergei had malaria at the time of his supposed primal scene exposure, a much more traumatic experience for an infant than witnessing his parents in sexual activity. In addition, modern research on memory has shown that it is impossible for an adult to recall events from the age of one and a half, as Freud insisted his patient did; in fact, an examination of the case shows Freud "educating" and "inducing" Sergei, who "very soon came to share my conviction that the causes of his infantile neurosis lay concealed behind [the dream]."

Sergei had several subsequent psychological breakdowns and was seen again by Freud before being turned over to one of his analysands, the young Ruth Mack Brunswick. He continued to have contact with psychoanalysis in one way or another for the rest of his life. In later years he earned money selling paintings of his wolf dream and would answer the telephone "Wolf Man here," revealing how his status as Freud's famous patient had given him an identity that helped him to survive.

Zionism

"Zionism," Freud wrote to J. Dwossis in Jerusalem, who was translating some of his writings into Hebrew, "has awakened my strongest sympathies, which still attach me to it. From the beginning," he noted, he had been concerned about it, "something the present-day situation seems to justify. I should like to be mistaken about this."

Einstein had asked Freud to make a public statement on the issue of Zionism, and Freud refused, writing to Einstein, "Whoever wants to influence a crowd, must have something resounding, enthusiastic to say, and my sober appraisal of Zionism does not permit this." He professed his sympathy for the movement, declared that he was "proud" of "our" University of Jerusalem, and took pleasure in the flourishing of "our" settlements. "On the other hand I do not believe that Palestine will ever become a Jewish state, and that the Christians or the Islamic world will ever be prepared to leave their shrines in Jewish hands. It would have seemed more comprehensible to me to found a Jewish fatherland on new, unencumbered soil." He was aware, he added, that such a "rational" attitude would never enlist "the enthusiasm of the masses and the resources of the rich." But he regretted to see the "unrealistic fanaticism" of his fellow Jews awakening the suspicion of the Arabs. "I can muster no sympathy whatever for the misguided piety that makes a national religion from a piece of a wall of Herod, and for its sake challenges the feelings of the local natives."

Bibliography

Allport, Gordon. *The Person in Psychology: Selected Essays.* Boston: Beacon Press, 1968.

Balmary, Marie. *Psychoanalyzing Psychoanalysis: Freud and the Hidden Fault of the Father.* Baltimore: Johns Hopkins University Press, 1979.

Binswanger, Ludwig. *Sigmund Freud: Reminiscences of a Friendship.* New York: Grune & Stratton, 1957.

Bonaparte, Marie, Anna Freud, and Ernst Kris, eds. *The Origin of Psychoanalysis: Letters of Sigmund Freud to Wilhelm Fliess, Drafts and Notes, 1887-1902.* New York: Basic Books, 1954.

Breger, Louis. *Freud: Darkness in the Midst of Vision.* New York: John Wiley & Sons, 2000.

Children's Bureau, Department of Labor. *Infant Care.* Washington, D.C.: Government Printing Office, 1951.

Clark, Ronald W. *Freud: The Man and the Cause.* New York: Random House, 1980.

Freud, Sigmund. "An Autobiographical Study." In *The Standard Edition of the Complete Psychological Works of Sigmund Freud,* Vol. 20, edited and translated by James Strachey. London: Hogarth, 1962.

———. *Beyond the Pleasure Principle.* In *The Standard Edition of the Complete Psychological Works of Sigmund Freud,* Vol. 18, edited and translated by James Strachey. London: Hogarth, 1955.

———. *Civilization and Its Discontents.* In *The Standard Edition of the Complete Psychological Works of Sigmund Freud,* Vol. 21, edited and translated by James Strachey. London: Hogarth, 1964.

————. *Civilized Sexual Morality and Modern Nervous Illness*. In *The Standard Edition of the Complete Psychological Works of Sigmund Freud*, Vol. 9, edited and translated by James Strachey. London: Hogarth, 1959.

————. "The Dissolution of the Oedipus Complex." In *The Standard Edition of the Complete Psychological Works of Sigmund Freud*, Vol. 19, edited and translated by James Strachey. London: Hogarth, 1962.

————. "A Disturbance of Memory on the Acropolis." In *The Standard Edition of the Complete Psychological Works of Sigmund Freud*, Vol. 22, edited and translated by James Strachey. London: Hogarth, 1963.

————. *Dora: An Analysis of a Case of Hysteria*. New York: Macmillan, 1963.

————. "Extracts from the Fliess Papers," Letter No. 70. In *The Standard Edition of the Complete Psychological Works of Sigmund Freud*, Vol. 1, edited and translated by James Strachey. London: Hogarth, 1966.

————. "Extracts from the Fliess Papers," Letter No. 71. In *The Standard Edition of the Complete Psychological Works of Sigmund Freud*, Vol. 1, edited and translated by James Strachey. London: Hogarth, 1966.

————. *Fragment of an Analysis of a Case of Hysteria*. In *The Standard Edition of the Complete Psychological Works of Sigmund Freud*, Vol. 7, edited and translated by James Strachey. London: Hogarth, 1962.

————. *Inhibition, Symptoms and Anxiety*. In *The Standard Edition of the Complete Psychological Works of Sigmund Freud*, Vol. 20, edited and translated by James Strachey. London: Hogarth, 1959.

————. *Instincts and Their Vicissitudes*. In *The Standard Edition of the Complete Psychological Works of Sigmund Freud*, Vol. 14, edited and translated by James Strachey. London: Hogarth, 1957.

————. *Interpretation of Dreams*. In *The Standard Edition of the Complete Psychological Works of Sigmund Freud*, Vols. 4 and 5, edited and translated by James Strachey. London: Hogarth, 1953.

————. *Introductory Lectures on Psychoanalysis*. In *The Standard Edition of the Complete Psychological Works of Sigmund Freud*, Vols. 15 and 16, edited and translated by James Strachey. London: Hogarth, 1963.

————. *Jokes and Their Relation to the Unconscious*. In *The Standard Edition of the Complete Psychological Works of Sigmund Freud*, Vol. 8, edited and translated by James Strachey. London: Hogarth, 1960.

————. "Letter No. 50." In *The Origin of Psychoanalysis: Letters of Sigmund Freud to Wilhelm Fliess, Drafts and Notes, 1887-1902*, edited by Marie Bonaparte, Anna Freud, and Ernst Kris. New York: Basic Books, 1954.

————. *The Letters of Sigmund Freud*. Edited and by Ernst L. Freud, translated by Tania Stern and James Stern. New York: Basic Books, 1960.

————. *Moses and Monotheism: Three Essays*. In *The Standard Edition of the Complete Psychological Works of Sigmund Freud*, Vol. 23, edited and translated by James Strachey. London: Hogarth, 1962.

————. "The Neuro-Psychoses of Defence." In *The Standard Edition of the Complete Psychological Works of Sigmund Freud*, Vol. 3, edited and translated by James Strachey. London: Hogarth, 1962.

————. *New Introductory Lectures on Psychoanalysis*. In *The Standard Edition of the Complete Psychological Works of Sigmund Freud*, Vol. 22, edited and translated by James Strachey. London: Hogarth, 1964.

————. "A Note on the Prehistory of the Technique of Analysis." In *The Standard Edition of the Complete Psychological Works of Sigmund Freud*, Vol. 18, edited and translated by James Strachey. London: Hogarth, 1955.

————. "On Beginning the Treatment." In *The Standard Edition of the Complete Psychological Works of Sigmund Freud*, Vol. 12, edited and translated by James Strachey. London: Hogarth, 1958.

————. *On Narcissism: An Introduction.* In *The Standard Edition of the Complete Psychological Works of Sigmund Freud,* Vol. 14, edited and translated by James Strachey. London: Hogarth, 1957.

————. *An Outline of Psychoanalysis.* New York: W.W. Norton, 1940.

————. "The Psychoanalytic View of Psychogenic Disturbance of Vision." In *The Standard Edition of the Complete Psychological Works of Sigmund Freud,* Vol. 11, edited and translated by James Strachey. London: Hogarth, 1957.

————. *The Psychopathology of Everyday Life.* In *The Standard Edition of the Complete Psychological Works of Sigmund Freud,* Vol. 6, edited and translated by James Strachey. London: Hogarth, 1960.

————. "Some Psychical Consequences of the Anatomical Distinction between the Sexes." In *The Standard Edition of the Complete Psychological Works of Sigmund Freud,* Vol. 19, edited and translated by James Strachey. London: Hogarth, 1962.

————. *Three Essays on a Theory of Sexuality.* In *The Standard Edition of the Complete Psychological Works of Sigmund Freud,* Vol. 7, edited and translated by James Strachey. London: Hogarth, 1962.

————. *Totem and Taboo.* In *The Standard Edition of the Complete Psychological Works of Sigmund Freud,* Vol. 13, edited and translated by James Strachey. London: Hogarth, 1958.

Freud to Dwossis, December 15, 1930. Typescript copy, Freud Museum, London.

Freud to Einstein, February 26, 1030. Freud Collection, B3, LC.

Goetz, Bruno. "Erinnerungen an Sigmund Freud," *Neue Schweizer Rundschau,* XX, May 1952.

Gay, Peter. *Freud: A Life for Our Time.* New York: W. W. Norton, 1988.

Goldman, Emma. *Living My Life.* New York: Knopf, 1931.

Guterl, Fred. "What Freud Got Right." *Newsweek,* November 11, 2002.

Hirschmüller, Albrecht. *The Life and Work of Josef Breuer: Physiology and Psychoanalysis.* New York: New York University Press, 1989.

Jones, Ernest. *The Life and Work of Sigmund Freud: The Formative Years and the Great Discoveries*, Vol. 1. New York: Basic Books, 1953.

———. *The Life and Work of Sigmund Freud: The Last Phase*, Vol. 3. New York: Basic Books, 1957.

Jung, C. G. *Memories, Dreams, and Reflections*. Edited by Ariela Jaffe; translated by Richard Winston and Clara Winston. New York: Vintage Books, 1965.

Kardiner, Abram. *My Analysis with Freud: Reminiscences*. New York: W. W. Norton, 1977.

LeDoux, Joseph. *The Emotional Brain: The Mysterious Underpinnings of Emotional Life*. New York: Simon & Schuster, 1996.

Marcus, S. "Freud and Dora: Story, History, Case History." In *Psychoanalysis and Contemporary Science*, edited by T. Shapiro. New York: International Universities Press, 1977.

Masson, Jeffrey. *The Assault on Truth: Freud's Suppression of the Seduction Theory*. New York: Farrar, Straus & Giroux, 1984.

Masters, W., and V. Johnson. *Human Sexual Response*. New York: Little Brown, 1966.

McGuire, William, ed. *The Freud/Jung Letters: The Correspondence between Sigmund Freud and C. G. Jung*. Translated by Ralph Manheim and R. F. C. Hull. Princeton, N.J.: Princeton University Press, 1974.

Oring, Elliott. *The Jokes of Sigmund Freud*. Philadelphia: University of Pennsylvania Press, 1984.

Pert, Candace. *Molecules of Emotion*. New York: Scribner, 1997.

Pfeiffer, Ernst, ed. *Sigmund Freud, and Lou Andreas-Salomé: Letters*. Translated by William Scott and Elaine Robson-Scott. New York: Harcourt Brace Jovanovich, 1972.

Prager, Jeffrey. "On the Abuses of Freud." *Contention* 4:1, 1994.

Roazen, Paul. *Freud and His Followers*. New York: Knopf, 1975.

Sachs, Hanns. *Freud: Master and Friend*. Cambridge, Mass.: Harvard University Press, 1944.

Sapolsky, Robert. *Why Zebras Don't Get Ulcers*. New York: W. H. Freeman, 1998.

Schur, Max. *Freud, Living and Dying*. New York: International Universities Press, 1972.

Spitz, Rene A. "Autoeroticism: Some Empirical Findings and Hypotheses on Three of Its Manifestations in the First Year of Life." *The Psychological Study of the Child*, Vols. 3 and 4. New York: International Universities Press, 1949.

Stekel, Wilhelm. *The Autobiography of Wilhelm Stekel: The Life Story of a Pioneer Psychoanalyst*. Edited by Emil A. Gutheil. New York: Liveright, 1950.

Weiss, Edoardo. "Meine Erinnerungen an Sigmund Freud," in *Freud-Weiss Briefe*.

Index